management
of organizational
behavior

management of

PAUL HERSEY

ohio university

KENNETH H. BLANCHARD

university of massachusetts

organizational

behavior

utilizing human resources

SECOND EDITION

PRENTICE-HALL, INC., Englewood Cliffs, New Jersey

Library of Congress Cataloging In Publication Data

Hersey, Paul.
    Management of organizational behavior.

    Bibliography: p.
    1. Psychology, Industrial.   2. Personnel
management.   3. Leadership.   I. Blanchard, Kenneth
H., joint author.   II. Title.
HF5548.8.H4   1972   658.31'4   76–38414
ISBN   C–0–13–548719–6   P–0–13–548743–9

To RALPH E. HERSEY, SR., a retired telephone pioneer with over fifty patents for Bell Laboratories, whose work made direct distance dialing a reality. In looking back over his thirty-nine years of work with the telephone industry, he once commented that of all his contributions, the most rewarding aspect to him personally was that he became known as a *developer of people*.

PAUL HERSEY AND KENNETH H. BLANCHARD

management of organizational behavior: utilizing human resources

Second Edition

10   9

PRENTICE-HALL INTERNATIONAL, INC., *London*
PRENTICE-HALL OF AUSTRALIA, PTY., LTD., *Sydney*
PRENTICE-HALL OF CANADA, LTD., *Toronto*
PRENTICE-HALL OF INDIA PRIVATE LIMITED, *New Delhi*
PRENTICE-HALL OF JAPAN, INC., *Tokyo*

contents

preface to the second edition   ix

preface to the first edition   xi

1   management: a behavioral approach   1

Successful versus Unsuccessful Sciences/2   *change*/2
a problem of investment/3   Management Defined/3
distinction between management and leadership/4
Management Process/4   Skills of a Manager/6
emphasis on human skills/7

2   motivation and behavior   9

Behavior/9   *motives/10   goals/11   motive strength/11
changes in motive strength/12*   Categories of
Activities/15   Motivating Situation/16   Expectancy
and Availability/19   Personality Development/21
changing personality/21   Hierarchy of Needs—Abraham
H. Maslow/22   Motivational Research/27   *physiological
needs/27   safety (security)/28   social (affiliation)/30
esteem/31   self-actualization/34   money motive/38*
What Do Workers Want from Their Jobs?/38

3   motivating environment   43

Hawthorne Studies—Elton Mayo/44   Theory X and
Theory Y—Douglas McGregor/46   Human Group—
George C. Homans/48   Immaturity–Maturity Theory—
Chris Argyris/50   Motivation–Hygiene Theory—
Frederick Herzberg/54   *hygiene factors/55   motivators/
55   example of job enrichment/58   a problem of
placement/59*   Management Systems—Rensis Likert/60
theory into practice/64   Summary and Conclusions/65

4   leader behavior   67

Leadership Defined/68   Trait Versus Situational
Approach to the Study of Leadership/68   Leadership
Process/69   *scientific management movement/69
human relations movement/70   authoritarian–
democratic–laissez faire leader behavior/70   Michigan
leadership studies/72   group dynamics studies/72
Ohio State leadership studies/73   managerial grid/75*
Is There A Best Style of Leadership?/77   Adaptive
Leader Behavior/79   *leadership contingency model/80*
The Tri-Dimensional Leader Effectiveness Model/81
*effectiveness dimension/83   attitudinal versus
behavioral models/86*

5 determining effectiveness   91

Management Effectiveness Versus Leadership
Effectiveness/91   Sources of Power/92   Successful
Leadership Versus Effective Leadership/93   What
Determines Organizational Effectiveness?/95   *causal
variables/96   intervening variables/96   output or end-
result variables/96   long-term goals versus short-term
goals/97   organizational dilemma/97*   Force Field
Analysis—Kurt Lewin/100   Integration of Goals and
Effectiveness/101   Participation and Effectiveness/103
management by objectives/104   Style and Effectiveness/
105

6 diagnosing the environment   109

Environmental Variables/109   *personality defined/110
expectations defined/111*   Personality and Expectations/
111   *leader's personality and expectations/112
followers' personalities and expectations/115   superiors'
personalities and expectations/116   associates'
personalities and expectations/118   organization's
personality and expectations/118*   Other Situational
Variables/119   *job demands/119   time/120*   Style
Adaptability/121   *determining style range/121   low
and high adaptability demands/122*   Developing
Strategies/123   *changing style/123   changes in
expectations versus changes in style/125   selection of
key subordinates/126   changing situational variables/
127*   Diagnosing the Environment—A Case/129   *anti-
Peter Principle vaccine/131*

7 managing for organizational effectiveness   133

Life Cycle Theory of Leadership/134   *maturity/134
parent-child relationship/135   management of research
and development personnel/138   educational setting and
life cycle theory/140*   The Influence of Cultural Change/
143   *span of control/144   narrow span at bottom/145
the role of the manager—a linking pin/146   two
responsibilities/146*   Summary/147

8   planning for change   149

Increasing Effectiveness/149   *breaking the ineffective
cycle/152*   Changing Maturity Through Behavior
Modification/152   Levels of Change/158   The Change
Cycles/159   *participative change/159   coerced change/
160*   Differences Between the Two Change Cycles/161
Change Process/161   *unfreezing/162   changing/162
refreezing/163   change process—some examples/164*
Managing Intergroup Conflict/167   *consequences of
group competition/167   preventing intergroup conflict/
168*   Impact of Change on Total System/169

9   management: a synthesis of theory   173

Life Cycle Theory of Leadership and Motivation/174
Life Cycle Theory of Leadership, Management Styles,
and the Nature of Man/175   Life Cycle Theory of
Leadership and Change/177   Conclusions/179

10   recommended supplementary reading   181

selected bibliography   183

index   201

preface

to the second edition

We appreciate the reaction to the first edition of *Management of Organizational Behavior*. It was our attempt to write a short, concise, easy-to-read text that would make the behavioral sciences "come alive" for practitioners and students alike. This goal seemed to be accomplished to the extent that the book was used in a variety of settings including psychology, sociology, political science, business, engineering, education, and agriculture as well as in training in industry, the military, and other professional organizations.

The emphasis in the first edition was on synthesizing significant behavioral findings into conceptual frameworks to help the manager understand why people behave as they do and to increase his effectiveness in predicting future behavior. In this second edition, while maintaining special attention on the diagnostic value of behavioral theory, we move more into how a manager can direct, change, and control behavior. Chapter 7, "Managing for Organizational Effectiveness," which has been thoroughly rewritten and expanded, and Chapter 8, "Planning for Change," one of three entirely new chapters, reflect this new emphasis.

This new edition also differs from the first in these ways: Chapter 2, "Motivation and Behavior," has been expanded to include more inputs on individual behavior with discussions on coping behavior, cognitive dissonance, and various expressions of frustration. Chapter 3, "Motivating Environment," now includes, among other things, a discussion of Homan's model of social systems. Chapter 4, "Leader Behavior," remains essentially the same, but Chapter 5, "Determining Effectiveness,' has been expanded significantly to include more material on sources of power, participation and effectiveness, what determines organizational effectiveness and a new section on force field analysis. Chapter 6, "Diagnosing the Environment," is a new chapter expanding the discussion of environmental variables and style adaptability presented in the first edition. As mentioned earlier, Chapter 7, "Managing for Organizational Effectiveness," has been essentially rewritten and now includes an extensive discussion of Life Cycle Theory of Leadership, an outgrowth of the Tri-Dimensional Leader Effectiveness Model presented in the first edition. Chapter 8, "Planning for Change," a totally new chapter, discusses the various kinds of change, the process of change, the implementation of change through behavior modification, the management of intergroup conflict, and the impact of change on the total system.

In Chapter 9, "Management: A Synthesis of Theory," the new concluding chapter, we make one final attempt to weave all the theories discussed in earlier chapters into a single integrated framework which will hopefully increase for the reader the usefulness of each. Two other changes might be worth mentioning. The footnotes in the second edition appear at the end of each chapter rather than at the end of the book. And in addition to the extensive bibliography, an authors' recommended reading list is provided for those interested in supplementing the text.

We hope this new edition is an improved book and better represents the present status of the behavioral sciences.

Our special thanks to colleagues, students, and practitioners, both on campus and in the field, who were helpful in providing feedback on the first edition.

PAUL HERSEY
KENNETH H. BLANCHARD

preface

to the first edition

For a long time management theory has been characterized by a search for universals—a preoccupation with discovering essential elements of all organizations. The discovering of common elements is necessary, but they do not really provide practitioners with "principles" that can be applied with universal success.

In the past decade there has appeared a relative maturity in this field as it begins to focus on "patterned variations"—situational differences. We assume that there are common elements in all organizations, but we also assume differences among them and in particular the managing of their human resources. As the inventory of empirical studies expands, making comparisons and contrasts possible, management theory will continue to emerge. Common elements will be isolated and important variables brought to light.

We believe that management theory is important to all categories of organizations—business, government, medicine, education, "voluntary" organizations such as the church, and even the home. We thus have drawn our illustrations and cases from a variety of these organizations and incorporated concepts from many disciplines. Our purpose is to identify a framework which may be helpful in integrating independent approaches from these various disciplines to the understanding of human behavior and management theory.

The focus of this book is on behavior within organizations and not between organizations. Our belief is that an organization is a unique living organism whose basic component is the individual and this individual is our fundamental unit of study. Thus, our concentration is on the interaction of people, motivation, and leadership.

Though this book is an outgrowth of the insights of many earlier writers, we hope it will make some contribution to management theory.

We owe much to colleagues and associates without whose guidance, encouragement, and inspiration this book would not have been written. In particular, we are indebted to Harry Evarts, Ted Hellebrandt, Dewey Johnson, Norman Martin, Don McCarty, Bob Melendes, Warren Ramshaw, and Franklin Williams.

We wish to make special mention of William J. Reddin, The University of New Brunswick, Fredericton, N.B., Canada, and Edgar H. Schein, The Massachusetts Institute of Technology. Their contributions to the field under discussion have been most valuable to us in the course of preparation of this book and we hereby express our appreciation to them.

Finally, we would like to thank our wives for their patience, support, and continued interest in the progress of this book.

management: a

behavioral approach

The transformation of American society since the turn of the century has been breathtaking. We have progressed from a basically agrarian society to a dynamic, industrial society with a higher level of education and standard of living than was ever thought possible. In addition, our scientific and technical advancement staggers the imagination.

This progress has not been without its "seamy side." At a time when we should be rejoicing in a golden age of plenty, we find ourselves wallowing in conflict—conflict between nations, conflict between races, conflict between management and workers, even conflict between neighbors. These problems that we face cannot be solved by scientific and technical skills alone; they will require social skills. Many of our most critical problems are not in the world of *things,* but in the world of *people.* Man's greatest failure has been his inability to secure cooperation and understanding with others. Shortly after World War II, Elton Mayo recognized this problem when he reflected that "the consequences for society of the unbalance between the development of technical and of social skill have been disastrous." [1]

SUCCESSFUL VERSUS UNSUCCESSFUL SCIENCES

In searching for reasons for this unbalance, Mayo suggested that a significant part of the problem might be traced to the difference between what he called "the successful sciences" (i.e., chemistry, physics, and physiology) and "the unsuccessful sciences" (i.e., psychology, sociology, and political science). He labeled the former "successful" because in studying these sciences, both theory and practice are provided. Pure knowledge is limited in value unless it can be applied in real situations. The implication of these profound conclusions is that in learning about chemistry or physics, a student or practitioner is given direct experience in using his new technical skills in the laboratory. But on the other hand, according to Mayo, the unsuccessful sciences

> do not seem to equip students with a single social skill that is usable in ordinary human situations . . . no continuous and direct contact with the social facts is contrived for the student. He learns from books, spending endless hours in libraries; he reconsiders ancient formulae, uncontrolled by the steady development of experimental skill, the equivalent of the clinic or indeed of the laboratory.[2]

change

Early contributions in the behavioral sciences, as Mayo suggests, seemed to provide knowledge without effecting changes in behavior. This book will focus on four levels of change in people: (1) knowledge changes, (2) attitudinal changes, (3) behavior changes, and (4) group or organizational performance changes.[3] The time relationship and the relative difficulty involved in making each of these levels of change are illustrated in Figure 1.1.

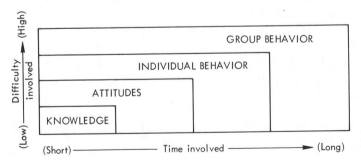

FIGURE 1.1 Time and difficulty involved in making various changes.

Changes in knowledge are the easiest to make, followed by changes in attitudes. Attitude structures differ from knowledge structures in that they are emotionally charged in a positive or a negative way. Changes in behavior are significantly more difficult and time consuming than either of the two previous levels. But the implementation of group or organizational performance change is perhaps the most difficult and time consuming. Man's destiny may in fact be dependent upon how well the behavioral sciences are able to resolve conflict through understanding and implementing change.

a problem of investment

A major obstacle to the practical application of the behavioral sciences has been the small amount of money allocated by government, business, and other agencies for research in these areas. In the United States only one of every thirty dollars spent on research and development is channeled to behavioral science areas. The remainder is spent for research in the "hard sciences" to be used in developing "things." However, more must be done than spend money on research in the behavioral sciences. Funds are also needed to support the practical application of this research. This is especially important since managers, to be effective, regardless of the type of organization in which they operate, need to develop know-how in human skills in addition to their knowledge of the technical aspects of their jobs.

MANAGEMENT DEFINED

It is obvious after a review of the literature that there are almost as many definitions of management as there are writers in the field. A common thread which appears in these definitions is the manager's concern for accomplishing organizational goals or objectives.[4] We shall define management as *working with and through individuals and groups to accomplish organizational goals.*

This definition, it should be noted, makes no mention of business or industrial organizations. Management, as defined, applies to organizations whether they are businesses, educational institutions, hospitals, political organizations, or even families. To be successful, these organizations require their management personnel to have interpersonal skills. The achievement of organizational objectives through leadership is management. Thus, everyone is a manager in at least certain portions of his life.

distinction between management and leadership

Management and leadership are often thought of as one and the same thing. We feel, however, that there is an important distinction between the two concepts.

In essence leadership is a broader concept than management. Management is thought of as a special kind of leadership in which the accomplishment of organizational goals is paramount. The key difference between the two concepts, therefore, lies in the word *organization*. While leadership also involves working with and through people to accomplish goals, these goals are not necessarily organizational goals. Many times an individual may attempt to accomplish his own personal goals with little concern for the organization's goals. Hence, one may be successful in accomplishing personal goals but may be ineffective in accomplishing organizational goals.

MANAGEMENT PROCESS

The managerial functions of *planning, organizing, motivating,* and *controlling* are considered central to a discussion of management by many authors. These functions are relevant, regardless of the type of organization or level of management with which one is concerned. As Harold Koontz and Cyril O'Donnell have said: "Acting in their managerial capacity, presidents, department heads, foremen, supervisors, college deans, bishops, and heads of governmental agencies all do the same thing." As managers they are all engaged in part in getting things done with and through people. As a manager, each must, at one time or another, carry out all the duties characteristic of managers." [5] Even a well-run household uses these managerial functions, although in many cases they are used intuitively.

Planning involves setting *goals* and *objectives* for the organization and developing "work maps" showing how these goals and objectives are to be accomplished. Once plans have been made, organizing becomes meaningful. This involves bringing together resources—people, capital, and equipment—in the most effective way to accomplish the goals. Organizing, therefore, involves an integration of resources.

Along with planning and organizing, motivating plays a large part in determining the level of performance of employees which, in turn, influences how effectively the organizational goals will be met. Motivating is sometimes included as part of directing along with communicating and leading.

In his research on motivation, William James of Harvard found that hourly employees could maintain their jobs, that is, not be fired, by working at approximately 20 to 30 percent of their ability. His study also showed that employees work at close to 80 to 90 percent of their ability if highly motivated. Both the minimum level at which employees might work and yet keep their jobs and the level at which they could be expected to perform with proper motivation are illustrated in Figure 1.2.

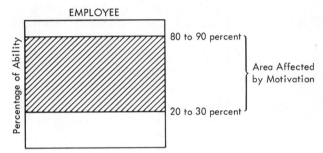

FIGURE 1.2   The potential influence of motivation on performance.

This illustration shows us that if motivation is low, employees' performance will suffer as much as if ability were low. For this reason, motivating is an extremely important function of management.

Another function of management is controlling. This involves feedback of results and follow-up to compare accomplishments with plans and to make appropriate adjustments where outcomes have deviated from expectations.

Even though these management functions are stated separately, and as presented seem to have a specific sequence, one must remember that they are interrelated, as illustrated in Figure 1.3. While these functions are interrelated, at any one time, one or more may be of primary importance.

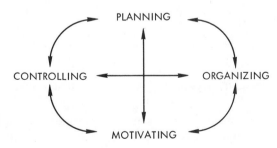

FIGURE 1.3   The process of management.

SKILLS OF A MANAGER

It is generally agreed that there are at least three areas of skill necessary for carrying out the process of management: technical, human, and conceptual.

> *Technical skill*—Ability to use knowledge, methods, techniques, and equipment necessary for the performance of specific tasks acquired from experience, education, and training.
> *Human skill*—Ability and judgment in working with and through people, including an understanding of motivation and an application of effective leadership.
> *Conceptual skill*—Ability to understand the complexities of the overall organization and where one's own operation fits into the organization. This knowledge permits one to act according to the objectives of the total organization rather than only on the basis of the goals and needs of one's own immediate group.[6]

The appropriate mix of these skills varies as an individual advances in management from supervisory to top management positions. This is illustrated in Figure 1.4.

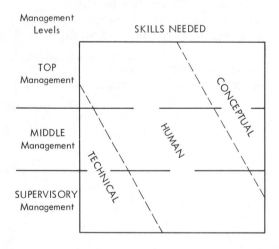

FIGURE 1.4   Management skills necessary at various levels of a business organization.

To be effective less technical skill tends to be needed as one advances from lower to higher levels in the organization, but more and more conceptual skill is necessary. Supervisors at lower levels need considerable technical skill because they are often required to train and develop technicians and other employees in their sections. At the other extreme, executives in a business organization do not need to know how to perform all the specific tasks at the operational level. However, they should be able to see how all these functions are interrelated in accomplishing the goals of the total organization.

While the amount of technical and conceptual skills needed at these different levels of management varies, *the common denominator that appears to be crucial at all levels is human skill.*

emphasis on human skills

The emphasis on human skills was considered important in the past, but it is of primary importance today. For example, one of the great entrepreneurs, John D. Rockefeller, stated: "I will pay more for the ability to deal with people than any other ability under the sun." [7] These words of Rockefeller are often echoed. According to a report by the American Management Association, an overwhelming majority of the two hundred managers who participated in a survey agreed that the most important single skill of an executive is his ability to get along with people.[8] In this survey, management rated this ability more vital than intelligence, decisiveness, knowledge, or job skills.

Since human skill involves working with and through other people, the main concern of this book will be to help the manager understand why people behave as they do and to increase his effectiveness in predicting future behavior and in directing, changing, and controlling behavior. Our intention is to provide a conceptual framework by which the reader can apply conclusions of the behavioral sciences while working with people in his own unique environment.

NOTES

1. Elton Mayo, *The Social Problems of an Industrial Civilization* (Boston: Harvard Business School, 1945), p. 23.
2. *Ibid.,* p. 20.
3. R. J. House discusses similar concepts in *Management Development: Design, Implementation and Evaluation* (Ann Arbor: Bureau of Industrial Relations, University of Michigan, 1967).
4. See as examples, Harold Koontz and Cyril O'Donnell, *Principles of Management,* 4th ed. (New York: McGraw-Hill Book Company, 1968); and William H. Newman, Charles E. Summer, and E. Kirby Warren, *The Process of Management* (Englewood Cliffs, N. J.: Prentice-Hall, Inc., 1967).
5. Koontz and O'Donnell, *Principles of Management,* p. 54.

6. These descriptions were adapted from a classification developed by Robert L. Katz, "Skills of an Effective Administrator," *Harvard Business Review,* January-February 1955, pp. 33–42.

7. John D. Rockefeller as quoted in Garret L. Bergen and William V. Haney, *Organizational Relations and Management Action* (New York: McGraw-Hill Book Company, 1966), p. 3.

8. Data as reported in Bergen and Haney, *Organizational Relations and Management Action.*

motivation

and behavior

The study of motivation and behavior is a search for answers to perplexing questions about the nature of man. Recognizing the importance of the human element in organizations, we will attempt in this chapter to develop a theoretical framework that may help managers to understand human behavior, not only to determine the "whys" of past behavior but to some extent to predict, to change, and even to control future behavior.

BEHAVIOR

Behavior is basically goal-oriented. In other words, our behavior is generally motivated by a desire to attain some goal. The specific goal is not always consciously known by the individual. All of us wonder many times, "Why did I do that?" The reason for our action is not always apparent to the conscious mind. The drives that motivate distinctive

9

individual behavioral patterns ("personality") are to a considerable degree subconscious and therefore not easily susceptible to examination and evaluation.

Sigmund Freud was one of the first to recognize the importance of subconscious motivation. He believed that people are not always aware of everything they want, and hence much of their behavior is affected by subconscious motives or needs. In fact, Freud's research convinced him that an analogy could be drawn between the motivation of most people and the structure of an iceberg. A significant segment of human motivation appears. below the surface where it is not always evident to the individual. Therefore, many times only a small portion of motivation is clearly visible or conscious to the individual himself.[1] This may be due to a lack of effort by individuals to gain self-insight. Yet, even with professional help, for example, psychotherapy, understanding oneself may be a difficult process yielding varying degrees of success.

The basic unit of behavior is an *activity*. In fact, all behavior is a series of activities. As human beings we are always doing something: walking, talking, eating, sleeping, working, and the like. In many instances we are doing more than one activity at a time, such as talking with someone as we walk or drive to work. At any given moment we may decide to change from one activity or combination of activities and begin to do something else. This raises some important questions. Why does a person engage in one activity and not another? Why does he change activities? How can we as managers understand, predict, and even control what activity or activities a person may engage in at a given moment in time? To predict behavior, managers must know which motives or needs of people evoke a certain action at a particular time.

motives

People differ not only in their ability to do but also in their "will to do," or *motivation*. The motivation of a person depends on the strength of his motives. *Motives* are sometimes defined as needs, wants, drives, or impulses within the individual. Motives are directed toward goals, which may be conscious or subconscious.

Motives are the "whys" of behavior. They arouse and maintain activity and determine the general direction of the behavior of an individual. In essence, motives, or needs, are the mainsprings of action. In our discussions we shall use these two terms—motives and needs—interchangeably. In this context, the term *need* should *not* be associated with urgency or any pressing desire for something. It simply means something within an individual that prompts him to action.

goals

Goals are *outside* an individual; they are sometimes referred to as "hoped for" rewards toward which motives are directed. These goals are often called *incentives* by psychologists. However, we prefer not to use this term since many people in our society tend to equate incentives with tangible financial rewards, such as increased pay, and yet most of us would agree that there are many intangible rewards, such as praise or power, which are just as important in evoking behavior. Managers who are successful in motivating employees are often providing an environment in which appropriate goals (incentives) are available for need satisfaction.

FIGURE 2.1   Motives are directed toward goals.

motive strength

We have said that motives, or needs, are the reasons underlying behavior. Every individual has many hundreds of needs. All of these needs compete for his behavior. What, then, determines which of these motives a person will attempt to satisfy through activity? The need with the *greatest strength* at a particular moment in time leads to activity, as illustrated in Figure 2.2. Satisfied needs decrease in strength and normally do not motivate individuals to seek goals to satisfy them.

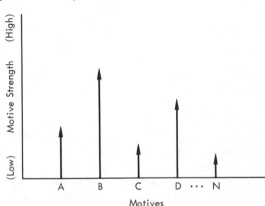

FIGURE 2.2   The most prepotent motive determines behavior (Motive B in this illustration).

In this illustration Motive B is the highest strength need and therefore it is this need that determines behavior. What can happen to change this situation?

changes in motive strength

A motive tends to decrease in strength if it is either satisfied or blocked from satisfaction.

NEED SATISFACTION.   When a need is satisfied, according to Abraham Maslow, it is no longer a motivator of behavior.[2] High strength needs that are satisfied are sometimes referred to as "satisfied," that is, the need has been satisfied to the extent that some competing need is now more potent. If a high strength need is thirst, drinking tends to lower the strength of this need and other needs may now become more important.

BLOCKING NEED SATISFACTION.   The satisfaction of a need may be blocked. While a reduction in need strength sometimes follows, it does not always occur initially. Instead, there may be a tendency for the person to engage in *coping behavior*. This is an attempt to overcome the obstacle by trial-and-error problem solving. The person may try a variety of behaviors to find one that will accomplish his goal or will reduce tension created by blockage, as illustrated in Figure 2.3.

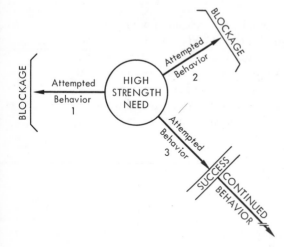

FIGURE 2.3   Coping behavior when blockage occurs in attempting to accomplish a *particular goal*.

Initially this coping behavior may be quite rational. Perhaps the person may even make several attempts in direction 1 before going to 2, and the same in direction 2 before moving in direction 3 where some degree of success and goal attainment are finally perceived.

If the person continues to strive for something with no success, he may substitute goals that can satisfy the need. For example, if a boy has a strong desire to play varsity basketball in high school but is continually cut from the squad, he may eventually be willing to settle for playing in the city recreation league.

COGNITIVE DISSONANCE.   Blocked motives and continually unsuccessful rational coping behavior may lead to forms of irrational coping behavior. Leon Festinger analyzes this phenomenon.[3] His theory of cognitive dissonance deals primarily with the relationships that exist between perceptions one has about himself and his environment. When individual perceptions have nothing to do with each other, they are considered irrelevant to each other. If one supports the other, they are said to be in a consonant relationship. Dissonance is created when two perceptions that are relevant to each other are in conflict. This creates tension which is psychologically uncomfortable and causes the individual to try to modify one of the incompatible knowledges so as to reduce the tension or dissonance. In a sense, he engages in coping behavior to regain a condition of consonance or equilibrium. For example, Festinger has done research that shows that "heavy smokers are less likely to believe that there is a relationship between smoking and lung cancer than non-smokers."[4] In other words, if one cannot give up smoking, he can at least remain skeptical about research that reports harmful effects. The same phenomenon is at work when a person goes out, fishes all day, doesn't catch anything, and remarks about the beautiful weather.

FRUSTRATION.   The blocking or thwarting of goal-attainment is referred to as *frustration*. This phenomenon is defined in terms of the condition of the individual, rather than in terms of the external environment. A person may be frustrated by an imaginary barrier and may fail to be frustrated by a real barrier.

As previously discussed, rational coping behavior can lead to alternative goal setting or decreasing need strength. Irrational behavior may occur in several forms when blockage to goal accomplishment continues and frustration develops. Frustration may increase to the extent that the individual engages in aggressive behavior. *Aggression* can lead to destructive behavior such as hostility and striking out. Freud was one of the first to demonstrate that hostility or rage can be exhibited by an individual in a variety of ways.[5] If possible, the individual will direct his hostility against the object or the person that he feels is the cause of frustration. The angry worker may try to hit his boss or may undermine his job and reputation through gossip and other malicious behavior. Often, though, a person cannot attack the cause of his frustration directly, and he may look for a "scapegoat" as a target for his hostility. For example, a worker may fear his boss because the boss holds his fate in his hands. In this case, "the resentful worker may pick a quarrel with his wife, kick the cat, beat his children, or, more constructively, work off his feelings by chopping wood, by cursing, and swearing, or engaging in violent exercises or horse-play of an aggressive nature." [6]

As Norman R. F. Maier has said, aggression is only one way in which frustration can be shown.[7] Other forms of frustrated behavior, such as rationalization, regression, fixation, and resignation, may develop if pressures continue and increase.

Rationalization simply means making excuses. For example, an individual might blame someone else for his inability to accomplish a given goal—"It was my boss's fault that I didn't get a raise." Or he talks himself out of the desirability of that particular goal—"I didn't want to do that anyway."

Regression is essentially not acting one's age. "Frustrated people tend to give up constructive attempts at solving their problems and regress to more primitive and childish behavior." [8] A person who cannot start his car and proceeds to kick it is demonstrating regressive behavior, and so is a manager who throws a temper tantrum when he is annoyed and frustrated. Barker, Dembo, and Lewin have shown experimentally that when children are exposed to mild frustration their play may resemble that of a child two or more years younger.[9]

Fixation occurs when a person continues to exhibit the same behavior pattern over and over again, although experience has shown that it can accomplish nothing. Thus, "frustration can freeze old and habitual responses and prevent the use of new and more effectual ones." [10] Maier has shown that although habits are normally broken when they bring no satisfaction or lead to punishment, a fixation actually becomes stronger under these circumstances.[11] In fact, he argued that it is possible to change a habit into a fixation by too much punishment. This phenomenon is seen in children who blindly continue to behave objectionably after being severely punished. Thus Maier concluded that punishment can have two effects on behavior. It may either eliminate the undesirable behavior or lead to fixation and other symptoms of frustration as well. It follows that punishment may be a dangerous management tool, since its effects are difficult to predict. According to J. A. C. Brown, common symptoms of fixation in industry are "the inability to accept change, the blind and stubborn refusal to accept new facts when experience has shown the old ones to be untenable, and the type of behavior exemplified by the manager who continues to increase penalties" even when this is only making conditions worse.[12]

Resignation or apathy occurs after prolonged frustration when a person loses hope of accomplishing his goal(s) in a particular situation and wants to withdraw from reality and the source of his frustration. This phenomenon is characteristic of people in boring, routine jobs where often they resign themselves to the fact that there is little hope for improvement within their environments.

A manager should remember that aggression, rationalization, regression, fixation, and resignation are all symptoms of frustration and may be indications that problems exist.

INCREASING MOTIVE STRENGTH. Behavior may change if an existing need increases in strength to the extent that it is now the high strength motive. The strength of some needs tends to appear in a cyclical pattern. For example, the need for food tends to recur regardless of how well it has been satisfied at a given movement. One can increase or delay the speed of this cyclical pattern by affecting the environment. For example, a person's need for food may not be high strength unless his immediate environment is changed such that his senses are exposed to the sight and the aroma of tempting food.

A person has a variety of needs at any given time. He may be hungry, thirsty, and tired, but the need with the highest strength will determine what he does. For example, he may eat, drink, and sleep, in that order, as shown in Figure 2.4.[13] All of these tend to be cyclical over time.

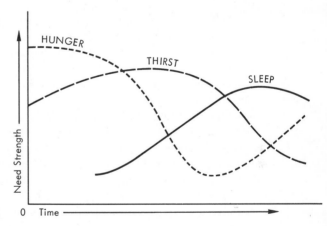

FIGURE 2.4 Multiple needs.

CATEGORIES OF ACTIVITIES

Activities resulting from high strength needs can generally be classified into two categories—goal-directed activity and goal activity. These concepts are important to practitioners because of their differing influence on need strength which can be useful in understanding human behavior.

Goal-directed activity, in essence, is motivated behavior directed at reaching a goal. If one's strongest need at a given moment is hunger, various activities such as looking for a place to eat, buying food, or preparing food would be considered goal-directed activities. On the other hand, *goal activity* is engaging in the goal itself. In the case of hunger, food is the goal and eating, therefore, is the goal activity.

An important distinction between these two classes of activities is their effect on the strength of the need. In goal-directed activity, the strength of the need tends to increase as one engages in the activity until goal behavior is reached or frustration sets in. As discussed earlier, frustration develops when one is continually blocked from reaching a goal. If the frustration becomes intense enough, the strength of the need for that goal may decrease until it is no longer potent enough to affect behavior—a person gives up.

The strength of the need tends to increase as one engages in goal-directed activity; however, once goal activity begins, the strength of the need tends to decrease as one engages in it. For example, as one eats more and more, the strength of the need for food declines for that particular time. At the point when another need becomes more potent than the present need, behavior changes.

On Thanksgiving Day, for example, as food is being prepared all morning (goal-directed activity), the need for food increases to the point of almost not being able to wait until the meal is on the table. As we begin to eat (goal activity), the strength of this need diminishes to the point where other needs become more important. As we leave the table, our need for food seems to be well satisfied. Our activity changes to that of watching football. This need for passive recreation has now become most potent, and we find ourselves in front of the television set. But gradually this need decreases, too. After several games, even though the competition is fierce, the need for passive recreation may also decline to the extent that other needs become more important—perhaps the need for fresh air and a walk, or better still, another piece of pumpkin pie. Several hours before we had sworn not to eat for a week, but now that pie looks very good. So once again hunger is the strongest need. Thus, it should be remembered that we never completely satiate a need. We satisfy it for only a period of time.

MOTIVATING SITUATION

The relationship between motives, goals, and activity can be shown in a simplified fashion, as illustrated in Figure 2.5.

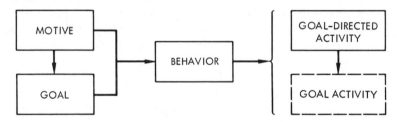

FIGURE 2.5   A motivating situation.

This schematic illustration shows a *motivating situation* in which the motives of an individual are directed toward goal attainment. The strongest motive produces behavior that is either goal-directed or goal activity. Since all goals are not attainable, individuals do not always reach goal activity, regardless of the strength of the motive. Thus goal activity is indicated by a dashed line.

An example of a tangible goal being used to influence behavior is illustrated in Figure 2.6.

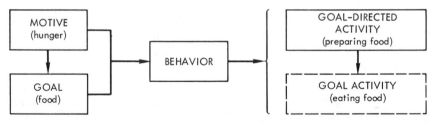

FIGURE 2.6   Use of a tangible incentive in a motivating situation.

With a broad goal such as food, it should be recognized that the type of food that satisfies the hunger motive varies from situation to situation. If an individual is starving he may eat anything, while at other times he may realign his goals and only a steak will satisfy his hunger motive.

A similar illustration could be given for an intangible goal. If an individual has a need for recognition—a need to be viewed as a contributing, productive person—praise is one incentive that will help satisfy this need. In a work situation, if the individual's need for recognition is strong enough, being praised by his manager or supervisor may be an effective incentive in influencing him to continue to do good work.

In analyzing these two examples, it should be remembered that if an individual wants to influence another person's behavior, he must first understand what motives or needs are most important to that person at that time. A goal, to be effective, must be appropriate to the need structure of the person involved.

A question that may be considered at this point is whether it is better to engage in goal-directed activity or in goal activity. Actually, maintenance at either level exclusively creates problems. If one stays at goal-directed activity too long, frustration will occur to the extent that the person may give up or other patterns of irrational behavior may be evoked. On the·other hand, if one engages exclusively in goal activity and the goal is not challenging, a lack of interest and apathy will develop, with motivation again tending to decrease. A more appropriate and effective pattern might be a continuous cycling function between goal-directed activity and goal activity.

FIGURE 2.7   Cycling function of goal-directed activity and goal activity.

What is an appropriate goal for a six-year-old may not be a meaningful goal for the same child when he is seven. Once he becomes proficient in attaining a particular goal, it becomes appropriate for the parent to provide an opportunity for the child to evaluate and set new goals. In the same light, what is an appropriate goal for a new employee may not be meaningful for an employee who has been with a corporation six months or a year. There may also be distinctions between employees who have been with an employer for only a few years and those who have been with him for longer periods of time.

This cycling process between goal-directed activity and goal activity is a continuous challenge for the parent or the manager. As employees increase in their ability to accomplish goals, it is appropriate that the superior reevaluate and provide an environment allowing continual realignment of goals and an opportunity for growth and development. The learning and developing process is not a phenomenon that should be confined to only one stage of a person's life. In this process, the role of a superior is not always that of setting goals for his followers. Instead, effectiveness may be increased by providing an environment where subordinates can play a role in setting their own goals. Research indicates that commitment increases when a person is involved in his own goal setting. If an individual is involved, he will tend to engage in much more goal-directed activity before he becomes frustrated and gives up. On the other hand, if the boss sets the goals for him, he is apt to give up more easily because he perceives these as his boss's goals and not as his own. Goals should be set high enough so that a person has to stretch to reach them, but low enough so that they can be attained. So often final goals are set, and the person is judged only in terms of success in relation to this terminal goal. For example, a student is doing poorly in school and his parents want him to raise his marks to a *B* average. Suppose that after the first semester he gets only *C*'s. The result is usually that the parents reprimand him; if this continues to occur there is a high probability that he may stop trying. His grades, instead of improving, may get worse. An alternative for the parents is setting interim goals—realistic goals that move in the direction of the final goals as they are attained. Now with a change in the desired direction, even though only moderate, positive reinforcement may be used rather than "zapping."

EXPECTANCY AND AVAILABILITY

We have already discussed the strength of needs. Two important factors that affect need strength are expectancy and availability. While these two concepts are interrelated, expectancy tends to affect motives, or needs, and availability tends to affect the perception of goals.

Expectancy is the perceived probability of satisfying a particular need of an individual based on his past experience. While expectancy is the technical term used by psychologists, it refers directly to the sum of the past experience. Experience can be either actual or vicarious. Vicarious experience comes from sources the person considers legitimate, such as parents, peer group, teachers, and books or periodicals. To illustrate the effect that past experience can have on behavior, let us look at an example. Suppose a boy's father was a basketball star and the boy wants to follow in his footsteps. Initially his expectancy may be high, and therefore the strength of the need is high. If he is cut from the eighth-grade team, it is difficult to determine whether this failure will discourage the boy. Since a single failure is usually not enough to discourage a person (in fact, it sometimes results in increased activity), little change in his expectancy is anticipated. But if he continues to get cut from the team year after year, eventually this motive will no longer be as strong or of such high priority. In fact, after enough unsuccessful experiences, he may completely give up on his goal.

Availability reflects the perceived limitations of the environment. It is determined by how accessible the goals that can satisfy a given need are perceived by an individual. For example, if the electricity goes off in a storm, one cannot watch television or read. These goal activities are no longer possible because of the limitations of the environment. One may have a high desire to read, but if there is no suitable substitute for the type of illumination required, he will soon be frustrated in his attempts to satisfy this desire and will settle for something else, like sleeping.

Consequently, availability is an environmental variable. Yet it should be stressed that it is not important whether the goals to satisfy a need are really available. It is the perception, or the interpretation of reality, that affects one's actual behavior. In other words, reality is what a person perceives.

An example of how perception can affect behavior was dramatically illustrated in an experiment with a fish. A pike was placed in an aquarium with many minnows swimming around him. After the fish became accustomed to the plentiful supply of food, a sheet of glass was placed between the pike and minnows. When the pike became hungry he tried to reach the minnows, but he continually hit his head on the glass. At first the strength of the need for food increased, and the pike tried harder than ever to get the minnows. But finally, his repeated failure of goal attainment resulted in enough frustration that he no longer attempted to eat the minnows. In fact, when the glass partition was finally removed, the minnows again swam all around the pike; but no further goal-directed activity took place. Eventually, the pike died of starvation while in the midst of plenty of food. In both cases, the fish operated according to the way he perceived reality and not on the basis of reality itself.

The expanded diagram of a motivating situation including expectancy and availability is presented in Figure 2.8.

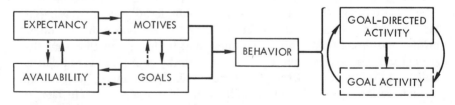

FIGURE 2.8   Expanded diagram of a motivating situation.

Motives, needs within an individual, are directed toward goals which are aspirations in the environment. These are interpreted by the individual as being available or unavailable. This affects expectancy. If expectancy is high, motive strength will increase. This tends to be a cyclical pattern moving in the direction of the prominent arrows. But to some extent these are interacting variables indicated by the secondary arrows. For example, experience may affect the way we perceive our feelings of availability. The presence of goals in the environment may affect the given strength of motives, and so forth.

PERSONALITY DEVELOPMENT

As an individual matures he develops habit patterns, or conditioned responses, to various stimuli. The sum of these habit patterns as perceived by others determines his *personality.*

habit *a,* habit *b,* habit *c,* . . . , habit *n* = *personality*

As an individual begins to behave in a similar fashion under similar conditions, this behavior is what others learn to recognize as that person, as his personality. They expect and can even predict certain kinds of behavior from him.

changing personality

Many psychologists contend that basic personality structures are developed quite early in life. In fact, some claim that few personality changes can be made after age seven or eight. Using a model similar to the one appearing in Figure 2.8, we can begin to understand why it tends

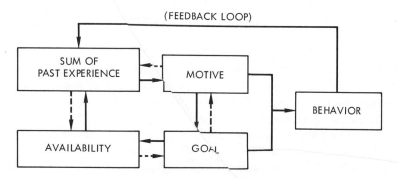

Figure 2.9   Feedback model.

to become more difficult to make changes in personality as people grow older.

Note that in this model we are using *sum of past experience* in place of the term *expectancy* used in the earlier model. These can be used interchangeably.

When a person behaves in a motivating situation, that behavior becomes a new input to his inventory of past experience, as the feedback loop in Figure 2.9 indicates. The earlier in life that this input occurs, the greater its potential effect on future behavior. The reason is that, early in life, this behavior represents a larger portion of the total past experience of a young person than the same behavior input will later in life. In addition, the longer behavior is reinforced, the more patterned it becomes and the more difficult it is to change. That is why it is easier to make personality changes early in life. The older a person gets, the more time and new experiences are necessary to effect a change in behavior.

While it is possible to change behavior in older people, it will be difficult to accomplish except over a long period of time under conducive conditions. It almost becomes a matter of economics—allocating limited resources in terms of unlimited human wants—how much we are willing to invest in implementing such a change. Not only may it be less expensive in terms of time necessary for training, but the potential payback period for younger people is much greater. An illustration might be helpful. Putting one new input, a drop of red coloring, into a half-pint bottle of clear liquid may be enough to change drastically the appearance of the total contents. Adding the same input, a drop of red coloring, to a gallon jug may make little, if any, noticeable change in its appearance to others. This example illustrates the relationship between the amount of past experience and the effect of any one new experience.

HIERARCHY OF NEEDS

We have argued that the behavior of an individual at a particular moment is usually determined by his strongest need. It would seem significant, therefore, for managers to have some understanding about the needs that are commonly most important to people.

An interesting framework that helps explain the strength of certain needs was developed by Abraham Maslow.[14] According to Maslow, there seems to be a hierarchy into which human needs arrange themselves, as illustrated in Figure 2.10.

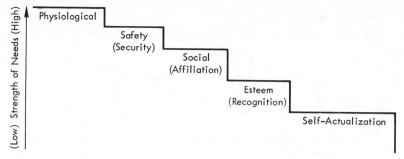

FIGURE 2.10   Maslow's hierarchy of needs.

The *physiological* needs are shown at the top of the hierarchy because they tend to have the highest strength until they are somewhat satisfied. These are the basic human needs to sustain life itself—food, clothing, shelter. Until these basic needs are satisfied to the degree needed for the sufficient operation of the body, the majority of a person's activity will probably be at this level, and the other levels will provide him with little motivation.

But what happens to a man's motivation when these basic needs begin to be fulfilled? Rather than physiological needs, other levels of needs become important and these motivate and dominate the behavior of the individual. And when these needs are somewhat satiated, other needs emerge, and so on down the hierarchy.

Once physiological needs become gratified the *safety,* or *security* needs become predominant, as illustrated in Figure 2.11. These needs are essentially the need to be free of the fear of physical danger and deprivation of the basic physiological needs. In other words, this is a need for self-preservation. In addition to the here and now, there is a concern for the future. Will an individual be able to maintain his property and/or job so he can provide food and shelter tomorrow and the next day? If a man's safety or security is in danger, other things seem unimportant.

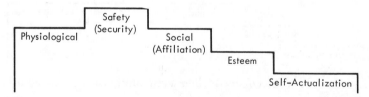

FIGURE 2.11   Safety need when dominant in the need structure.

Once physiological and safety needs are fairly well satisfied, *social* or *affiliation* will emerge as dominant in the need structure, as illustrated in Figure 2.12. Since man is a social being, he has a need to belong and to

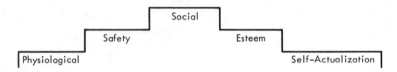

FIGURE 2.12   Social need when dominant in the need structure.

be accepted by various groups. When social needs become dominant a person will strive for meaningful relations with others.

After an individual begins to satisfy his need to belong, he generally wants to be more than just a member of his group. He then feels the need for *esteem*—both self-esteem and recognition from others. Most people have a need for a high evaluation of themselves that is firmly based in reality—recognition and respect from others. Satisfaction of these esteem needs produces feelings of self-confidence, prestige, power, and control. One begins to feel that he is useful and has some effect on his environment. There are other occasions, though, when persons are unable to satisfy their need for esteem through constructive behavior. When this need is dominant an individual may resort to disruptive or immature behavior to satisfy his desire for attention—a child may throw a temper tantrum, an employee may engage in work restriction or arguments with his co-workers or boss. Thus, recognition is not always obtained through mature or adaptive behavior. It is sometimes garnered by disruptive and irresponsible actions. In fact, some of the social problems we have today may have their roots in the frustration of esteem needs.

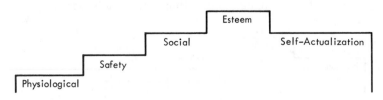

FIGURE 2.13   Esteem need when dominant in the need structure.

Once esteem needs begin to be adequately satisfied, the *self-actualization* needs become more prepotent, as shown in Figure 2.14. Self-actualization is the need to maximize one's potential, whatever it may be: A musician must play music, a poet must write, a general must win battles, a professor must teach. As Maslow expressed it, "What a man *can* be, he *must* be." Thus self-actualization is the desire to become what one is capable of becoming. Individuals satisfy this need in different ways. In one person it may be expressed in the desire to be an ideal mother; in another it may be expressed in managing an organization; in another it may be expressed athletically; in still another, by playing the piano.

In combat, a soldier may put his life on the line and rush a machine-gun nest in an attempt to destroy it, knowing full well that his chances for survival are low. He is not doing it for affiliation or recognition, but rather for what he thinks is important. In this case, you may consider the soldier to have self-actualized—to be maximizing the potential of what is important to him.

The way self-actualization is expressed can change over the life cycle. For example, the self-actualized athlete may eventually look for other areas in which to maximize his potential as his physical attributes change over time or as his horizons broaden. In addition, the hierarchy does not necessarily follow the pattern described by Maslow. It was not his intent to say that this hierarchy applies universally. Maslow felt this was a *typical* pattern that operates most of the time. He realized, however, that there were numerous exceptions to this general tendency. For example, the late Indian leader, Mahatma Gandhi, frequently sacrificed his physiological and safety needs for the satisfaction of other needs when India was striving for independence from Great Britain. In his historical fasts, Gandhi went weeks without nourishment to protest governmental injustices. He was operating at the self-actualization level while some of his other needs were unsatisfied.

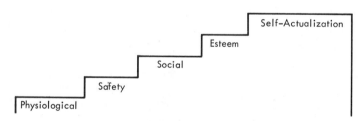

FIGURE 2.14 Self-actualization needs when dominant in the need structure.

In discussing the preponderance of one category of need over another, we have been careful to speak in such terms as "if one level of needs has been somewhat gratified, then other needs emerge as dominant." This was done because we did not want to give the impression that one level of needs has to be completely satisfied before the next level emerges as the most important. In reality, most people in our society tend to be partially satisfied at each level and partially unsatisfied, with greater satisfaction tending to occur at the physiological and safety levels than at the social, esteem, and self-actualization levels. For example, people in an emerging society where much of the behavior engaged in tends to be directed toward satisfying physiological and safety needs still operate to some extent at other levels. Therefore Maslow's hierarchy of needs is not intended to be an all-or-none framework, but rather one that may be useful in predicting behavior on a high or a low probability basis. Figure 2.15 attempts to portray how people in an emerging nation may be categorized.

FIGURE 2.15   Need mix when physiological and safety needs are high strength.

Many people in our own society at this time might be characterized by very strong social, or affiliation needs, relatively strong esteem and safety needs, with self-actualization and physiological needs somewhat less important, as shown in Figure 2.16.

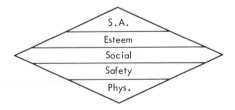

FIGURE 2.16   Need mix when social needs are high strength and self-actualization and physiological needs are less important.

Some people, however, can be characterized as having satisfied to a large extent the physiological, safety, and social needs, and their behavior tends to be dominated by esteem and self-actualizing activities, as shown in Figure 2.17. This will tend to become more characteristic if standards of living and levels of education continue to rise.

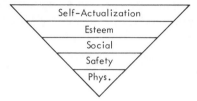

FIGURE 2.17 Need mix when esteem and self-actualization needs are high strength.

These are intended only as examples. For different individuals, varying configurations may be appropriate. In reality they would fluctuate tremendously from one individual or group to another.

MOTIVATIONAL RESEARCH

Having discussed Maslow's hierarchy of needs, we can now examine what researchers say about some of our motives and the incentives that tend to satisfy them.

physiological needs

The satisfaction of physiological needs (shelter, food, clothing) is usually associated in our society with *money*. It is obvious that most people are not interested in dollars as such, but only as a means to be used to satisfy other motives. Thus, it is what money can buy, not money itself, that satisfies one's physiological needs. To suggest that money as a tool is useful *only* to satisfy physiological needs would be shortsighted because money can play a role in the satisfaction of needs at every level. Extensive studies of the impact of money have found that money is so complicated an incentive that it is entangled with all kinds of needs besides physiological ones, and its importance is difficult to ascertain. Consequently, we will discuss the money motive in a separate section later in the chapter. It is clear, however, that the ability of a given amount of money to satisfy *seems* to diminish as one moves from physiological and safety needs to other needs on the hierarchy. In many cases, money can buy the satisfaction of physiological and safety needs and even social needs, if, for example, it provides entry into a desired group, such as a country club. But as one becomes concerned about esteem, recognition, and eventually self-actualization, money becomes a less-appropriate tool to satisfy these needs and, therefore, less effective. The more an individual becomes involved with esteem and self-actualization needs, the more he will have to earn his satisfaction directly, and thus the less important money will be in their attainment.

safety (security)

We mentioned earlier that motives are not always apparent to the individual. Although some motives appear above the surface, many are largely subconscious and are not obvious or easy to identify. According to Saul W. Gellerman, security needs appear in both forms.[15]

The conscious security needs are quite evident and very common among most people. We all have a desire to remain free from the hazards of life—accidents, wars, diseases, and economic instability. Therefore, individuals and organizations are interested in providing some assurance that these catastrophes will be avoided if possible. Gellerman suggests that many organizations tend to overemphasize the security motive by providing elaborate programs of fringe benefits, such as health, accident, and life insurance and retirement plans. While such emphasis on security may make people more docile and predictable, it does not mean they will be more productive. In fact, if creativity or initiative is necessary in their jobs, an overemphasis on security can thwart desired behavior.

While concern for security can affect major decisions, such as remaining in or leaving an organization, Gellerman indicates it is not likely to be an individual's dominant motive. Conscious security needs usually play a background role, often inhibiting or restraining impulses rather than initiating outward behavior. For example, if a particular course of action, such as disregarding a rule or expressing an unpopular position, might endanger one's job, then security considerations motivate a person *not* to take this course of action. Organizations can influence these security needs either positively—through pension plans, insurance programs, and the like—or negatively by arousing fears of being fired or laid off, demoted, or passed over. In both cases, the effect can be to make behavior too cautious and conservative.

Peter F. Drucker suggests that one's attitude toward security is important to consider in choosing a job.[16] He raises some interesting questions: Do you belong in a job calling primarily for faithfulness in the performance of routine work and promising security? Do you find real satisfaction in the precision, order, and system of a clearly laid out job? Do you prefer the security not only of knowing what your work is today and what it is going to be tomorrow, but also security in your job, in your relationship to the people above, below, and next to you? Or do you belong in a job that offers a challenge to imagination and ingenuity—with the attendant penalty for failure? Are you one of those people who tend to grow impatient with anything that looks like a "routine" job? The answers to these questions are not always easy even though we all understand ourselves to some degree. But the answers are involved with how important the security motive is for that particular individual.

To reiterate, security needs can be conscious or subconscious. A strong subconscious orientation toward security is often developed early in childhood. Gellerman discusses several ways in which it can be implanted. A common way is through identification with security-minded parents who are willing to accept whatever fate comes along. This often occurs in depressed economic areas where the prospects for improvement are poor.[17]

The world seems uncertain and uncontrollable to people raised in a security-minded home. As a result, such people may not feel they are competent enough to be able to influence their environment.

The security-minded person we have been describing is often very likable. He is not competitive and, therefore, does not put people on the defense. Others tend to expect little of him and thus are seldom critical of his work. This, combined with the fact that he is pleasant to have around, often enables him to obtain a secure, nonthreatening position in an organization.

Subconscious security motives may also develop in a child through interaction with overprotective parents. Such parents are constantly trying to shield their children from heartache, disappointment, or failure. The supportive attitude of these parents in many instances permits their children to have their own way. Conflict is avoided at all costs. As a result, the child is given a distorted picture of reality and gains little insight into what he can expect of other people and what they will expect of him. In some cases, he becomes unrealistic in his optimism about life. Even in the face of disaster, when he should be threatened, he seems to believe that all is well until too late.

When this type of security-minded person leaves home after high school to seek his way in the world, he quickly wakes up to reality. Often he finds himself unequipped to handle the hardships of life because he has *not* been permitted the opportunity to develop the capacity to handle frustration, tension, and anxiety. As a result, even a minor setback may throw him for a loss. Drucker suggests that getting fired from their first job might be the best thing that could happen to such young people. He feels that getting fired from the first job is the least painful and least damaging way to learn how to take a setback and that this is a lesson well worth learning. If a person learns how to recover from seeming disaster when he is young, he will be better equipped to handle worse fate as he gets older.

To many people, the security motive carries with it a negative connotation. A strong security need is frowned upon, for some reason, as if it were less respectable than other motives. This seems unjust, especially since nearly everyone has some conscious and subconscious security motives. Life is never so simple or clear-cut that one does not maintain some concern for security. In addition, many segments of our society often cater to these needs to the exclusion of such important needs as affiliation and self-actualization. We have already mentioned how industry concentrates on security needs by providing elaborate fringe benefits. Unions have a similar effect with their emphasis on seniority, and the government does much the same thing with welfare and other similar support programs.

social (affiliation)

After the physiological and safety needs have become somewhat satisfied, the social needs may become predominant. Since man is a social animal, most people like to interact and be with others in situations where they feel they belong and are accepted. While this is a common need, it tends to be stronger for some people than for others and stronger in certain situations. In other words, even such a commonplace social need as belongingness is, upon examination, quite complex.

In working toward a better understanding of our need to belong, Stanley Schachter of the University of Minnesota has made a significant contribution.[18] His efforts, in particular, have been directed toward studying the desire to socialize as an end in itself—that is, when people interact simply because they enjoy it. In some of these situations no apparent reward such as money or protection was gained from this affiliation.

Schachter found that it was not always simply good fellowship that motivated affiliation. In many instances, people seek affiliation because they desire to have their beliefs confirmed. People who have similar beliefs tend to seek each other out, especially if a strongly held belief has been shattered. In this case, they tend to assemble and try to reach some common understanding about what happened and what they should believe (even if it is the same as before). In this instance, the need for affiliation was prompted by a desire to make one's life *seem* a little more under control. When alone, the world seems "out of whack," but if one can find an environment where others hold the same beliefs, it somehow makes order out of chaos. This attitude hints at some of the problems inherent in any change.

In pursuing this question further, it was found that when people are excited, confused, or unhappy, they do not just seek out anyone, they tend to want to be with others "in the same boat." Misery does not just love company, it loves other miserable company. These conclusions suggest that the strong informal work groups that Elton Mayo found developing in the factory system might have been a reaction to the boredom, insignificance, and lack of competence that the workers felt.[19] As a result, workers congregated because of mutual feelings of being beaten by the system.

In observing "loners" and "rate-busters" in similar factory situations, it became apparent that there is not some universal need for affiliation as an end in itself. It was found, however, that these exceptions to the affiliation tendency were special types of people. They tended not to join informal work groups because they felt either suspicious or contemptuous of them, or secure and competent enough to fend for themselves.

Management is often suspicious of informal groups that develop at work because of the potential power these groups have to lower productivity. Schachter found that such work-restricting groups were sometimes formed as a reaction to the insignificance and impotence that workers tend to feel when they have no control over their working environment. Such environments develop where the work is routine, tedious, and oversimplified. This situation is made worse when, at the same time, the workers are closely supervised and controlled but have no clear channels of communication with management.

In this type of environment, workers who cannot tolerate this lack of control over their environment depend on the informal group for support of unfulfilled needs such as affiliation or achievement. Work restriction follows not from an inherent dislike for management, but as a means to preserve the identification of individuals within the group and the group itself. Rate-busters are not tolerated because they weaken the group and its power with management, and to weaken the group destroys the only dignity, security, and significance the worker feels he has.

Lowering productivity is not always the result of informal work groups. In fact, informal groups can be a tremendous asset to management if their internal organization is understood and fully utilized. The productivity of a work group seems to depend on how the group members see their own goals in relation to the goals of the organization. For example, if they perceive their own goals as being in conflict with the goals of the organization, then productivity will tend to be low. However, if these workers see their own goals as being the same as the goals of the organization or as being satisfied as a direct result of accomplishing organizational goals, then productivity will tend to be high. Work restriction is therefore not a necessary aspect of informal work groups.

esteem

The need for esteem or recognition appears in a number of forms. In this section we shall discuss two motives related to esteem—prestige and power.

PRESTIGE.   The prestige motive is becoming more evident in our society today, especially as we move more toward a middle-class society. People with a concern for prestige want to "keep up with the Joneses"; in fact, given the choice, they would like to stay ahead of the Joneses. Vance Packard [20] and David Riesman [21] probably had the greatest impact in exposing prestige motivation. Packard wrote about the status seekers and their motives, while Riesman unveiled "other-directed" individuals who were part of "the lonely crowd."

What exactly is prestige? Gellerman describes it as "a sort of unwritten definition of the kinds of conduct that other people are expected to show in one's presence: what degree of respect or disrespect, formality or informality, reserve or frankness." [22] Prestige seems to have an effect on how comfortably or conveniently one can expect to get along in life.

Prestige is something intangible bestowed upon an individual by society. In fact, at birth a child inherits the status of his parents. In some cases, this is enough to carry him through life on "a prestige-covered wave." For example, a Rockefeller or a Ford inherits instant prestige with his family background.

People seek prestige throughout their lives in various ways. Many tend to seek only the material symbols of status, while others strive for personal achievement or self-actualization which might command prestige in itself. Regardless of the way it is expressed, there seems to be a widespread need for people to have their importance clarified and, in fact, set at a level that each feels he deserves. As discussed earlier, people normally want to have a high evaluation of themselves that is firmly based in reality as manifested by the recognition and respect accorded them by others.

The need for prestige is more or less self-limiting. People tend to seek prestige only to a preconceived level. When they feel they have gained this level, the strength of this need tends to decline and prestige becomes a matter of maintenance rather than of further advancement. Some people can become satisfied with their level of importance in their company and community. In their own evaluation, "they have arrived." Only the exceptional seek national or international recognition. Prestige motivation therefore often appears in young people who tend not to be satisfied yet with their status in life. Older people tend to have reached a level of prestige that satisfies them, or they become resigned to the fact that they can do little to improve their status. [23]

POWER.   The ability to induce or influence behavior is *power*. There tend to be two kinds of power—position and personal. An individual who is able to influence the behavior of another because of his position in the organization has *position* power, while an individual who derives his influence from his personality and behavior has *personal* power. Some people are endowed with both types of power. Still others seem to have no power at all.

Alfred Adler, a one-time colleague of Freud, became very interested in this power motive.[24] By power Adler essentially meant the ability to manipulate or control the activities of others to suit one's own purposes. He found that this ability starts at an early age when a baby realizes that if he cries he influences his parents' behavior. The child's position as a baby gives him considerable power over his parents.

According to Adler, this manipulative ability is inherently pleasurable. A child, for example, often has a hard time adjusting to the continuing reduction in his position power. In fact, he might spend a significant amount of time as an adult trying to recapture the power he had as a child. However, Adler did not feel that a child seeks power for its own sake as often as he does out of necessity. Power, for a child, is often a life-and-death matter because he is helpless and needs to count on his parents' availability. Parents are a child's lifeline. Thus, power acquires an importance in children that they somehow never lose, even though they are later able to fend for themselves.

After childhood, the power motive again becomes very potent in individuals who feel somehow inadequate in winning the respect and recognition of others. These people go out of their way to seek attention to overcome this weakness which is often felt but not recognized. In this connection, Adler introduced two interesting and now well-known concepts in his discussion—*inferiority complex* and *compensation.*

A person with an inferiority complex has underlying fears of inadequacy which may or may not have some basis in reality. In some cases, individuals compensate for this inferiority complex by exerting extreme efforts to achieve goals or objectives which (they feel) inadequacy would deny. In many cases extreme effort seems to be an overcompensation for something not clearly perceived although felt. Once accurately perceived, the frame of reference can be realigned with reality and can result in more realistic behavior.

Adler found another interesting thing. If a child does not encounter too much tension as he matures, his need for power gradually transforms itself into a desire to perfect his social relationships. He wants to be able to interact with others without fear or suspicion in an open and trusting atmosphere. Thus, an individual often moves from the *task* aspect of power, wanting to structure and manipulate his environment and the people in it, to a concern for *relationships,* developing trust and respect for others. This transformation is often delayed with individuals who have had tension-filled childhoods and have not learned to trust. In these cases, the power motive would not only persist but might even become stronger. Thus Adler, like Freud, felt that the personality of an individual is developed early in life and is often a result of the kind of experiences the child had with adults in his world.

self-actualization

Of all the needs discussed by Maslow, the one that social and behavioral scientists know least about is self-actualization. Perhaps this is because people satisfy this need in different ways. Thus, self-actualization is a difficult need to pin down and identify.

While little research has been done on the concept of self-actualization, extensive research has been done on two motives which the authors feel are related to it—*competence* and *achievement.*

COMPETENCE. According to Robert W. White, one of the mainsprings of action in a human being is a desire for competence.[25] Competence implies control over environmental factors—both physical and social. People with this motive do not wish to wait passively for things to happen; they want to be able to manipulate their environment and make things happen.

The competence motive can be identified in young children as they move from the early stage of wanting to touch and handle everything in reach to the later stage of wanting not only to touch but to take things apart and put them back together again. The child begins to learn his way around his world. He becomes aware of what he can do and cannot do. This is not in terms of what he is allowed to do, but in terms of what he is able to do. During these early years a child develops a feeling of competence.

This feeling of competence is closely related to the concept of expectancy discussed earlier. Whether a child's sense of competence is strong or weak depends on his successes and failures in the past. If his successes overshadow his failures, then his feeling of competence will tend to be high. He will have a positive outlook toward life, seeing almost every new situation as an interesting challenge that he can overcome. If, however, his failures carry the day, his outlook will be more negative and expectancy for satisfying various needs may become low. Since expectancy tends to influence motives, people with low feelings of competence will not often be motivated to seek new challenges or take risks. These people would rather let their environment control them than attempt to change it.

The sense of competence, while established early in life, is not necessarily permanent. White found that unexpected good or bad fortune may influence one's feelings of competence in a positive or negative way. Thus, the competence motive tends to be cumulative. For example, a person can get off to a bad start and then develop a strong sense of competence because of new successes. There is, however, a point in time when a sense of competence seems to stabilize itself. When this occurs, the sense of competence almost becomes a self-fulfilling prophecy, influencing whether a given experience will be a success or a failure. After a person reaches a certain age, he seldom achieves more than he thinks he can, because he does not attempt things he thinks he cannot achieve.

According to White, the competence motive reveals itself in adults as a desire for job mastery and professional growth. An individual's job is one arena where he can match his ability and skills against his environment in a contest that is challenging but not overwhelming. In jobs where such a contest is possible, the competence motive in an individual can be expressed freely and significant personal rewards can be gained. But in routine, closely supervised jobs, this contest is often impossible. Such situations make the worker dependent on the system and therefore completely frustrate people with high competence needs.

ACHIEVEMENT.   Over the years behavioral scientists have observed that some people have an intense need to achieve; others, perhaps the majority, do not seem to be as concerned about achievement. This phenomenon has fascinated David C. McClelland. For over twenty years he and his associates at Harvard University have been studying this urge to achieve.[26]

McClelland's research has led him to believe that the need for achievement is a distinct human motive that can be distinguished from other needs. More important, the achievement motive can be isolated and assessed in any group.

What are some of the characteristics of people with a high need for achievement? McClelland illustrates some of these characteristics in describing a laboratory experiment. Participants were asked to throw rings over a peg from any distance they chose. Most men tended to throw randomly, now close, now far away; but individuals with a high need for achievement seemed to carefully measure where they were most likely to get a sense of mastery—not too close to make the task ridiculously easy or too far away to make it impossible. They set moderately difficult but potentially achievable goals. In biology, this is known as the *overload principle*. In weight lifting, for example, strength cannot be increased by tasks that can be performed easily or that cannot be performed without injury to the organism. Strength can be increased by lifting weights that are difficult but realistic enough to "stretch" the muscles.

Do people with a high need for achievement behave like this all the time? No. Only if they can influence the outcome. Achievement-motivated people are not gamblers. They prefer to work on a problem rather than leave the outcome to chance.

In terms of a manager, setting moderately difficult but potentially achievable goals may be translated into an attitude toward risks. Many people tend to be extreme in their attitude toward risks, either favoring wild speculative gambling or minimizing their exposure to losses. The gambler seems to choose the big risk because the outcome is beyond his power and, therefore, he can easily rationalize away his personal responsibility if he loses. The conservative individual chooses tiny risks where the gain is small but secure, perhaps because there is little danger of anything going wrong for which he might be blamed. The achievement-motivated person takes the middle ground, preferring a moderate degree of risk because he feels his efforts and abilities will probably influence the outcome. In business, this aggressive realism is the mark of the successful entrepreneur.

Another characteristic of the achievement-motivated person is that he seems to be more concerned with personal achievement than with the rewards of success. While he does not reject rewards, they are not as essential to him as the accomplishment itself. He gets a bigger "kick" out of winning or solving a difficult problem than he gets from any money or praise he receives. Money, to the achievement-motivated person, is valuable to him primarily as a measurement of his performance. It provides him with a means of assessing his progress and comparing his achievements with those of other people. He normally does not seek money for status or economic security.

A desire by people with a high need for achievement to seek situations in which they get concrete feedback on how well they are doing is closely related to this concern for personal accomplishment. Consequently, achievement-motivated people are often found in sales jobs or as owners and managers of their own business. In addition to concrete feedback, the nature of the feedback is important to achievement-motivated people. They respond favorably to information about their work. They are not interested in comments about their personal characteristics, such as how cooperative or helpful they are. Affiliation-motivated people might want "social" or attitudinal feedback. Achievement-motivated people might want task-relevant feedback. They want to know the score.

Why do achievement-motivated people behave as they do? McClelland claims because they habitually spend time thinking about doing things better. He has found, in fact, that wherever people start to think in achievement terms, things start to happen. Examples can be cited. College students with a high need for achievement will generally get better grades than equally bright students with weaker achievement needs. Achievement-motivated men tend to get more raises and are promoted faster because they are constantly trying to think of better ways of doing things. Companies with many such men grow faster and are more profitable. McClelland has even extended his analysis to countries where he related the presence of a large percentage of achievement-motivated individuals to the national economic growth.

McClelland has found that achievement-motivated people are more likely to be found in certain groups or classes of society than in others. He found that middle-class families (the merchants, managers, professionals, and salaried specialists of all kinds) seem to breed these kinds of children more than the other socio-economic classes. Perhaps this is why our country continues to grow economically and socially. After all, we are gradually becoming a nation of middle-class people.

McClelland discovered that middle-class parents hold different expectations for their children than do other parents. More importantly, they expect their children to start showing some independence between the ages of six and eight, making choices and doing things without help, such as knowing the way around the neighborhood and taking care of themselves around the house. Other parents tend to either expect this too early, before the child is ready, or smother the development of the personality of the child. One extreme seemed to foster a passive, defeated attitude, as the child felt unwanted at home and incompetent away from home. He was just not ready for that kind of independence so early. The other extreme yielded either an overprotected or an overdisciplined child. The child became very dependent on his parents and found it difficult to break away and make his own decisions.

Given all we know about the need for achievement, can this motive be taught and developed in people? McClelland is convinced that this can be done. In fact, he has also developed training programs for businessmen that are designed to increase their achievement motivation. He is also in the process of developing similar programs for other segments of the population. These programs could have tremendous implications for training and developing human resources.

While achievement-motivated people can be the backbone of most organizations, what can we say about their potential as managers? As we know, a person with a high need for achievement gets ahead because as an individual he is a producer. He gets things done. However, when he is promoted to a position where his success depends not only on his own work but on the activities of others, he may be less effective. Since he is highly task-oriented and works to his capacity, he tends to expect others to do the same. As a result, he sometimes lacks the human skills and patience necessary for being an effective manager of people who are competent but have a higher need for affiliation than he does. In this situation his high task–low relationships behavior frustrates and prohibits these people from maximizing their own potentials. Thus, while achievement-motivated people are needed in organizations, they do not always make the best managers.

money motive

As stated earlier, money is a very complicated motive which is entangled in such a way with all kinds of needs besides physiological needs
that its importance is often difficult to ascertain. For example, in some
cases, money can provide an individual with certain material things, such
as a fancy sports car, from which he can gain a feeling of affiliation (joins
a sports car club), recognition (status symbol), and even self-actualization
(becomes an outstanding sports car driver). Consequently, we delayed our
discussion of the money motive until other basic concepts were clarified.

From extensive research on incentive pay schemes, William F. Whyte
has found that money, the "old reliable" motivational tool, is not as "al-
mighty" as it is supposed to be, particularly for production workers.[27]
For each of these workers, another key factor, as Mayo discovered, is his
work group. Using the ratio of high-producing "rate-busters" to low-
producing "restrictors" as an index, Whyte estimates that only about 10
percent of the production workers in the United States will ignore group
pressure and produce as much as possible in response to an incentive plan.
It seems that while the worker *is* interested in advancing his own financial
position, there are many other considerations, such as the opinions of
his fellow workers, his comfort and enjoyment on the job, and his long-
range security, which prevent him from making a direct, automatic, positive response to an incentive plan.

According to Gellerman, the most subtle and most important characteristic of money is its power as a symbol. Its most obvious symbolic power
is its market value. It is what money can buy, not money itself, that gives
it value. But money's symbolic power is not limited to its market value.
Since money has no intrinsic meaning of its own, it can symbolize almost
any need an individual wants it to represent. In other words, money can
mean whatever people want it to mean.[28]

WHAT DO WORKERS WANT FROM THEIR JOBS?

In talking about motives it is important to remember that people have
many needs, all of which are continually competing for their behavior.
No one person has exactly the same mixture or strength of these needs.
There are some people who are driven mainly by money; others who are
concerned primarily with security, and so on. While we must recognize
individual differences, this does not mean that, as managers, we cannot
make some predictions about which motives seem to be currently more
prominent among our employees than others. According to Maslow, these

are prepotent motives—those that are still *not* satisfied. An important question for managers to answer is, What do workers really want from their jobs?

Some interesting research has been conducted among employees in American industry in an attempt to answer this question. In one such study, supervisors were asked to try to put themselves in a *worker's* shoes by ranking in order of importance a series of items which describe things workers may want from their jobs. It was emphasized that in ranking the items the supervisors should *not* think in terms of what they want but what they think a worker wants. In addition to the supervisors, the workers themselves were asked to rank these same items in terms of what *they* wanted most from their jobs. The results are given in Table 2.1. (1 = highest and 10 = lowest in importance.)

TABLE 2.1 What do workers want from their jobs?

	Supervisors	Workers
Good working conditions	4	9
Feeling "in" on things	10	2
Tactful disciplining	7	10
Full appreciation for work done	8	1
Management loyalty to workers	6	8
Good wages	1	5
Promotion and growth with company	3	7
Sympathetic understanding of personal problems	9	3
Job security	2	4
Interesting work	5	6

As is evident from the results, supervisors generally ranked good wages, job security, promotion, and good working conditions as the things workers want most from their jobs. On the other hand, workers felt that what they wanted most was full appreciation for work done, feeling "in" on things, and sympathetic understanding of personal problems—all incentives that seem to be related to affiliation and recognition motives. It is interesting to note that those things that workers indicated they wanted most from their jobs were rated by their foremen as least important. In some cases, there seems to be very little sensitivity by supervisors as to what things are really most important to workers. Supervisors seem to think that incentives directed to satisfy physiological and safety motives tend to be most important to their workers. Since supervisors perceive workers as having these motives, supervisors act as if they were true.

Therefore, supervisors use the "old reliable" incentives—money, fringe benefits, and security—to motivate workers.

One might generalize at this point that individuals act on the basis of their perceptions and *not* on reality. By bringing his perception closer and closer to reality—what his men really want—a manager can often increase his effectiveness in working with employees. A manager has to know his people to understand what motivates them; he cannot just make assumptions. Even if a manager asked an employee how he felt about something, this does not necessarily result in relevant feedback. The quality of communications a manager receives from his employees is often based upon the rapport that has been established between his men and himself over a long period of time.

It is becoming clearer that many managers do not realize or understand that what people want from their jobs today is different from what they wanted a few decades ago. Today in the United States, few people, with the exception of those in some of the urban ghettos and poverty belts, have to worry about where their next meal will come from or whether they will be protected from the elements or physical dangers. The satisfaction of physiological and safety needs has been the result of the tremendous rise in our standard of living, dramatic increases in pay and fringe benefits at all levels of work, and extensive aid from governmental programs—welfare, social security, medicare, and unemployment insurance. In addition, the union movement and labor laws have made significant strides in assuring safe working conditions and job security.

Our society almost has a built-in guarantee of physiological and safety needs for large segments of the population. Since many physiological and safety needs have been provided for, it is understandable why people today have become more concerned with social, recognition, and self-actualization motives. Managers must become aware of this fact. Because of employees' changing need priorities, today's organizations should provide the kind of environment that will motivate and satisfy more than just physiological and security needs. In Chapter 3 we will describe some of the research that may be helpful to a manager in building a motivating environment that will increase organizational effectiveness.

NOTES

1. Sigmund Freud, *The Ego and the Id* (London: Hogarth Press, 1927). See also *New Introductory Lectures on Psychoanalysis* (New York: W. W. Norton & Company, Inc., 1933).
2. Abraham H. Maslow, *Motivation and Personality* (New York: Harper & Row Publishers, 1954).

3. Leon Festinger, *A Theory of Cognitive Dissonance* (Stanford, Calif.: Stanford University Press, 1957).

4. *Ibid.*, p. 155.

5. Freud, *The Ego and the Id.*

6. J. A. C. Brown, *The Social Psychology of Industry* (Baltimore: Penguin Books, Inc., 1954), p. 249.

7. Norman R. F. Maier, *Frustration* (Ann Arbor: The University of Michigan Press, 1961).

8. Brown, *The Social Psychology*, p. 252.

9. H. Barker, T. Dembo, and K. Lewin, *Frustration and Aggression* (Iowa City: University of Iowa Press, 1942).

10. Brown, *The Social Psychology*, p. 253.

11. Maier, *Frustration.*

12. Brown, *The Social Psychology*, p. 254.

13. Dewey E. Johnson, *Concepts of Air Force Leadership* (Washington, D.C.: Air Force ROTC, 1970), p. 209.

14. Maslow, *Motivation and Personality.*

15. Saul W. Gellerman, *Motivation and Productivity* (New York: American Management Association, 1963). See also Gellerman, *Management by Motivation* (New York: American Management Association, 1968).

16. Peter F. Drucker, "How to be an Employee," *Psychology Today,* March 1968, a reprint from *Fortune* magazine.

17. Gellerman, *Motivation and Productivity,* pp. 154–55.

18. Stanley Schachter, *The Psychology of Affiliation* (Stanford, Calif.: Stanford University Press, 1959).

19. Elton Mayo, *The Social Problems of an Industrial Civilization* (Boston: Harvard Business School, 1945); see also Mayo, *The Human Problems of an Industrial Civilization* (New York: The Macmillan Company, 1933).

20. Vance Packard, *The Status Seekers* (New York: David McKay Co., Inc., 1959).

21. David Reisman, *The Lonely Crowd* (New Haven, Conn.: Yale University Press, 1950).

22. Gellerman, *Motivation and Productivity,* p. 151.

23. *Ibid.*, pp. 150–54.

24. Alfred Adler, *Social Interest* (London: Faber & Faber Ltd., 1938). See also H. L. Ansbacher and R. R. Ansbacher, eds., *The Individual Psychology of Alfred Adler* (New York: Basic Books, Inc., Publishers, 1956).

25. Robert W. White, "Motivation Reconsidered: The Concept of Competence," *Psychological Review,* LXVI, No. 5 (1959).

26. David C. McClelland, J. W. Atkinson, R. A. Clark, and E. L. Lowell, *The Achievement Motive* (New York: Appleton-Century-Crofts, 1953); and *The Achieving Society* (Princeton, N.J.: D. Van Nostrand Co., Inc., 1961).

27. William F. Whyte, ed., *Money and Motivation* (New York: Harper & Row, Publishers, 1955).

28. Gellerman, *Motivation and Productivity,* pp. 160–69.

motivating

environment

3

In 1924 efficiency experts at the Hawthorne, Illinois, plant of the Western Electric Company designed a research program to study the effects of illumination on productivity. At first, nothing about this program seemed exceptional enough to arouse any unusual interest. After all, efficiency experts had long been trying to find the ideal mix of physical conditions, working hours, and working methods which stimulate workers to produce at maximum capacity. Yet, by the time these studies were completed (over a decade later), there was little doubt that the work at Hawthorne would stand the test of time as one of the most exciting and important research projects ever done in an industrial setting. For it was at Western Electric's Hawthorne plant that the Human Relations Movement began to gather momentum, and one of its early advocates, Elton Mayo of the Harvard Graduate School of Business Administration, gained recognition.[1]

HAWTHORNE STUDIES

Elton Mayo

In the initial study at Hawthorne, efficiency experts assumed that increases in illumination would result in higher output. Two groups of employees were selected: an *experimental* or *test group* which worked under varying degrees of light, and a *control group* which worked under normal illumination conditions in the plant. As lighting power was increased, the output of the test group went up as anticipated. Unexpectedly, however, the output of the control group went up also—without any increase in light.

Determined to explain these and other surprising test results, the efficiency experts decided to expand their research at Hawthorne. They felt that in addition to technical and physical changes, some of the behavioral considerations should be explored, so Mayo and his associates were called in to help.

Mayo and his team started their experiments with a group of girls who assembled telephone relays, and, like the efficiency experts, the Harvard men uncovered astonishing results. For over a year and a half during this experiment, Mayo's researchers improved the working conditions of the girls by implementing such innovations as scheduled rest periods, company lunches, and shorter work weeks. Baffled by the results, the researchers suddenly decided to take everything away from the girls, returning the working conditions to the exact way they had been at the beginning of the experiment. This radical change was expected to have a tremendous negative psychological impact on the girls and reduce their output. Instead, their output jumped to a new *all-time high*. Why?

The answers to this question were *not* found in the production aspects of the experiment (i.e., changes in plant and physical working conditions), but in the *human* aspects. As a result of the attention lavished upon them by experimenters, the girls were made to feel they were an important part of the company. They no longer viewed themselves as isolated individuals, working together only in the sense that they were physically close to each other. Instead they had become participating members of a congenial, cohesive work group. The relationships that developed elicited feelings of affiliation, competence, and achievement. These needs, which had long gone unsatisfied at work, were now being fulfilled. The girls worked harder and more effectively than they had worked previously.

Realizing that they had uncovered an interesting phenomenon, the Harvard team extended their research by interviewing over twenty thousand employees from every department in the company. Interviews were designed to help researchers find out what the workers thought about their jobs, their working conditions, their supervisors, their company, and anything that bothered them, and how these feelings might be related to their productivity. After several interview sessions, Mayo's group found that a structured question-and-answer-type interview was useless for eliciting the information they wanted. Instead, the workers wanted to talk freely about what *they* thought was important. So the predetermined questions were discarded, and the interviewer allowed the worker to ramble as he chose.

The interviews proved valuable in a number of ways. First of all, they were therapeutic; the workers got an opportunity to get a lot off their chests. Many felt this was the best thing the company had ever done. The result was a wholesale change in attitude. Since many of their suggestions were being implemented, the workers began to feel that management viewed them as important, both as individuals and as a group; they were now participating in the operation and future of the company and not just performing unchallenging, unappreciated tasks.

Second, the implications of the Hawthorne studies signaled the need for management to study and understand relationships among people. In these studies, as well as in the many that followed, the most significant factor affecting organizational productivity was found to be the inter-personal relationships that are developed on the job, not just pay and working conditions. Mayo found that when informal groups identified with management, as they did at Hawthorne through the interview program, productivity rose. The increased productivity seemed to reflect the workers' feelings of competence—a sense of mastery over the job and work environment. Mayo also discovered that when the group felt that their own goals were in opposition to those of management, as often happened in situations where the workers were closely supervised and had no significant control over their job or environment, productivity remained at low levels or was even lowered.

These findings were important because they helped answer many of the questions that had puzzled management about why some groups seemed to be high producers while others hovered at a minimal level of output. The findings also encouraged management to involve workers in planning, organizing, and controlling their own work in an effort to secure their positive cooperation.

Mayo saw the development of informal groups as an indictment of an entire society which treated human beings as insensitive machines that were concerned only with economic self-interest. As a result, workers had been taught to look at work merely as an impersonal exchange of money for labor. Work in American industry meant humiliation—the performance of routine, tedious, and oversimplified tasks in an environment over which one had no control. This environment denied satisfaction of esteem and self-actualization needs on the job. Instead only physiological and safety needs were satisfied. The lack of avenues for satisfying other needs led to tension, anxiety, and frustration in workers. Such feelings of helplessness were called "anomie" by Mayo. This condition was characterized by workers' feeling unimportant, confused, and unattached—victims of their own environment.

While anomie was a creation of the total society, Mayo felt its most extreme application was found in industrial settings where management held certain negative assumptions about the nature of man. According to Mayo, too many managers assumed that society consisted of a horde or mob of unorganized individuals whose only concern was self-preservation or self-interest. It was assumed that people were primarily dominated by physiological and safety needs, wanting to make as much money as they could for as little work as possible. Thus, management operated and organized work on the basic assumption that workers, on the whole, were a contemptible lot. Mayo called this assumption the "Rabble Hypothesis." He deplored the authoritarian, task-oriented management practices that it created.

THEORY X AND THEORY Y

Douglas McGregor

The work of Mayo and particularly his exposure of the Rabble Hypothesis may have paved the way for the development of the now classic "Theory X–Theory Y" by Douglas McGregor.[2] According to McGregor, traditional organization with its centralized decision making, superior-subordinate pyramid, and external control of work is based upon assumptions about human nature and human motivation. These assumptions are very similar to the view of man defined by Mayo in the Rabble Hypothesis. Theory X assumes that most people prefer to be directed, are not interested in assuming responsibility, and want safety above all. Accompanying this philosophy is the belief that people are motivated by money, fringe benefits, and the threat of punishment.

Managers who accept Theory X assumptions attempt to structure, control, and closely supervise their employees. These managers feel that external control is clearly appropriate for dealing with unreliable, irresponsible, and immature people.

After describing Theory X, McGregor questioned whether this view of man is correct and if management practices based upon it are appropriate in many situations today: Isn't man in a democratic society, with its increasing level of education and standard of living, capable of more mature behavior? Drawing heavily on Maslow's hierarchy of needs, McGregor concluded that Theory X assumptions about the nature of man are generally inaccurate and that management approaches that develop from these assumptions will often fail to motivate individuals to work toward organizational goals. Management by direction and control may not succeed, according to McGregor, because it is a questionable method for motivating people whose physiological and safety needs are reasonably satisfied and whose social, esteem, and self-actualization needs are becoming predominant.

McGregor felt that management needed practices based on a more accurate understanding of the nature of man and human motivation. As a result of his feeling, McGregor developed an alternate theory of human behavior called Theory Y. This theory assumes that people are *not*, by nature, lazy and unreliable. It postulates that man can be basically self-directed and creative at work if properly motivated. Therefore, it should be an essential task of management to unleash this potential in man. The properly motivated worker can achieve his own goals *best* by directing *his own* efforts toward accomplishing organizational goals.

TABLE 3.1   List of assumptions about nature of man which underline McGregor's Theory X and Theory Y.

Theory X	*Theory Y*
1. Work is inherently distasteful to most people.	1. Work is as natural as play, if the conditions are favorable.
2. Most people are not ambitious, have little desire for responsibility, and prefer to be directed.	2. Self-control is often indispensable in achieving organizational goals.
3. Most people have little capacity for creativity in solving organizational problems.	3. The capacity for creativity in solving organizational problems is widely distributed in the population.
4. Motivation occurs only at the physiological and safety levels.	4. Motivation occurs at the social, esteem, and self-actualization levels, as well as physiological and security levels.
5. Most people must be closely controlled and often coerced to achieve organizational objectives.	5. People can be self-directed and creative at work if properly motivated.

Managers who accept the Theory Y image of human nature do *not* usually structure, control, or closely supervise the work environment for employees. Instead they attempt to help their employees mature by exposing them to progressively less external control, allowing them to assume more and more self-control. Employees are able to achieve the satisfaction of social, esteem, and self-actualization needs within this kind of environment, often neglected on the job. To the extent that the job does not provide need satisfaction at every level, today's employee will usually look elsewhere for significant need satisfaction. This helps explain some of the current problems management is facing in such areas as turnover and absenteeism. McGregor argues that this does not have to be the case.

Management is interested in work, and McGregor feels that work is as natural and can be as satisfying for people as play. After all, both work and play are physical and mental activities; consequently, there is no inherent difference between work and play. In reality, though, particularly under Theory X management, a distinct difference in need satisfaction is discernible. Whereas play is internally controlled by the individual (he decides what he wants to do), work is externally controlled by others (the worker has no control over his job). Thus, management and its assumptions about the nature of man have built in a difference between work and play that seems unnatural. As a result, people are stifled at work and hence look for excuses to spend more and more time away from the job in order to satisfy their esteem and self-actualization needs (provided they have enough money to satisfy their physiological and safety needs). Because of their conditioning to Theory X types of management, most employees consider work a *necessary evil* rather than a source of personal challenge and satisfaction.

Does work really have to be a necessary evil? No—especially in organizations where cohesive work groups have developed and where the goals parallel organizational goals. In such organizations there is high productivity, and people come to work gladly because work is inherently satisfying.

HUMAN GROUP

George C. Homans

Management is often suspicious of strong informal work groups because of their potential power to control the behavior of their members and, as a result, the level of productivity. Where do these groups get their power to control behavior? George C. Homans has developed a model of social systems which may be useful to the practitioner trying to answer this question.[3]

There are three elements in a social system. *Activities* are the tasks that people perform. *Interactions* are the behaviors that occur between people in performing these tasks. And *sentiments* are the attitudes that develop between individuals and within groups. Homans argues that while these concepts are separate, they are closely related. In fact, as Figure 3.1 illustrates, they are mutually dependent upon each other.

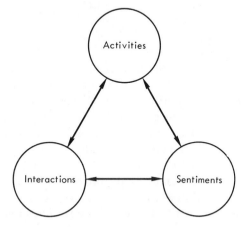

FIGURE 3.1 The mutual dependence of activities, interactions, and sentiments.

A change in any of these three elements will produce some change in the other two.

In an organization certain activities, interactions, and sentiments are essential, or required from its members, if it is to survive. In other words, jobs (activities) have to be done that require people to work together (interactions). These jobs must be sufficiently satisfying (sentiments) for people to continue doing them. As people interact on their jobs, they develop sentiments toward each other. As people increase interaction with each other, more positive sentiments will tend to develop toward each other. The more positive the sentiment, the more people will tend to interact with each other. It can become a spiraling process until some equilibrium is reached. As this spiraling process continues, there is a tendency for the group members to become more alike in their activities and sentiments—in what they do and how they feel about things. As this happens, the group tends to develop expectations or norms that specify how people in the group "might" tend to behave under specific circumstances. For example, a group of workers might have a norm that "you should not talk to the boss, or help him, any more than necessary." If the group is cohesive enough, that is, the group is attractive to its members and they are reluctant to leave it, then it will have little trouble in getting members to conform. People who deviate significantly from group norms usually incur sanctions from the group. "The group has at its disposal a variety of penalties, ranging from gentle kidding to harsh ostracism, for pressuring deviant members into line." [4] The group member may react in several ways. He may decide to go ahead and continue to deviate from group norms. If the resulting pressure from his peers becomes too great, he may leave the group.

The influence group pressures can have in achieving conformity in the perceptions and behavior of people is well documented. For example, S. E. Asch conducted a classic experiment in which groups of eight college men were each asked to match the length of a line with one of three unequal lines.[5] Seven members of each group were privately told to give the same incorrect answer. The uninstructed member was the last one asked to give his answer and was thus confronted with the dilemma of either reporting what he saw as being correct or reporting what all the others had said in order to be congruent with the group. Asch reported that "one-third of all the estimates were errors identical with or in the direction of the distorted estimates of the majority." [6] If pressure can cause distorted behavior in this kind of exercise, imagine what peer group pressure can induce with more subjective judgments.

It should be reiterated that strong informal work groups do not have to be a detriment to organizations. In fact, as Mayo discovered at Hawthorne, these groups can become powerful driving forces in accomplishing organizational goals if they see their own goals as being satisfied by working for organizational goals.

IMMATURITY–MATURITY THEORY

Chris Argyris

Even though management based on the assumptions of Theory X is perhaps no longer appropriate in the opinion of McGregor and others, it is still widely practiced. Consequently, a large majority of the people in the United States today are treated as immature human beings in their working environments. It is this fact that has produced many of our current organizational problems. Chris Argyris, while at Yale University, examined industrial organizations to determine what effect management practices have had on individual behavior and personal growth within the work environment.[7]

According to Argyris, seven changes should take place in the personality of an individual if he is to develop into a mature person over the years.

First, an individual moves from a passive state as an infant to a state of increasing activity as an adult. Second, an individual develops from a state of dependency upon others as an infant to a state of relative independence as an adult. Third, an individual behaves in only a few ways as an infant, but as an adult, he is capable of behaving in many ways. Fourth, an individual has erratic, casual, and shallow interests as an infant but develops deeper and stronger interests as an adult. Fifth, a child's time perspective is very short, involving only the present, but as he matures, his time perspective increases to include the past and the future. Sixth, an individual as an infant is subordinate to everyone, but he moves to equal or superior position with others as an adult. Seventh, as a child, an individual lacks an awareness of a "self," but as an adult, he is not only aware of, but he is able to control "self." Argyris postulates that these changes reside on a continuum and that the "healthy" personality develops along the continuum from "immaturity" to "maturity."

TABLE 3.2   Immaturity-maturity continuum.

Immaturity ——————————————→ *Maturity*

Passive ————————————————	Active
Dependence ————————————————	Independence
Behave in a few ways ——————————	Capable of behaving in many ways
Erratic shallow interests ————————	Deeper and stronger interests
Short time perspective ———————	Long time perspective (past and future)
Subordinate position ———————	Equal or superordinate position
Lack of awareness of self ———————	Awareness and control over self

These changes are only general tendencies, but they give some light to the matter of maturity. Norms of the individual's culture and personality inhibit and limit maximum expression and growth of the adult, yet the tendency is to move toward the "maturity" end of the continuum with age. Argyris would be the first to admit that few, if any, develop to full maturity.

In examining the widespread worker apathy and lack of effort in industry, Argyris questions whether these problems are simply the result of individual laziness. He suggests that this is *not* the case. Argyris contends that, in many cases, when people join the work force, they are kept from maturing by the management practices utilized in their organizations. In these organizations, they are given minimal control over their environment and are encouraged to be passive, dependent, and subordinate; therefore, they behave immaturely. The worker in many organizations is expected to act in immature ways rather than as a mature adult.

According to Argyris, keeping people immature is built into the very nature of the formal organization. He argues that because organizations are usually created to achieve goals or objectives that can best be met collectively, the formal organization is often the architect's conception of how these objectives may be achieved. In this sense the individual is fitted to the job. The design comes first. This design is based upon four concepts of scientific management: task specialization, chain of command, unity of direction, and span of control. Management tries to increase and enhance organizational and administrative efficiency and productivity by making workers "interchangeable parts."

Basic to these concepts is that power and authority should rest in the hands of a few at the top of the organization, and thus those at the lower end of the chain of command are strictly controlled by their superiors or the system itself. Task specialization often results in the oversimplification of the job so that it becomes repetitive, routine, and unchallenging. This implies directive, task-oriented leadership where decisions about the work are made by the superior, with the workers only carrying out those decisions. This type of leadership evokes managerial controls such as budgets, some incentive systems, time and motion studies, and standard operating procedures which can restrict the initiative and creativity of workers.

Argyris feels that these concepts of formal organization lead to assumptions about human nature that are incompatible with the proper development of maturity in human personality. He sees a definite incongruity between the needs of a mature personality and the formal organizations as they now exist. Since he implies that the classical theory of management (based on Theory X assumptions) usually prevails, management creates childlike roles for workers that frustrate natural development.

An example of how work is often designed at this extremely low level was dramatically illustrated by the successful use of mentally retarded workers in such jobs. Argyris cites two instances, one in a knitting mill and the other in a radio manufacturing corporation in which mentally retarded people were successfully employed on unskilled jobs. In both cases, the managers praised these workers for their excellent performance. In fact, a manager in the radio corporation reported:

> The girls proved to be exceptionally well-behaved, particularly obedient, and strictly honest and trustworthy. They carried out work required of them to such a degree of efficiency that *we were surprised they were classed as subnormals for their age*. Their attendance was good, and their behavior was, if anything, certainly better than that of any other employee of the same age.[8]

Disturbed by what he finds in many organizations, Argyris, as did McGregor, challenges management to provide a work climate in which everyone has a chance to grow and mature as an individual, as a member of a group by satisfying his own needs, while working for the success of the organization. Implicit here is the belief that man can be basically self-directed and creative at work if properly motivated, and, therefore, management based on the assumption of Theory Y will be more profitable for the individual and the organization.

More and more companies are starting to listen to the challenge that Argyris is directing at management. For example, the president of a large company asked Argyris to show him how to better motivate his workers. Together they went into one of his production plants where a product similar to a radio was being assembled. There were twelve girls involved in assembling the product, each doing a small segment of the job as designed by an industrial engineer. The group also had a foreman, an inspector, and a packer.

Argyris proposed a one-year experiment during which each of the girls would assemble the total product in a manner of her own choice. At the same time they would inspect, sign their name to the product, pack it, and handle any correspondence involving complaints about it. The girls were assured that they would receive no cut in pay if production dropped but would receive more pay if production increased.

Once the experiment began, production dropped 70 percent during the first month. By the end of six weeks it was even worse. The girls were upset, morale was down. This continued until the eighth week, when production started to rise. By the end of the fifteenth week production was higher than it had ever been before. And this was without an inspector, a packer, or an industrial engineer. More important than increased productivity, costs due to errors and waste decreased 94 percent; letters of complaint dropped 96 percent.

Experiments like this are being duplicated in numerous other situations.[9] It is being found over and over again that broadening individual responsibility is beneficial to both the workers and the company. Giving people the opportunity to grow and mature on the job helps them satisfy more than just physiological and safety needs, which, in turn, motivates them and allows them to use more of their potential in accomplishing organizational goals. While all workers do *not* want to accept more responsibility or deal with the added problems responsibility inevitably brings, Argyris contends that the number of employees whose motivation can be improved by increasing and upgrading their responsibility is much larger than most managers would suspect.

MOTIVATION–HYGIENE THEORY

Frederick Herzberg

As people mature, we have noted that needs such as esteem and self-actualization seem to become more important. One of the most interesting series of studies that concentrates heavily on these areas was directed by Frederick Herzberg of Case-Western Reserve University.[10] Out of these studies has developed a theory of work motivation which has broad implications for management and its efforts toward effective utilization of human resources.

Herzberg, in developing his motivation-hygiene theory, seemed to sense that scholars like McGregor and Argyris were touching on something important. Knowledge about the nature of man, his motives and needs, could be invaluable to organizations and individuals.

> To industry, the payoff for a study of job attitudes would be increased productivity, decreased absenteeism, and smoother working relations. To the individual, an understanding of the forces that lead to improved morale would bring greater happiness and greater self-realization.[11]

Herzberg set out to collect data on job attitudes from which assumptions about human behavior could be made. The motivation-hygiene theory resulted from the analysis of an initial study by Herzberg and his colleagues at the Psychological Service of Pittsburgh. This study involved extensive interviews with some two hundred engineers and accountants from eleven industries in the Pittsburgh area. In the interviews, they were asked about what kinds of things on their job made them unhappy or dissatisfied and what things made them happy or satisfied.

In analyzing the data from these interviews, Herzberg concluded that man has two different categories of needs which are essentially independent of each other and affect behavior in different ways. He found that when people felt dissatisfied with their jobs, they were concerned about the environment in which they were working. On the other hand, when people felt good about their jobs, this had to do with the work itself. Herzberg called the first category of needs *hygiene factors* because they describe man's environment and serve the primary function of preventing job dissatisfaction. He called the second category of needs *motivators* since they seemed to be effective in motivating people to superior performance.

hygiene factors

Company policies and administration, supervision, working conditions, interpersonal relations, money, status, and security may be thought of as hygiene factors. These are not an intrinsic part of a job, but they are related to the conditions under which a job is performed. Herzberg relates his use of the word "hygiene" to its medical meaning (preventative and environmental). Hygiene factors produce no growth in worker output capacity; they only prevent losses in worker performance due to work restriction.

motivators

Satisfying factors that involve feelings of achievement, professional growth, and recognition that one can experience in a job that offers challenge and scope are referred to as motivators. Herzberg used this term because these factors seem capable of having a positive effect on job satisfaction often resulting in an increase in one's total output capacity.

TABLE 3.3   Motivation and hygiene factors.

HYGIENE FACTORS	*MOTIVATORS*
Environment	*The Job Itself*
Policies and administration Supervision Working conditions Interpersonal relations Money, status, security	Achievement Recognition for accomplishment Challenging work Increased responsibility Growth and development

In recent years motivation-hygiene research has been extended well beyond scientists and accountants to include every level of an organization from top management all the way down to hourly employees. For example, in an extensive study of Texas Instruments, Scott Meyers concluded that Herzberg's motivation-hygiene theory "is easily translatable to supervisory action at all levels of responsibility. It is a framework on which supervisors can evaluate and put into perspective the constant barrage of 'helpful hints' to which they are subjected, and hence serves to increase their feelings of competence, self-confidence, and autonomy." [12]

Herzberg's framework seems compatible with Maslow's hierarchy of needs. Maslow refers to needs or motives, while Herzberg seems to deal with the goals or incentives that tend to satisfy these needs. Examples can be cited. Money and benefits tend to satisfy needs at the physiological and security levels; interpersonal relations and supervision are examples of hygiene factors that tend to satisfy social needs, while increased responsibility, challenging work, and growth and development are motivators that tend to satisfy needs at the esteem and self-actualization levels.

Figure 3.2 shows the relationship between these two frameworks.

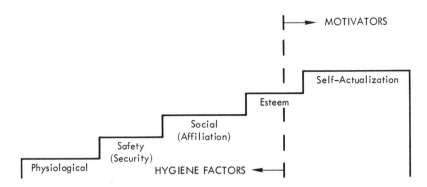

FIGURE 3.2   The relationships between the motivation-hygiene theory and Maslow's hierarchy of needs.

We feel that the physiological, safety, social, and part of the esteem needs are all hygiene factors. The esteem needs are divided because there are some distinct differences between status per se and recognition. Status tends to be a function of the position one occupies. One may have gained this position through family ties or social pressures, and thus this position is not a reflection of personal achievement or earned recognition. Recognition is gained through competence and achievement. It is earned and granted by others. Consequently, status is classified with physiological, safety, and social needs as a hygiene factor, while recognition is classified with self-actualization as a motivator.

Perhaps an example will further differentiate between hygiene factors and motivators. This might help explain the reason for classifying needs as Herzberg has done as well as in a hierarchical arrangement.

Let us assume that a man is highly motivated and is working at 90 percent of capacity. He has a good working relationship with his supervisor, is well satisfied with his pay and working conditions, and is part of a congenial work group. Suppose his supervisor is suddenly transferred and replaced by a person he is unable to work with, or he finds out that someone whose work he feels is inferior to his own is receiving more pay. How do these factors affect a man's behavior? Since we know performance or productivity depends on both ability and motivation, these unsatisfied hygiene needs (supervision and money) may lead to restriction of output. In some cases this is intentional, while in others the individual may not be consciously aware that he is holding back. In either case, though, productivity will be lowered as illustrated in Figure 3.3.

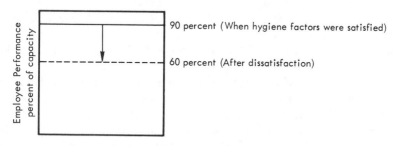

FIGURE 3.3 Effect of dissatisfying hygienes.

In this illustration, even if his former supervisor returns and his salary is readjusted well above his expectations, his productivity will probably increase only to its original level.

Conversely, let us take the same person and assume that dissatisfaction has not occurred; he is working at 90 percent capacity. Suppose he is given an opportunity to mature and satisfy his motivational needs in an environment where he is free to exercise some initiative and creativity, to make decisions, to handle problems, and to take responsibility. What effect will this situation have on this individual? If he is able to successfully fulfill his supervisor's expectations in performing these new responsibilities, he may still work at 90 percent capacity, but as a person he may have matured and grown in his ability and may be capable now of more productivity, as illustrated in Figure 3.4.

FIGURE 3.4 Effect of satisfying motivators.

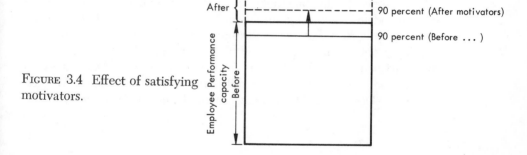

Hygiene needs, when satisfied, tend to eliminate dissatisfaction and work restriction but do little to motivate an individual to superior performance or increased capacity. Satisfaction of the motivators, however, will permit an individual to grow and develop in a mature way, often implementing an increase in ability. Herzberg encourages management to design into the work environment an opportunity to satisfy the motivators.

Prior to Herzberg's work, many other behavioral scientists were concerned with worker motivation. For several years there was an emphasis on what was termed "job enlargement." This was purported to be an answer to the overspecialization that had characterized many industrial organizations. The assumption was that a worker could gain more satisfaction at work if his job was enlarged, that is, if the number of operations in which he engaged was increased.

Herzberg makes some astute observations about this trend. He claims that doing a snippet of this and a snippet of that does not necessarily result in motivation. Washing dishes, then silverware, and then pots and pans does no more to satisfy and provide an opportunity to grow than washing only dishes. What we really need to do with work, Herzberg suggests, is to *enrich* the job. By job enrichment is meant the deliberate upgrading of responsibility, scope, and challenge in work.

example of job enrichment

An example of job enrichment may be illustrated by the experience an industrial relations superintendent had with a group of janitors. When the superintendent was transferred to a new plant, he soon found, much to his amazement, that in addition to his duties, fifteen janitors in plant maintenance reported directly to him. There was no foreman over these men. Upon browsing through the files one day, the superintendent noticed there was a history of complaints about housekeeping around the plant. After talking to others and observing for himself, it took the superintendent little time to confirm the reports. The janitors seemed to be lazy, unreliable, and generally unmotivated. They were walking examples of Theory X assumptions about human nature.

Determined to do something about the behavior of the janitors, the superintendent called a group meeting of all fifteen men. He opened the meeting by saying that he understood there were a number of housekeeping problems in the plant, but confessed that he did not know what to do about them. Since he felt they, as janitors, were experts in the housekeeping area, he asked if together they would help him solve these problems. "Does anyone have a suggestion?" he asked. There was a deadly silence. The superintendent sat down and said nothing; the janitors said nothing. This lasted for almost twenty minutes. Finally one janitor spoke up and related a problem he was having in his area and made a suggestion. Soon others joined in, and suddenly the janitors were involved in a lively discussion while the superintendent listened and jotted down their ideas. At the conclusion of the meeting the suggestions were summarized with tacit acceptance by all, including the superintendent.

After the meeting, the superintendent referred any housekeeping problems to the janitors, individually or as a group. For example, when any cleaning equipment or material salesmen came to the plant the superintendent did not talk to them, the janitors did. In fact, the janitors were given an office where they could talk to salesmen. In addition, regular meetings continued to be held where problems and ideas were discussed.

All of this had a tremendous influence on the behavior of these men. They developed a cohesive productive team that took pride in its work. Even their appearance changed. Once a grubby lot, now they appeared at work in clean, pressed work clothes. All over the plant, people were amazed how clean and well kept everything had become. The superintendent was continually stopped by supervisors in the plant and asked, "What have you done to those lazy, good-for-nothing janitors, given them pep pills?" Even the superintendent could not believe his eyes. It was not uncommon to see one or two janitors running floor tests to see which wax or cleaner did the best job. Since they had to make all the decisions including committing funds for their supplies, they wanted to know which were the best. Such activities, while taking time, did not detract from their work. In fact, these men worked harder and more efficiently than ever before in their lives.

This example illustrates that even at low levels in an organization, people can respond in responsible and productive ways to a work environment in which they are given an opportunity to grow and mature. People begin to satisfy their esteem and self-actualization needs by participating in the planning, organizing, motivating, and controlling of their own tasks.

a problem of placement

It should be pointed out that the problem of motivation is not always a question of enriching jobs. As Chris Argyris dramatically showed in his successful use of mentally retarded workers on the assembly line, some organizations have a tendency to hire people with ability far in excess of the demands of the work.

An example of overhiring happened in the start-up operation of a large plant. As in the case of most new plants, one of the first work groups to be assembled was security. The supervisor of plant security set, as hiring criteria, a high school education and three years of police or plant protection experience as minimal requirements for applicants. Being the first large industrial plant in a relatively agricultural area, the company was able to hire people not at the minimum level but well over these standards.

When these people began their jobs—which consisted simply of checking badges on the way in and lunch pails on the way out—boredom, apathy, and lack of motivation soon characterized their performance. This resulted in a high rate of turnover. When the problem was re-evaluated, the reverse of the hiring procedures was found to be appropriate. Those applicants with a high school education were considered overqualified. Those with police or security experience were also considered overqualified. Rather than experienced workers, applicants with fourth- and fifth-grade educations were hired for these positions. Their performance was found to be much superior, and the turnover, absenteeism, and tardiness rates were cut to a minimum. Why? For these workers, a new uniform, a badge, and some power were important, but they also found the job as one incorporating opportunities for more responsibility and challenging work.

MANAGEMENT SYSTEMS

Rensis Likert

Most managers, if asked what they would do if they suddenly lost half of their plant, equipment, or capital resources, are quick to answer. Insurance or borrowing are often avenues open to refurbish plant, equipment, or capital. Yet when these same managers are asked what they would do if they suddenly lost half of their human resources—managers, supervisors, and hourly employees—they are at a loss for words. There is no insurance against outflows of human resources. Recruiting, training, and developing large numbers of new personnel into a working team takes years. In a competitive environment this is almost an impossible task. Organizations are only beginning to realize that their most important assets are human resources and that the managing of these resources is one of their most crucial tasks.

Rensis Likert and his colleagues of the Institute for Social Research at the University of Michigan emphasized the need to consider both human resources and capital resources as assets requiring proper management.[13] As a result of behavioral research studies of numerous organizations, Likert implemented organizational change programs in various industrial settings. It appears these programs were intended to help organizations move from Theory X to Theory Y assumptions, from fostering immature behavior to encouraging and developing mature behavior, from emphasizing only hygiene factors to recognizing and helping workers to satisfy the motivators.

Likert in his studies found that the prevailing management styles of organization can be depicted on a continuum from System 1 through System 4. These systems might be described as follows.

System 1—Management is seen as having no confidence or trust in subordinates, since they are seldom involved in any aspect of the decision-making process. The bulk of the decisions and the goal setting of the organization are made at the top and issued down the chain of command. Subordinates are forced to work with fear, threats, punishment, and occasional rewards and need satisfaction at the physiological and safety levels. The little superior-subordinate interaction that does take place is usually with fear and mistrust. While the control process is highly concentrated in top management, an informal organization generally develops which opposes the goals of the formal organization.

System 2—Management is seen as having condescending confidence and trust in subordinates, such as master has toward servant. While the bulk of the decisions and goal setting of the organization are made at the top, many decisions are made within a prescribed framework at lower levels. Rewards and some actual or potential punishment are used to motivate workers. Any superior-subordinate interaction takes place with some condescension by superiors and fear and caution by subordinates. While the control process is still concentrated in top management, some is delegated to middle and lower levels. An informal organization usually develops, but it does not always resist formal organizational goals.

System 3—Management is seen as having substantial but not complete confidence and trust in subordinates. While broad policy and general decisions are kept at the top, subordinates are permitted to make more specific decisions at lower levels. Communication flows both up and down the hierarchy. Rewards, occasional punishment, and some involvement are used to motivate workers. There is a moderate amount of superior-subordinate interaction, often with a fair amount of confidence and trust. Significant aspects of the control process are delegated downward with a feeling of responsibility at both higher and lower levels. An informal organization may develop, but it may either support or partially resist goals of the organization.

System 4—Management is seen as having complete confidence and trust in subordinates. Decision making is widely dispersed throughout the organization, although well integrated. Communication flows not only up and down the hierarchy but among peers. Workers are motivated by participation and involvement in developing economic rewards, setting goals, improving methods, and appraising progress toward goals. There is extensive, friendly superior-subordinate interaction with a high degree of confidence and trust. There is widespread responsibility for the control process, with the lower units fully involved. The informal and formal organizations are often one and the same. Thus, all social forces support efforts to achieve stated organizational goals.[14]

In summary, System 1 is a task-oriented, highly structured authoritarian management style, while System 4 is a relationships-oriented management style based on teamwork, mutual trust, and confidence. Systems 2 and 3 are intermediate stages between two extremes which approximate closely Theory X and Theory Y assumptions.

To expedite the analysis of a company's present behavior, Likert's group developed an instrument which enables members to rate their organization in terms of its management system. This instrument is designed to gather data about a number of operating characteristics of an organization. These characteristics include leadership, motivation, communication, decision making, interaction and influence, goal setting, and the control process used by the organization. Sample items from this instrument are presented in Figure 3.5. The complete instrument includes over twenty such items.[15]

In testing this instrument, Likert asked hundreds of managers from many different organizations to indicate where the *most* productive department, division, or organization they have known would fall between System 1 and System 4. Then these same managers were asked to repeat this process and indicate the position of the *least* productive department, division, or organization they have known. While the ratings of the most and the least productive departments varied among managers, almost without exception each manager rated the high-producing unit closer to System 4 than the low-producing department. In summary, Likert has

FIGURE 3.5 (right) Examples of items from Likert's table of organizational and performance characteristics of different management systems.

Organizational variable	System 1	System 2	System 3	System 4
Leadership processes used				
Extent to which superiors have confidence and trust in <u>subordinates</u>	Have no confidence and trust in subordinates	Have condescending confidence and trust, such as master has to servant	Substantial but not complete confidence and trust; still wishes to keep control of decisions	Complete confidence and trust in all matters
Character of motivational forces				
Manner in which motives are used	Fear, threats, punishment, and occasional rewards	Rewards and some actual or potential punishment	Rewards, occasional punishment, and some involvement	Economic rewards based on compensation system developed through participation; group participation and involvement in setting goals, improving methods, appraising progress toward goals, etc.
Character of interaction-influence process				
Amount and character of interaction	Little interaction and always with fear and distrust	Little interaction and usually with some condescension by superiors; fear and caution by subordinates	Moderate interaction, often with fair amount of confidence and trust	Extensive, friendly interaction with high degree of confidence and trust

found that the closer the management style of an organization approaches System 4, the more likely it is to have a continuous record of high productivity. Similarly, the closer this style reflects System 1, the more likely it is to have a sustained record of low productivity.

Likert has also used this instrument not only to measure what an individual believes are the present characteristics of his organization but also to find out what he would like these characteristics to be. Data generated from this use of the instrument with managers of well-known companies have indicated a large discrepancy between the management system they feel their company is now using and the management system they feel would be most appropriate. System 4 is seen as being most appropriate, but few see their companies presently utilizing this approach. These implications have led to attempts by some organizations to adapt their management system to more closely approximate System 4. Changes of this kind are not easy. They involve a massive reeducation of all concerned from the top management to the hourly workers.

theory into practice

One instance of a successful change in the management style of an organization occurred with a leading firm in the pajama industry.[16] After being unprofitable for several years this company was purchased by another corporation. At the time of the transaction, the purchased company was using a management style falling between System 1 and System 2. Some major changes were soon implemented by the new owners. The changes that were put into effect included extensive modifications in how the work was organized, improved maintenance of machinery, and a training program involving managers and workers at every level. Managers and supervisors were exposed in depth to the philosophy and understanding of management approaching System 4. All of these changes were supported by the top management of the purchasing company.

Although productivity dropped in the first several months after the initiation of the change program, productivity had increased by almost 30 percent within two years. Although it is not possible to calculate exactly how much of the increased productivity resulted from the change in management system, it was obvious to the researchers that the impact was considerable. In addition to increases in productivity, manufacturing costs decreased 20 percent, turnover was cut almost in half, and morale rose considerably (reflecting a more friendly attitude of workers toward the organization). The company's image in the community was enhanced, and for the first time in years the company began to show a profit.

SUMMARY AND CONCLUSIONS

We have tried through the material presented to examine what is known today about understanding and motivating employees. The attempt has been to review theoretical literature, empirical research, and case examples with the intention of integrating these sources into frameworks which may be useful to managers for analyzing and understanding behavior. Analyzing and understanding are necessary, but the real value of the application of the behavioral sciences will be their usefulness in directing, changing, and controlling behavior. Beginning with Chapter 4 a framework for applying leader behavior will be presented.

NOTES

1. For detailed descriptions of this research see F. J. Roethlisberger and W. J. Dickson, *Management and the Worker* (Cambridge: Harvard University Press, 1939); T. N. Whitehead, *The Industrial Worker,* 2 vols. (Cambridge: Harvard University Press, 1938); Elton Mayo, *The Human Problems of an Industrial Civilization* (New York: The Macmillan Company, 1933).

2. Douglas McGregor, *The Human Side of Enterprise* (New York: McGraw-Hill Book Company, 1960). See also McGregor, *Leadership and Motivation* (Boston: MIT Press, 1966).

3. George C. Homans, *The Human Group* (New York: Harcourt, Brace & World, Inc., 1950).

4. Anthony G. Athos and Robert E. Coffey, *Behavior in Organizations: A Multidimensional View* (Englewood Cliffs, N.J.: Prentice-Hall, Inc., 1968), p. 101.

5. S. E. Asch, "Effects of Group Pressure upon the Modification and Distortion of Judgments," in *Groups, Leadership and Men,* ed. Harold Guetzkow (New York: Russell and Russell, Publishers, 1963), pp. 177–90. Also in Dorwin Cartwright and Alvin Zander, *Group Dynamics,* 2nd ed. (Evanston, Ill.: Row, Peterson & Company, 1960), pp. 189–200.

6. *Ibid.*

7. Chris Argyris, *Personality and Organization* (New York: Harper & Row, Publishers, 1957); *Interpersonal Competence and Organizatioanl Effectiveness* (Homewood, Ill.: Dorsey Press, 1962); and *Integrating the Individual and the Organization* (New York: John Wiley & Sons, Inc., 1964).

8. N. Breman, *The Making of a Moron* (New York: Sheed & Ward, 1953).

9. For other examples of successful interventions, see Argyris, *Intervention Theory and Method: A Behavioral Science View* (Reading, Mass.: Addison-Wesley Publishing Company, 1970).

10. Frederick Herzberg, Bernard Mausner, and Barbara Synderman, *The Motivation to Work* (New York: John Wiley & Sons, Inc., 1959); and Herzberg, *Work and the Nature of Man* (New York: World Publishing Co., 1966).

11. Herzberg, Mausner, and Snyderman, *The Motivation to Work,* p. ix.

12. Scott M. Meyers, "Who Are Your Motivated Workers," in David R. Hampton, *Behavioral Concepts in Management* (Belmont, Calif.: Dickenson Publishing Co., Inc., 1968), p. 64. Originally published in *Harvard Business Review,* January-February 1964, pp. 73–88.

13. Rensis Likert, *The Human Organization* (New York: McGraw-Hill Book Company 1967); see also Likert, *New Patterns of Management* (New York: McGraw-Hill Book Company, 1961).

14. Descriptions adapted from Likert, *The Human Organization,* pp. 4–10.

15. *Ibid.*

16. A. J. Marrow, D. G. Bowers, and S. E. Seashore, eds., *Strategies of Organizational Change* (New York: Harper and Row, Publishers, 1967).

leader

behavior

4

The successful organization has one major attribute that sets it apart from unsuccessful organizations: dynamic and effective leadership. Peter F. Drucker points out that managers (business leaders) are the basic and scarcest resource of any business enterprise.[1] Statistics from recent years make this point more evident: "Of every 100 new business establishments started, approximately 50, or one half go out of business within two years. By the end of five years, only one third of the original 100 will still be in business." [2] Most of the failures can be attributed to ineffective leadership.

On all sides there is a continual search for persons who have the necessary ability to enable them to lead effectively. This shortage of effective leadership is not confined to business but is evident in the lack of able administrators in government, education, foundations, churches, and every other form of organization. Thus, when we decry the scarcity of leadership talent in our society, we are not talking about a lack of people to fill administrative or executive positions; we have plenty of administrative "bodies." What we are agonizing over is a scarcity of people who are willing to assume significant leadership roles in our society and can get the job done effectively.

LEADERSHIP DEFINED

According to George R. Terry, "Leadership is the activity of influencing people to strive willingly for group objectives."[3] Robert Tannenbaum, Irving R. Weschler, and Fred Massarik define leadership as "interpersonal influence exercised in a situation and directed, through the communication process, toward the attainment of a specialized goal or goals."[4] Harold Koontz and Cyril O'Donnell state that "leadership is *influencing* people to follow in the achievement of a common goal."[5]

A review of other writers reveals that most management writers agree that leadership is *the process of influencing the activities of an individual or a group in efforts toward goal achievement in a given situation.* From this definition of leadership, it follows that the leadership process is a function of the *leader*, the *follower*, and other *situational* variables—$L = f(l,f,s)$.

TRAIT VERSUS SITUATIONAL APPROACH TO THE STUDY OF LEADERSHIP

For many years the most common approach to the study of leadership concentrated on leadership traits per se, suggesting that there were certain characteristics, such as physical energy or friendliness, that were essential for effective leadership. These inherent personal qualities, like intelligence, were felt to be transferable from one situation to another. Since all individuals did not have these qualities, only those who had them would be considered to be potential leaders. Consequently this approach seemed to question the value of training individuals to assume leadership positions. It implied that if we could discover how to identify and measure these leadership qualities (which are inborn in the individual), we should be able to screen leaders from nonleaders. Leadership training would then be helpful only to those with inherent leadership traits.

A review of the research literature using this trait approach to leadership has revealed few significant or consistent findings.[6] As Eugene E. Jennings concluded, "Fifty years of study have failed to produce one personality trait or set of qualities that can be used to discriminate leaders and non-leaders."[7] Empirical studies suggest that leadership is a dynamic process, varying from situation to situation with changes in leaders, followers, and situations. Current literature seems to support this situational or leader behavior approach to the study of leadership.[8]

The focus in the situational approach to leadership is on observed behavior, not on any hypothetical inborn or acquired ability or potential for leadership. The emphasis is on the behavior of leaders and their group members (followers) and various situations. With this emphasis upon behavior and environment, more encouragement is given to the possibility of training individuals in adapting styles of leader behavior to varying situations. Therefore it is believed that most people can increase their effectiveness in leadership roles through education, training, and development. From observations of the frequency (or infrequency) of certain leader behavior in numerous types of situations, theoretical models can be developed to help a leader make some predictions about the most appropriate leader behavior for his present situation. For these reasons, in this chapter we will talk in terms of leader behavior rather than leadership traits, thus emphasizing the situational approach to leadership.

LEADERSHIP PROCESS

We have defined leadership as the process of influencing the activities of an individual or a group in efforts toward goal achievement in a given situation. In essence, leadership involves accomplishing goals with and through people. Therefore a leader must be concerned about tasks and human relationships. Although using different terminology, Chester I. Barnard identified these same leadership concerns in his classic work *The Functions of the Executive* in the late 1930s.[9] These leadership concerns seems to be a reflection of two of the earliest schools of thought in organizational theory—scientific management and human relations.

scientific management movement

In the early 1900s one of the most widely read theorists on administration was Frederick Winslow Taylor. The basis for his *scientific management* was technological in nature. It was felt that the best way to increase output was to improve the techniques or methods used by workers. Consequently, he has been interpreted as considering people as instruments or machines to be manipulated by their leaders. Accepting this assumption, other theorists of the scientific management movement proposed that an organization as rationally planned and executed as possible be developed to create more efficiency in administration and consequently increase production. Management was to be divorced from human affairs and emotions. The result was that the people or workers had to adjust to the management and not the management to the people.

To accomplish this plan, Taylor initiated time and motion studies to analyze work tasks in order to improve performance in every aspect of the organization. Once jobs had been reorganized with efficiency in mind, the economic self-interest of the workers could be satisfied through various incentive work plans (piece rates, etc.).

The function of the leader under scientific management or classical theory was quite obviously to set up and enforce performance criteria to meet organizational goals. His main focus was on the needs of the organization and not on the needs of the individual.[10]

human relations movement

In the 1920s and early 1930s, the trend initiated by Taylor was to be replaced at center stage by the *human relations* movement. This was initiated by Elton Mayo and his associates. These theorists argued that in addition to finding the best technological methods to improve output, it was beneficial to management to look into human affairs. It was claimed that the real power centers within an organization were the interpersonal relations that developed within the working unit. The study of these human relations was the most important consideration for management and the analysis of organization. The organization was to be developed around the workers and had to take into consideration human feelings and attitudes.[11]

The function of the leader under human relations theory was to facilitate cooperative goal attainment among his followers while providing opportunities for their personal growth and development. His main focus, contrary to scientific management theory, was on individual needs and not the needs of the organization.

In essence, then, the scientific management movement emphasized a concern for task, while the human relations movement stressed a concern for relationships (people). The recognition of these two concerns has characterized the writings on leadership ever since the conflict between the scientific management and the human relations schools of thought became apparent.

authoritarian–democratic–laissez faire leader behavior

Past writers have felt that concern for task tends to be represented by authoritarian leader behavior, while a concern for relationships is represented by democratic leader behavior. This feeling was popular because it was generally agreed that a leader influences his followers by either of two ways: (1) he can tell his followers what to do and how to do it, or (2) he can share his leadership responsibilities with his followers by involving them in the planning and execution of the task. The former is the traditional authoritarian style which emphasizes task concerns. The latter is the more nondirective democratic style which stresses the concern for human relationships.

The differences in the two styles of leader behavior are based on the assumptions the leader makes about the source of his power or authority and human nature. The authoritarian style of leader behavior is often based on the assumption that the leader's power is derived from the position he occupies and that man is innately lazy and unreliable (Theory X), whereas the democratic style assumes that the leader's power is granted by the group he is to lead and that men can be basically self-directed and creative at work if properly motivated (Theory Y). As a result, in the authoritarian style, all policies are determined by the leader, while in the democratic style, policies are open for group discussion and decision.

There are, of course, a wide variety of styles of leader behavior between these two extremes. Robert Tannenbaum and Warren H. Schmidt depicted a broad range of styles on a continuum moving from authoritarian leader behavior at one end to democratic leader behavior at the other end,[12] as illustrated in Figure 4.1.

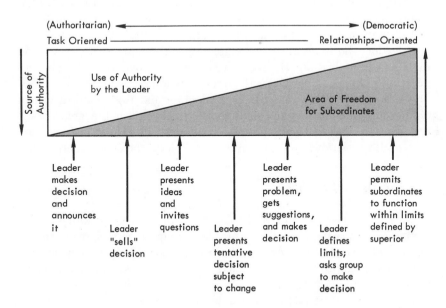

FIGURE 4.1   Continuum of leader behavior.

Leaders whose behavior is observed to be at the authoritarian end of the continuum tend to be task-oriented and use their power to influence their followers, while leaders whose behavior appears to be at the democratic end tend to be group-oriented and thus give their followers considerable freedom in their work. Often this continuum is extended beyond democratic leader behavior to include a laissez faire style. This style of behavior permits the members of the group to do whatever they want to do. No policies or procedures are established. Everyone is let alone. No one attempts to influence anyone else. As is evident, this style is not included in the continuum of leader behavior illustrated in Figure 4.1. This was done because it was felt that in reality, a laissez faire atmosphere represents an absence of leadership. The leadership role has been abdicated, and therefore no leader behavior is being exhibited.

The recognition of two leadership styles, one emphasizing task and the other stressing relationships, has been given support in several leadership studies.

Michigan leadership studies

In the early studies of the Survey Research Center at the University of Michigan there was an attempt to approach the study of leadership by locating clusters of characteristics that seemed to be related to each other and tests of effectiveness. The studies identified two concepts which they called *employee orientation* and *production orientation.*

A leader who is described as employee-oriented stresses the relationships aspect of his job. He feels that every employee is important. He takes interest in everyone, accepting their individuality and personal needs. Production orientation emphasizes production and the technical aspects of the job, viewing employees as tools to accomplish the goals of the organization. These two orientations parallel the authoritarian (task) and democratic (relationships) concepts of the leader behavior continuum.[13]

group dynamics studies

Dorwin Cartwright and Alvin Zander, based on the findings of numerous studies at the Research Center for Group Dynamics, claim that all group objectives fall into one of two categories: (1) the achievement of some specific group goal, or (2) the maintenance or strengthening of the group itself.[14]

According to Cartwright and Zander, the type of behavior involved in goal achievement is illustrated by these examples: The manager "initiates action . . . keeps members' attention on the goal . . . clarifies the issue and develops a procedural plan." [15]

On the other hand, characteristic behaviors for group maintenance are: The manager "keeps interpersonal relations pleasant . . . arbitrates disputes . . . provides encouragement . . . gives the minority a chance to be heard . . . stimulates self-direction . . . and increases the interdependence among members." [16]

Goal achievement seems to coincide with the task concepts discussed earlier (authoritarian and production orientation), while group maintenance parallels the relationships concepts (democratic and employee orientation).

In recent years, research findings indicate that leadership styles vary considerably from leader to leader. Some leaders emphasize the task and can be described as authoritarian leaders, while others stress interpersonal relationships and may be viewed as democratic leaders. Still others seem to be both task-oriented and relationships-oriented. There are even some individuals in leadership positions who are not concerned about either. No dominant style appears. Instead various combinations are evident. Thus task and relationships are not either/or leadership styles as the preceding continuum suggests. They are separate and distinct dimensions that can be plotted on two separate axes rather than a single continuum.

Ohio State leadership studies

The leadership studies initiated in 1945 by the Bureau of Business Research at Ohio State University attempted to identify various dimensions of leader behavior.[17] The staff, defining leadership as the behavior of an individual when he is directing the activities of a group toward a goal attainment, eventually narrowed the description of leader behavior to two dimensions: *Initiating Structure* and *Consideration.* Initiating Structure refers to "the leader's behavior in delineating the relationship between himself and members of the work-group and in endeavoring to establish well-defined patterns of organization, channels of communication, and methods of procedure." On the other hand, Consideration refers to "behavior indicative of friendship, mutual trust, respect, and warmth in the relationship between the leader and the members of his staff." [18]

To gather data about the behavior of leaders, the Ohio State staff developed the Leader Behavior Description Questionnaire (LBDQ), an instrument designed to describe *how* a leader carries out his activities.[19] The LBDQ contains fifteen items pertaining to Consideration and an equal number for Initiating Structure. Respondents judge the frequency with which their leader engages in each form of behavior by checking one of five descriptions—always, often, occasionally, seldom, or never—as it relates to each particular item of the LBDQ. Thus Consideration and Initiating Structure are dimensions of observed behavior as perceived by others. Examples of items used in the LBDQ for both these dimensions are given below.

Consideration	*Initiating Structure*
The leader finds time to listen to group members	The leader assigns group members to particular tasks
The leader is willing to make changes	The leader asks the group members to follow standard rules and regulations
The leader is friendly and approachable	The leader lets group members know what is expected of them

In studying leader behavior the Ohio State staff found that Initiating Structure and Consideration were separate and distinct dimensions. High on one dimension does not necessitate being low on the other. The behavior of a leader could be described as any mix of both dimensions. Thus it was during these studies that leader behavior was first plotted on two separate axes rather than on a single continuum. Four quadrants were developed to show various combinations of Initiating Structure (task behavior) and Consideration (relationships behavior), as illustrated in Figure 4.2.

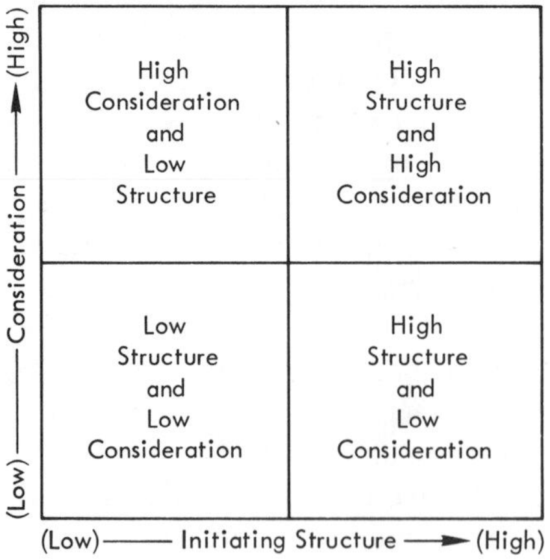

FIGURE 4.2 The Ohio State leadership quadrants.

managerial grid

In discussing the Ohio State, Michigan, and Group Dynamics leadership studies, we have been concentrating on two theoretical concepts, one emphasizing *task* accomplishment and the other stressing the development of personal *relationships*. Robert R. Blake and Jane S. Mouton have popularized these concepts in their Managerial Grid and have used them extensively in organization and management development programs.[20]

In the Managerial Grid, five different types of leadership based on concern for production (task) and concern for people (relationships) are located in the four quadrants identified by the Ohio State studies.

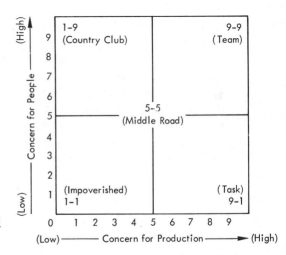

FIGURE 4.3   The Managerial Grid leadership styles.

Concern for production is illustrated on the horizontal axis. Production becomes more important to the leader as his rating advances on the horizontal scale. A leader with a rating of 9 on the horizontal axis has a maximum concern for production.

Concern for people is illustrated on the vertical axis. People become more important to the leader as his rating progresses up the vertical axis. A leader with a rating of 9 on the vertical axis has maximum concern for people.

The five leadership styles are described as follows:

Impoverished—Exertion of minimum effort to get required work done is appropriate to sustain organization membership.

Country Club—Thoughtful attention to needs of people for satisfying relationships leads to a comfortable friendly organization atmosphere and work tempo.

Task—Efficiency in operations results from arranging conditions of work in such a way that human elements interfere to a minimum degree.

Middle-of-the-Road—Adequate organization performance is possible through balancing the necessity to get out work while maintaining morale of people at a satisfactory level.

Team—Work accomplishment is from committed people; interdependence through a "common stake" in organization purpose leads to relationships of trust and respect.[21]

In essence, the Managerial Grid has given popular terminology to five points within the four quadrants of the Ohio State studies. However, one significant difference between the two frameworks should be noted. "Concern for" is a predisposition about something or an attitudinal dimension. Therefore, the Managerial Grid tends to be an attitudinal model which measures the predispositions of a manager, while the Ohio State framework tends to be a behavioral model which examines how leader actions are perceived by others. A diagram combining the two frameworks could be illustrated as shown in Figure 4.4.

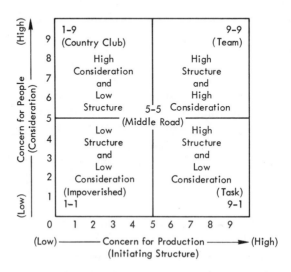

FIGURE 4.4   Merging of the Ohio State and the Managerial Grid theories of leadership.

IS THERE A BEST STYLE OF LEADERSHIP?

After identifying the two central concerns of any leadership situation, task and relationships, the researchers discussed earlier have recognized the potential conflict in satisfying both concerns. Consequently, an attempt has been made to find a middle ground which will encompass both concerns. Chester Barnard recognized this fact when he purposely included both concerns as necessary factors for the survival of any organization.[22]

According to Warren G. Bennis, theorists like Barnard who express concern for both task and relationships are called "revisionists."

> The revisionists are now concerned with external, economic factors, with productivity, with formal status, and so on, but not to the exclusion of the human elements that the traditional theorists so neglected. So what we are observing now is the pendulum swinging just a little farther to the middle from its once extreme position to balance and modulate with more refinement in the human organization requirements.[23]

Andrew W. Halpin, using the Leader Behavior Description Questionnaire in a study of school superintendents, found that the administrators he interviewed had a tendency to view Consideration and Initiating Structure as either/or forms of leader behavior. "Some administrators act as if they were forced to emphasize one form of behavior at the expense of the other." [24] Halpin stressed that this conflict between Initiating Structure and Consideration should not necessarily exist. He points out that according to his findings, "effective or desirable leadership behavior is characterized by high scores on both Initiating Structure and Consideration. Conversely, ineffective or undesirable leadership behavior is marked by low scores on both dimensions." [25]

From these observations, Halpin concludes that a successful leader "must contribute to both major group objectives: goal achievement and group maintenance (in Cartwright and Zander's terms); or in Barnard's terms, he must facilitate cooperative group action that is both effective and efficient." [26] Thus the Ohio State leadership studies seem to conclude that the high Consideration and Initiating Structure style is theoretically the ideal or "best" leader behavior, while the style low on both dimensions is theoretically the "worst."

The Managerial Grid also implies that the most desirable leader behavior is "team management" (maximum concern for production and people). In fact, Blake and Mouton have developed training programs to change managers toward a 9–9 management style.[27]

Using the earlier Michigan studies as a starting place, Rensis Likert did some extensive research to discover the general pattern of management used by high-producing managers in contrast to that used by the other managers. He found that "supervisors with the best records of performance focus their primary attention on the human aspects of their subordinates' problems and on endeavoring to build effective work groups with high performance goals." [28] These supervisors were called "employee-centered." Other supervisors who kept constant pressure on production were called "job-centered" and were found more often to have low-producing sections.[29] Figure 4.5 presents the findings from one study.

NUMBER OF FIRST-LINE SUPERVISORS WHO ARE

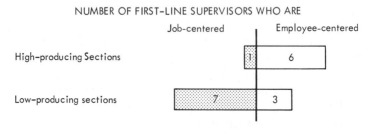

FIGURE 4.5   Employee-centered supervisors are higher producers than job-centered supervisors.

Likert also discovered that high-producing supervisors "make clear to their subordinates what the objectives are and what needs to be accomplished and then give them freedom to do the job." [30] Thus he found that general rather than close supervision tended to be associated with high productivity. This relationship, found in a study of clerical workers,[31] is illustrated in Figure 4.6.

NUMBER OF FIRST-LINE SUPERVISORS WHO ARE

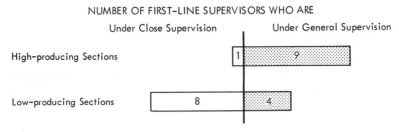

FIGURE 4.6   Low-production section heads are more closely supervised than high-production heads.

The implication throughout Likert's writings is that the ideal and most productive leader behavior for industry is employee-centered or democratic. Yet his own findings raise questions as to whether there can be an ideal or single normatively good style of leader behavior which can apply in all leadership situations. As the preceding figures revealed, one of the eight job-centered supervisors and one of the nine supervisors using close supervision had high-producing sections; also three of the nine employee-centered supervisors and four of the thirteen supervisors who used general supervision had low-producing sections. In other words, in almost 35 percent of the low-producing sections, the suggested ideal type of leader behavior produced undesirable results and almost 15 percent of the high-producing sections were supervised by the suggested "undesirable" style.

Similar findings and interpretations were made by Halpin and Winer in a study of the relationship between the aircraft commander's leadership pattern and the proficiency rating of his crew.[32] Using the LBDQ, they found that eight of ten commanders with high proficiency ratings were described as using above average Consideration and Initiating Structure, while six of seven commanders with low ratings were seen as below average in Consideration and Initiating Structure. As Likert did, Halpin and Winer reported only that the leaders above average in both *Consideration* and *Initiating Structure* are likely to be effective and did not discuss the two high proficiency low Consideration-low Initiating Structure commanders and the one low-producing high Consideration-High Initiating Structure commander.

Further evidence suggesting that a single ideal or normative style of leader behavior is unrealistic was provided when a study was done in an industrial setting in Nigeria.[33] The results were almost the exact opposite of Likert's findings. In that country the tendency is for job-centered supervisors who provide close supervision to have high-producing sections, while the low-producing sections tend to have employee-centered supervisors who provide general supervision. Thus a single normative leadership style does not take into consideration cultural differences, particularly customs and traditions as well as the level of education and the standard of living. These are examples of cultural differences in the followers and the situation which are important in determining the appropriate leadership style to be used. Therefore, based on the definition of leadership process as a function of the leader, the followers, and other situational variables, the desire to have *a single ideal type of leader behavior seems unrealistic.*

ADAPTIVE LEADER BEHAVIOR

This desire to have an ideal type of leader behavior is common. Many managers appear to want to be told how to act. It is also clear from the preceding discussion that many writers in the field of leadership suggest some normative style. Most of these writers have supported either an integrated leadership style (high concern for both task and relationships) or a permissive, democratic, human relations approach. These styles might be appropriate in some industrial or educational settings in the United States, but they also may be limited to them. Effective leader behavior in other institutions, such as the military, hospitals, prisons, churches, might very well be entirely different. Perhaps our formula should be modified to read: $E = f(l,f,s)$. The E stands for effectiveness. An effective leader is able to adapt his style of leader behavior to the needs of situation and the followers. Since these are not constants, the use of an appropriate style of leader behavior is a challenge to the effective leader. "The manager must be much like the musician who changes his techniques and approaches to obtain the shadings of total performance desired." [34] The concept of *adaptive leader behavior* might be stated as follows:

> The more a manager adapts his style of leader behavior to meet the particular situation and the needs of his followers, the more effective he will tend to be in reaching personal and organizational goals. [35]

leadership contingency model

The concept of adaptive leader behavior questions the existence of a "best" style of leadership: It is not a matter of the best style, but of the most effective style for a particular situation. The suggestion is that a number of leader behavior styles may be effective or ineffective depending on the important elements of the situation.

According to a Leadership Contingency Model developed by Fred E. Fiedler, three major situational variables seem to determine whether a given situation is favorable or unfavorable to a leader: (1) his personal relations with the members of his group (leader-member relations); (2) the degree of structure in the task that the group has been assigned to perform (task structure); and (3) the power and authority that his position provides (position power). [36] Leader-member relations seem to parallel the relationships concepts discussed earlier, while task structure and position power, which measure very closely related aspects of a situation, seem to be related to task concepts. Fiedler defines the *favorableness of a situation* as "the degree to which the situation enables the leader to exert his influence over his group." [37]

In this model, eight possible combinations of these three situational variables can occur. As a leadership situation varies from high to low on these variables, it will fall into one of the eight combinations (situations). The most favorable situation for a leader to influence his group is one in which he is well liked by the members (good leader-member relations), has a powerful position (high position power), and is directing a well-defined job (high task structure): for example, a well-liked general making inspection in an army camp. On the other hand, the most unfavorable situation is one in which the leader is disliked, has little position power, and faces an unstructured task: an unpopular chairman of a voluntary hospital fund-raising committee.

Having developed this model for classifying group situations, Fiedler has attempted to determine what the most effective leadership style—task-oriented or relationships-oriented—seems to be for each of the eight situations. In a reexamination of old leadership studies and an analysis of new studies, in terms of his model, Fiedler has concluded that:

1. *Task-oriented* leaders tend to perform best in group situations that are either very favorable or very unfavorable to the leader.
2. *Relationships-oriented* leaders tend to perform best in situations that are intermediate in favorableness.

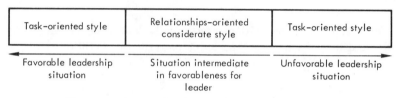

FIGURE 4.7   Leadership styles appropriate for various group situations.[38]

While Fiedler's model is useful to a leader, he seems to be reverting to a single continuum of leader behavior, suggesting that there are only two basic leader behavior styles, task-oriented and relationships-oriented. It is felt that most evidence indicates that leader behavior must be plotted on two separate axes rather than on a single continuum. Thus a leader who has a high concern for tasks does not necessarily have a high or a low concern for relationships. Any combination of the two dimensions may occur.

THE TRI-DIMENSIONAL LEADER EFFECTIVENESS MODEL

In the Tri-Dimensional Leader Effectiveness model which we will be discussing, the terms *task behavior* and *relationships behavior* will be used to describe the same concepts that the Ohio State studies defined as *Consideration* and *Initiating Structure*. The four basic leader behavior quadrants will be labeled as high task and low relationships, high task and high relationships, high relationships and low task, and low task and low relationships, as illustrated in Figure 4.8.

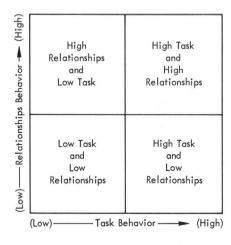

FIGURE 4.8 The basic leader behavior styles.

These four basic styles depict essentially leader personalities. As an individual matures he develops habit patterns or conditioned responses to various stimuli.

habit *a,* habit *b,* habit c, . . . , habit *n* = *personality*

An individual begins to behave in a similar fashion under similar conditions. This behavior is what others learn to recognize as that person, as his *personality.* They expect and can even predict certain kinds of behavior from him.

In the context of leader behavior, we are concerned about the portion of the total personality of an individual that we will call his *leader personality.* This is what some authors refer to as style. In the context of this book we will use the words "personality" and "style" interchangeably. The leader personality, or style, of an individual is the behavior pattern he exhibits when he is involved in directing the activities of others. The pattern generally involves either task behavior or relationships behavior or some combination of both. The two types of behavior, task and relationships, which are central to the concept of leader personality, are defined as follows:

Task Behavior—The extent to which a leader is likely to organize and define the roles of the members of his group (followers); to explain what activities each is to do and when, where, and how tasks are to be accomplished; characterized by endeavoring to establish well-defined patterns of organization, channels of communication, and ways of getting jobs accomplished.

Relationships Behavior—The extent to which a leader is likely to maintain personal relationships between himself and the members of his group (followers) by opening up channels of communication, delegating responsibility, giving subordinates an opportunity to use their potential; characterized by socioemotional support, friendship, and mutual trust.[39]

effectiveness dimension

Recognizing that the effectiveness of a leader depends on how his leader personality interrelates with the situation in which he operates, an effectiveness dimension should be added to the two-dimensional model. This is illustrated in Figure 4.9.

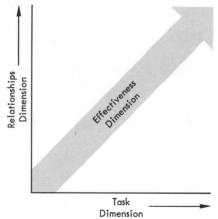

FIGURE 4.9   Adding an effectiveness dimension.

In his 3-D Management Style Theory, William J. Reddin was the first to add an effectiveness dimension to the task and relationships dimensions of earlier models.[40] Reddin, whose pioneer work influenced greatly the development of the Tri-Dimensional Leader Effectiveness Model presented in this text, felt that a useful theoretical model "must allow that a variety of styles may be effective or ineffective depending on the situation." [41]

By adding an effectiveness dimension to the task and relationships dimensions of earlier leadership models, we are attempting to integrate the concepts of leader style with situational demands of a specific environment. When the style of a leader is appropriate to a given situation, it is termed *effective;* when his style is inappropriate to a given situation, it is termed *ineffective.*

If the effectiveness of a leader behavior style depends upon the situation in which it is used, it follows that any of the basic styles may be effective or ineffective depending on the situation. The difference between the effective and the ineffective styles is often not the actual behavior of the leader, but the appropriateness of this behavior to the situation in which it is used. You might think of the leader's basic style as a particular stimulus, and it is the response to this stimulus that can be considered effective or ineffective. This is an important point because theorists and practitioners who argue that there is one best style of leadership are making value judgments about the stimulus, while those taking a situational approach to leadership are evaluating the response or the results rather than the stimulus. This concept is illustrated in the diagram of the Tri-Dimensional Leader Effectiveness Model presented in Figure 4.10.

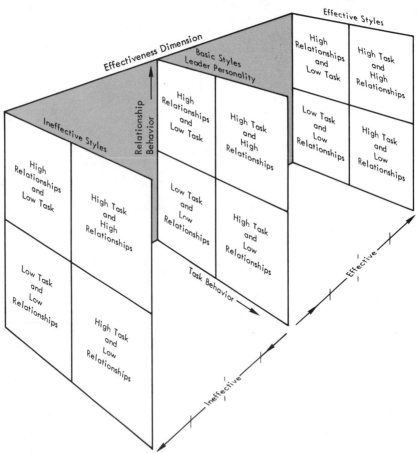

FIGURE 4.10   The tri-dimensional leader effectiveness model.

Although effectiveness appears to be an either/or situation in this model, in reality it should be represented as a continuum. Any given style in a particular situation could fall somewhere on this continuum from extremely effective to extremely ineffective. Effectiveness, therefore, is a matter of degree, and there could be an infinite number of faces in the effectiveness dimension rather than only three. To illustrate this fact, the effectiveness dimension has been divided into quartiles ranging on the effective side from +1 to +4 and on the ineffective side from −1 to −4.

The four effective and the four ineffective styles are, in essence, how appropriate a leader's basic style is to a given situation as seen by his followers, his superiors, or his associates. Table 4.1 describes briefly how each style might be perceived by others.[42]

TABLE 4.1   How the basic leader behavior styles are seen by others when they are effective or ineffective.

Basic Styles	Effective	Ineffective
High Task and Low Relationships	Often seen as knowing what he wants and imposing his methods for accomplishing this without creating resentment.	Often seen as having no confidence in others, unpleasant, and interested only in short-run output.
High Task and High Relationships	Often seen as satisfying the needs of the group for setting goals and organizing work, but also providing high levels of socioemotional support.	Often seen as initiating more structure than is needed by the group and spends more time on socioemotional support than necessary.
High Relationships and Low Task	Often seen as having implicit trust in people and as being primarily concerned with developing their talents.	Often seen as primarily interested in harmony and being seen as "a good person," and being unwilling to risk disruption of a relationship to accomplish a task.
Low Task and Low Relationships	Often seen as appropriately permitting his subordinates to decide how the work should be done and playing only a minor part in their social interaction.	Often seen as uninvolved and passive, as a "paper shuffler," who cares little about the task at hand or the people involved.

A model such as the Tri-Dimensional Leader Effectiveness Model is distinctive because it does not depict a single ideal leader behavior style that is suggested as being appropriate in all situations. For example, the high task and high relationships style is appropriate only in certain situations. In basically crisis-oriented organizations like the military or the police, there is considerable evidence that the most appropriate style would be high task and low relationships, since under combat, riot, or emergency conditions success often depends upon immediate response to orders. Time demands do not permit talking things over or explaining decisions. But once the crisis is over, other styles might become appropriate. For example, although the fire chief may have to initiate a high level of structure at the scene of a fire, upon returning to the firehouse it may be appropriate for the chief to engage in other styles while his men are participating in auxiliary functions, such as maintaining the equipment or studying new firefighting techniques.

attitudinal versus behavioral models

In examining the dimensions of the Managerial Grid (concern for production and concern for people), one can see that these are *attitudinal* dimensions. Concern is a feeling or an emotion toward something. On the other hand, the dimensions of the Ohio State Model (Initiating Structure and Consideration) and the Tri-Dimensional Leader Effectiveness Model (task behavior and relationships behavior) are dimensions of *observed* behavior. Thus, the Ohio State and the Leader Effectiveness models measure *how* people behave, while the Managerial Grid measures *predisposition* toward production and people.[43] As discussed earlier, the Tri-Dimensional Leader Effectiveness Model is different from the Ohio State Model in that it adds an effectiveness dimension.

Although the Managerial Grid and the Leader Effectiveness Model measure different aspects of leadership, they are not incompatable. A conflict develops, however, because behavioral assumptions have often been drawn from analysis of the attitudinal dimensions of the Managerial Grid. While high *concern* for both production and people is desirable in organizations, managers having a high concern for both people and production do not always find it appropriate in all situations to initiate a high degree of structure and provide a high degree of socioemotional support. For example, if a manager's subordinates are emotionally mature and can take responsibility for themselves, his appropriate style of leadership may be low task and low relationships. In this case, the manager permits these subordinates to participate in the planning, organizing, and controlling of their own operation. He plays a background role, providing socioemotional support only when necessary. Consequently, it is assumptions about behavior drawn from the Managerial Grid and not the Grid itself that are inconsistent with the Leader Effectiveness Model.

In summary, empirical studies tend to show that there is no normative (best) style of leadership; successful leaders do adapt their leader behavior to meet the needs of the group and of the particular situation. Effectiveness depends upon the *leader,* the *follower(s),* and other *situational* variables—$E = f(l,f,s)$. Therefore, anyone who is interested in increasing his own success as a leader must give serious thought to these behavioral and environmental considerations.

We have now discussed a number of approaches to the study of leader behavior, concluding with a Tri-Dimensional Leader Effectiveness Model. In Chapter 5 we will discuss the effectiveness dimension in this model.

NOTES

1. Peter F. Drucker, *The Practice of Management* (New York: Harper & Row, Publishers, 1954).
2. George R. Terry, *Principles of Management,* 3rd ed. (Homewood, Ill.: Richard D. Irwin, Inc., 1960), p. 5.
3. Terry, *Principles of Management,* p. 493.
4. Robert Tannenbaum, Irving R. Weschler, and Fred Massarik, *Leadership and Organization: A Behavioral Science Approach* (New York: McGraw-Hill Book Company, 1959).
5. Harold Koontz and Cyril O'Donnell, *Principles of Management,* 2nd ed. (New York: McGraw-Hill Book Company, 1959), p. 435.
6. Cecil A. Gibb, "Leadership," in *Handbook of Social Psychology,* Gardner Lindzey, ed. (Cambridge, Mass.: Addison-Wesley Publishing Company, Inc., 1954). See also Roger M. Stogdill, "Personal Factors Associated with Leadership: A Survey of the Literature," *Journal of Psychology,* 25 (1948), 35–71.
7. Eugene E. Jennings, "The Anatomy of Leadership," *Management of Personnel Quarterly,* I, No. 1 (Autumn 1961).
8. John K. Hemphill, *Situational Factors in Leadership,* Monograph No. 32 (Columbus, Ohio: Bureau of Educational Research, The Ohio State University, 1949).
9. Chester I. Barnard, *The Functions of the Executive* (Cambridge: Harvard University Press, 1938).
10. Frederick W. Taylor, *The Principles of Scientific Management* (New York: Harper & Brothers, 1911).
11. Elton Mayo, *The Social Problems of an Industrial Civilization* (Boston: Harvard Business School, 1945), p. 23.
12. This figure was adapted from Exhibit 1 in Robert Tannenbaum and Warren H. Schmidt, "How to Choose a Leadership Pattern," *Harvard Business Review,* March-April 1957, pp. 95–101.
13. D. Katz, N. Maccoby, and Nancy C. Morse, *Productivity, Supervision, and Morale in an Office Situation* (Ann Arbor, Mich.: Survey Research Center, 1950); D. Katz, N. Maccoby, G. Gurin, and Lucretia G. Floor, *Productivity, Supervision, and*

Morale among Railroad Workers (Ann Arbor, Mich.: Survey Research Center, 1951).

14. Dorwin Cartwright and Alvin Zander, eds., *Group Dynamics: Research and Theory,* 2nd ed. (Evanston, Ill.: Row, Peterson & Company, 1960).

15. *Ibid.,* p. 496.

16. *Ibid.*

17. Roger M. Stogdill and Alvin E. Coons, eds., *Leader Behavior: Its Description and Measurement,* Research Monograph No. 88 (Columbus, Ohio: Bureau of Business Research, The Ohio State University, 1957).

18. Andrew W. Halpin, *The Leadership Behavior of School Superintendents* (Chicago: Midwest Administration Center, The University of Chicago, 1959), p. 4.

19. *Ibid.,* pp. 6–9.

20. Robert R. Blake and Jane S. Mouton, *The Managerial Grid* (Houston, Tex.: Gulf Publishing, 1964).

21. Robert R. Blake *et al.,* "Breakthrough in Organization Development," *Harvard Business Review,* November-December 1964, p. 136.

22. Barnard, *The Functions of the Executive.*

23. Warren G. Bennis, "Leadership Theory and Administrative Behavior: The Problems of Authority," *Administrative Science Quarterly,* IV, No. 3 (December 1959), p. 274.

24. Halpin, *The Leadership Behavior of School Superintendents,* p. 79.

25. *Ibid.*

26. *Ibid.,* p. 6.

27. Blake *et al.,* "Breakthrough," p. 135.

28. Rensis Likert, *New Patterns of Management* (New York: McGraw-Hill Book Company, 1961), p. 7.

29. *Ibid.*

30. *Ibid.,* p. 9.

31. *Ibid.*

32. Andrew W. Halpin and Ben J. Winer, *The Leadership Behavior of Airplane Commanders* (Columbus, Ohio: The Ohio State University Research Foundation, 1952).

33. Paul Hersey, an unpublished research project, 1965.

34. Koontz and O'Donnell, *Principles of Management.*

35. Paul Hersey, *Management Concepts and Behavior: Programmed Instruction for Managers* (Little Rock, Ark.: Marvern Publishing Co., 1967), p. 15.

36. Fred E. Fiedler, *A Theory of Leadership Effectiveness* (New York: McGraw-Hill Book Company, 1967).

37. *Ibid.,* p. 13.

38. Adapted from Fiedler, *A Theory of Leadership Effectiveness,* p. 14.

39. Since our model is an outgrowth of the Ohio State Leadership Studies these definitions have been adapted from their definitions of "Initiating Structure" (task) and "Consideration" (relationships), Stogdill and Coons, *Leader Behavior: Its Description and Measurement,* pp. 42–43.

40. William J. Reddin, "The 3-D Management Style Theory," *Training and Development Journal,* April 1967, pp. 8–17; see also *Managerial Effectiveness* (New York: McGraw-Hill Book Company, 1970).

41. Reddin, "The 3-D Management Style Theory," p. 13.

42. Parts of this table were adapted from the managerial style descriptions of William J. Reddin, *The 3-D Management Style Theory,* Theory Paper #2—Managerial Styles (Fredericton, N.B., Canada: Social Science Systems, 1967), pp. 5–6.

43. Reddin's 3-D Management Style Theory seems to be attitudinal in nature rather than behavioral. The dimensions of his model are task orientation and relationships orientation. See Reddin, "The 3-D Management Style Theory," *Training and Development Journal.* Fiedler in his Contingency Model of Leadership Effectiveness (Fiedler, *A Theory of Leadership Effectiveness*) also tends to make behavioral assumptions from data gathered from an attitudinal measure of leadership style. A leader is asked to evaluate his least preferred co-worker (LPC) on a series of Semantic Differential type scales. Leaders are classified as high or low LPC depending on the favorableness with which they rate their LPC.

determining

effectiveness

5

The most important aspect of the Tri-Dimensional Leader Effectiveness Model is that it adds *effectiveness* to the task and relationships dimensions of earlier leadership models. For this reason, it seems appropriate to examine closely the concept of effectiveness.

MANAGEMENT EFFECTIVENESS
VERSUS LEADERSHIP EFFECTIVENESS

In discussing effectiveness it is important once again to distinguish between *management* and *leadership*. In essence, leadership is a broader concept than management. Management is thought of as a special kind of leadership in which the accomplishment of organizational goals is paramount. While leadership also involves working with and through people to accomplish goals, these goals are not necessarily organizational goals.

For example, a vice-president may have a strong personal goal to become the company president. In attempting to achieve this goal, he may not be concerned with organizational goals at all, but only with undermining the plans of the president and other executives who may be contenders for the job. He may accomplish his goals and, in that sense, be a successful leader. However, he cannot be considered an effective manager, since his actions are probably disruptive to the effective operation of the firm. Thus, in discussing effectiveness we must recognize the difference between *individual goals, organizational goals, leadership,* and *management.*

SOURCES OF POWER

One of the characteristics of leadership is that leaders exercise power. Amitai Etzioni discusses the difference between *position power* and *personal power.* His distinction springs from his concept of power as the ability to induce or influence behavior. He claims that power is derived from an organizational office, personal influence, or both. An individual who is able to induce another individual to do a certain job because of his position in the organization is considered to have position power, while an individual who derives his power from his followers is considered to have personal power. Some individuals can have both position and personal power.[1]

Etzioni postulates that the best situation for a leader is when he has both personal and position power. But in some cases it is not possible to build a relationship on both. Then the question becomes whether it is more important to have personal power or position power. Happiness and human relations have been culturally reinforced over the past several decades. With this emphasis, most people would pick personal power as being the most important. But there may be another side of the coin.

In his fifteenth century treatise *The Prince,* Machiavelli presents an interesting viewpoint when he raises the question whether it is better to have a relationship based upon love (personal power) or fear (position power).[2] Machiavelli, as Etzioni, contends that it is best to be both loved and feared. If, however, one cannot have both, he suggests that a relationship based on love alone tends to be volatile, short run, and easily terminated when there is no fear of retaliation. On the other hand, Machiavelli contends that a relationship based upon fear tends to be longer lasting in that the individual must be willing to incur the sanction (pay the price) before terminating the relationship. This is a difficult concept for many people to accept, and yet one of the most difficult roles for a leader, whether he be a boss, teacher, or parent, is disciplining someone about whom he cares. Yet to be effective one sometimes has to sacrifice short-term friendship for long-term respect if he is interested in the growth and development of the people with whom he is working. Machiavelli warns, however, that one should be careful that fear does not lead to hatred. For hatred often evokes overt behavior in terms of retaliation, undermining, and attempts to overthrow.

SUCCESSFUL LEADERSHIP
VERSUS EFFECTIVE LEADERSHIP

If an individual attempts to have some effect on the behavior of an-other, we call this stimulus *attempted* leadership. The response to this leadership attempt can be successful or unsuccessful. Since a manager's basic responsibility in any type of organization is to get work done with and through people, his success is measured by the output or productivity of the group he leads. With this thought in mind, Bernard M. Bass suggests a clear distinction between *successful* and *effective* leadership or manage-ment.[3]

Suppose manager A attempts to influence individual B to do a certain job. A's attempt will be considered successful or unsuccessful depending on the extent that B accomplishes the job. It is not really an either/or situation. A's success could be depicted on a continuum (Figure 5.1) ranging from very successful to very unsuccessful with gray areas in be-tween which would be difficult to ascertain as either.

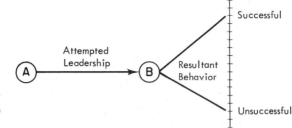

FIGURE 5.1   Successful-unsuccessful   leadership continuum.

Let us assume that A's leadership is successful. In other words, B's response to A's leadership stimulus falls on the successful side of the continuum. This still does not tell the whole story of effectiveness.

If A's leader style is not compatible with the expectations of B, and if B is antagonized and does the job only because of A's position power, then we can say that A has been successful but not effective. B has responded as A intended because A has control of rewards and punishment, and not because B sees his own needs being accomplished by satisfying the goals of the manager or the organization.

On the other hand, if A's attempted leadership leads to a successful response, and B does the job because he wants to do it and finds it rewarding, then we consider A as having not only position power but also personal power. B respects A and is willing to cooperate with him, realizing that A's request is consistent with his own personal goals. In fact, B sees his own goals as being accomplished by this activity. This is what is meant by effective leadership, keeping in mind that effectiveness also appears as a continuum which can range from very effective to very ineffective, as illustrated in Figure 5.2.

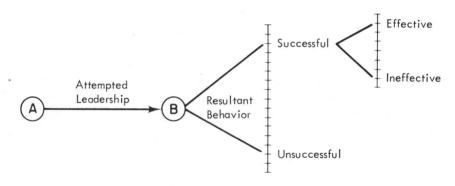

FIGURE 5.2   Successful and effective leadership continuums.

Success has to do with how the individual or the group behaves. On the other hand, effectiveness describes the internal state or predisposition of an individual or a group and thus is attitudinal in nature. If an individual is interested only in success, he tends to emphasize his position power and uses close supervision. However, if he is effective he will depend also on personal power and be characterized by more general supervision. Position power tends to be delegated down though the organization, while personal power is generated upward from below through follower acceptance.

In the management of organizations, the difference between successful and effective often explains why many supervisors can get a satisfactory level of output only when they are right there, looking over the worker's shoulder. But as soon as they leave output declines and often such things as horseplay and scrap loss increase.

The phenomenon described applies not only to business organizations but also to less formal organizations like the family. If parents are successful and effective, have both position and personal power, their children accept family goals as their own. Consequently, if the husband and wife leave for the weekend, the children behave no differently than if their parents were there. If, on the other hand, the parents continually use close supervision and the children view their own goals as being stifled by their parents' goals, the parents have only position power. They maintain order because of the rewards and the punishments they control. If these parents went away on a trip leaving the children behind, upon returning they might be greeted by havoc and chaos.

In summary, a manager could be successful, but ineffective, having only short-run influence over the behavior of others. On the other hand, if a manager is both successful and effective, his influence tends to lead to long-run productivity and organizational development.

It should be pointed out that this successful versus effective framework is a way of evaluating the response to a specific behavioral event and not of evaluating behavior over time. The evaluation of a leader or an organization over time will be discussed in the following section.

WHAT DETERMINES
ORGANIZATIONAL EFFECTIVENESS?

In discussing effectiveness we have concentrated on evaluating the results of individual leaders or managers. While these results are significant, perhaps the most important aspect of effectiveness is its relationship to an entire organization. Here we are concerned not only with the outcome of a given leadership attempt but with the effectiveness of the organizational unit over a period of time. Rensis Likert identifies three variables—causal, intervening, and end-result—which are useful in discussing effectiveness over time.[4]

causal variables

Causal variables are those factors that influence the course of develop-
ments within an organization and its results or accomplishments. These
variables are those independent variables that can be altered or changed
by the organization and its management, and not variables that are beyond
the control of the organization, like general business conditions. Leadership strategies, skills, and behavior, management's decisions, and the
policies and structure of the organization are examples of causal variables.

intervening variables

Leadership strategies, skills, and behavior and other causal variables
affect the human resources or intervening variables in an organization.
According to Likert, intervening variables represent the current condition
of the internal state of the organization and are reflected in its skills,
loyalty, commitment to objectives, motivations, communications, decision
making, and capacity for effective interaction.[5]

output or end-result variables

Output or end-result variables are the dependent variables that reflect
the achievements of the organization. In evaluating effectiveness, perhaps
more than 90 percent of managers in organizations look at measures of
output alone. Thus, the effectiveness of a business manager is often determined by net profits, the effectiveness of a college professor may be
determined by the number of articles and books he has published, and
the effectiveness of a basketball coach may be determined by his won-lost
record.

Many researchers talk about effectiveness by emphasizing similar output variables. Fred E. Fiedler, for example, in his studies evaluated
"leader effectiveness in terms of group performance on the group's primary
assigned task." [6] William J. Reddin, in discussing management styles,
thinks in similar terms about effectiveness. He argues that the effectiveness
of a manager should be measured "objectively by his profit center performance"—maximum output, market share, or other similar criteria.[7]

One might visualize the relationship between the three classes of variables as stimuli (causal variables) acting upon the organism (intervening
variables) and creating certain responses (output variables), as illustrated
in Figure 5.3.[8]

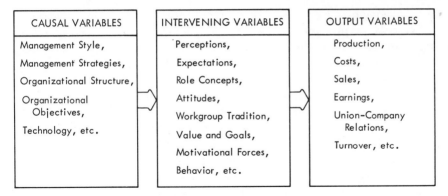

FIGURE 5.3   Relationship between causal, intervening, and output variables.

The level or condition of the intervening variables are produced largely by the causal variables and in turn have influence upon the end-result variables. Attempts by members of the organization to improve the intervening variables by endeavoring to alter these variables directly will be much less successful usually than efforts directed toward modifying them through altering the causal variables. Similarly, efforts to improve the end-result variables by attempting to modify the intervening variables will usually be less effective than changing the causal variables.[9]

long-term goals versus short-term goals

Intervening variables are concerned with building and developing the organization and tend to be long-term goals. Managers are often promoted, however, on the basis of short-run output variables such as increased production and earnings, without concern for the long-run and organizational development. This creates a dilemma.

organizational dilemma

One of the major problems in industry today is that there is a shortage of successful managers. Therefore, it is not uncommon for a manager to be promoted in six months or a year if he is a "producer." Since the basis on which top management promotes is often short-run output, managers attempt to achieve high levels of productivity and often overemphasize tasks, placing extreme pressure on everyone, even when it is inappropriate.

We have all probably had some experience with coming into an office or a home and raising the roof with subordinates. The immediate or short-run effect is probably increased productivity. We also know that if this style is inappropriate for those concerned, and if it continues over a long period of time, the morale and climate of the organization will deteriorate. Some indications of deterioration of these intervening variables at work may be turnover, absenteeism, increased accidents, scrap loss, and numerous grievances. Not only the number of grievances but the nature of grievances is important. Are grievances really significant problems or do they reflect pent-up emotions due to anxieties and frustration? Are they settled at the complaint stage between the employee and the supervisor or are they pushed up the hierarchy to be settled at higher levels or by arbitration? The organizational dilemma is that in many instances, a manager who places pressure on everyone and produces in the short run is promoted out of this situation before the disruptive aspects of the intervening variables catch up.

There tends to be a time lag between declining intervening variables and significant restriction of output by employees under such management climate. Employees tend to feel "things will get better." Thus, when the manager is promoted rapidly, he often stays "one step ahead of the wolf."

The real problem is faced by the next manager. Although productivity records are high, he has inherited many problems. Merely the introduction of a new manager may be enough to collapse the slowly deteriorating intervening variables. A tremendous drop in morale and motivation leading almost immediately to significant decrease in output can occur. Change by its very nature is frightening; to a group whose intervening variables are declining, it can be devastating. Regardless of this new manager's style, the present expectations of the followers may be so distorted that much time and patience will be needed to close the now apparent "credibility gap" between the goals of the organization and the personal goals of the group. No matter how effective this manager may be in the long run, his superiors, in reviewing a productivity drop, may give him only a few months to improve performance. But as Likert's studies indicate, rebuilding a group's intervening variables in a small organization may take one to three years, and in a large organization, it may extend to seven years. This dilemma is not restricted to business organizations.

In one of Fiedler's studies he examined the leadership in basketball teams. The criterion he used in evaluating the effectiveness of these leaders was percentage of games—won and lost. Most people also tend to evaluate coaches on won-and-lost records.

Charlie, a high school coach, has had several good seasons. He knows if he has one more such season he will have a job offer with a better salary at a more prestigious school. Under these conditions, he may decide to concentrate on the short-run potential of the team. He may play only his seniors and he may have an impressive record at the end of the season. Short-run output goals have been maximized, but the intervening variables of the team have not been properly used. If Charlie leaves this school and accepts another job, a new coach will find himself with a tremendous rebuilding job. But because developing the freshmen and sophomores and rebuilding a good team takes time and much work, the team could have a few poor seasons in the interim. When the alumni and fans see the team losing, they soon forget that old adage "It's not whether you win or lose, it's how you play the game." They immediately consider the new coach "a bum." After all, "We had some great seasons with good ole Charlie." It is difficult for them to realize that the previous coach concentrated only on short-run winning at the expense of building for the future. The problem is that the effectiveness of a new coach is judged immediately on the same games won basis as his predecessor. He may be doing an excellent job of rebuilding and may have a winning season in two or three years, but the probability of his being given the opportunity to build a future winner is low.

It should be clear that we do not think this is an either/or process. It is often a matter of determining how much to concentrate on each. In our basketball example, suppose a team has good potential, having a large number of experienced senior players, but as the season progresses it does not look as if it is going to be an extremely good year. There comes a point in this season when the coach must make a basic decision. Will he continue to play his experienced seniors and hope to win a majority of his final games, or should he forget about concentrating on winning the last games and play his sophomores and juniors to give them experience, in hopes of developing and building a winning team for future years? The choice is between short- and long-term goals. If the accepted goal is building and developing the team for the future, then the coach should be evaluated on these terms and not entirely on his present won-lost record.

While intervening variables do not appear on won-lost records, balance sheets, sales reports, or accounting ledgers, we feel that these long-term considerations are just as important to an organization as short-term output variables. Therefore, although difficult to measure, intervening variables should not be overlooked in determining organizational effectiveness. One of the instruments used by Likert to measure these variables was discussed in Chapter 3.

In summary, we feel that effectiveness is actually determined by whatever the manager and the organization decide are their goals and objectives, but they should consider these factors: *output variables, intervening variables, short-range goals,* and *long-range goals.*

FORCE FIELD ANALYSIS

Kurt Lewin

Force field analysis, a technique for diagnosing situations, developed by Kurt Lewin, may be useful in looking at the variables involved in determining effectiveness.[10]

Lewin assumes that in any situation there are both driving and restraining forces which influence any change that may occur. *Driving forces* are those forces affecting a situation that are "pushing" in a particular direction; they tend to initiate a change and keep it going. In terms of improving productivity in a work group, pressure from a supervisor, incentive earnings, and competition may be examples of driving forces. *Restraining forces* are forces acting to restrain or decrease the driving forces. Apathy, hostility, and poor maintenance of equipment may be examples of restraining forces against increased production. Equilibrium is reached when the sum of the driving forces equals the sum of the restraining forces. In our example, equilibrium represents the present level of productivity, as shown in Figure 5.4.

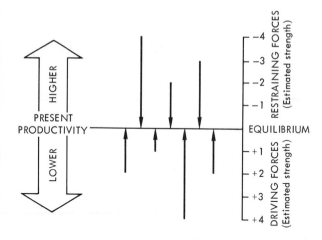

FIGURE 5.4   Driving and restraining forces in equilibrium.

This equilibrium, or present level of productivity, can be raised or lowered by changes in the relationship between the driving and the restraining forces. For illustrations, let us look again at the dilemma of the new manager who takes over a work group where productivity is high but his predecessor drained the human resources (intervening variables). The former manager had upset the equilibrium by increasing the driving forces (i.e., being autocratic and keeping continual pressure on his men) and thus achieving increases in output in the short run. By doing this, though, new restraining forces developed, such as increased hostility and antagonism, and at the time of his departure the restraining forces were beginning to increase and the results manifested themselves in turnover, absenteeism, and other restraining forces which lowered productivity shortly after the new manager arrived. Now a new equilibrium at a significantly lower productivity is faced by the new manager.

Now just assume that our new manager decides not to increase the driving forces but to reduce the restraining forces. He may do this by taking time away from the usual production operation and engaging in problem solving and training and development. In the short run, output will tend to be lowered still further. However, if commitment to objectives, and technical know-how of his group, are increased in the long run, they may become new driving forces, and that, along with the elimination of the hostility and the apathy, which were restraining forces, will now tend to move the balance to a higher level of output.

A manager is often in a position where he must consider not only output but also intervening variables, not only short-term but also long-term goals, and a framework that is useful in diagnosing these interrelationships is available through force field analysis.

INTEGRATION OF GOALS AND EFFECTIVENESS

The extent that individuals and groups perceive their own goals as being satisfied by the accomplishment of organizational goals is the degree of integration of goals. When organizational goals are shared by all, this is what McGregor calls a true "integration of goals." [11]

To illustrate this concept we can divide an organization into two groups, management and subordinates. The respective goals of these two groups and the resultant attainment of the goals of the organization to which they belong are illustrated in Figure 5.5.

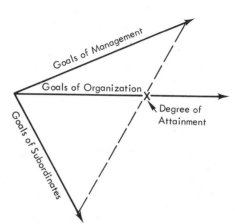

FIGURE 5.5 Directions of goals of management, subordinates, and the organization—*moderate* organizational accomplishment.

In this instance, the goals of management are somewhat compatible with the goals of the organization but are not exactly the same. On the other hand, the goals of the subordinates are almost at odds with those of the organization. The result of the interaction between the goals of management and the goals of subordinates is a compromise, and actual performance is a combination of both. It is at this approximate point that the degree of attainment of the goals of the organization can be pictured. This situation can be much worse where there is little accomplishment of organizational goals, as illustrated in Figure 5.6.

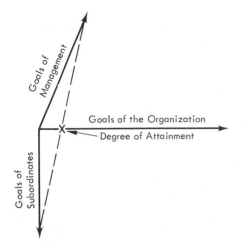

FIGURE 5.6 Little organizational accomplishment.

In this situation, there seems to be a general disregard for the welfare of the organization. Both managers and workers see their own goals conflicting with the organization's. Consequently, both morale and performance will tend to be low and organizational accomplishment will be negligible. In some cases, the organizational goals can be so opposed that no positive progress is obtained. The result often is substantial losses, or draining off of assets. (See Figure 5.7.) In fact, organizations are going out of business every day because of these very reasons.

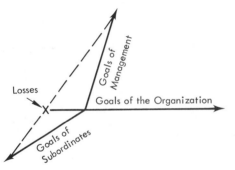

FIGURE 5.7 No positive organizational accomplishment.

The hope in an organization is to create a climate in which one of two things occurs. The individuals in the organization (both managers and subordinates) either perceive their goals as being the same as the goals of the organization or, although different, see their own goals being satisfied as a direct result of working for the goals of the organization. Consequently, the closer we can get the individual's goals and objectives to the organization's goals, the greater will be the organizational performance, as illustrated in Figure 5.8.

FIGURE 5.8   An integration of the goals of management, subordinates, and the organization—*high* organizational accomplishment.

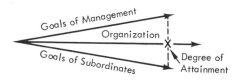

One of the ways in which the effective leader bridges the gap between the individual's and the organization's goals is by creating a loyalty to himself among his men. He does this by being an influential spokesman for them with higher management.[12]

The leader then has no difficulty in communicating organizational goals to his men, and his men do not find it difficult to associate the acceptance of these goals with accomplishment of their own need satisfaction.

PARTICIPATION AND EFFECTIVENESS

In an organizational setting, it is urged that the criteria for an individual or a group's performance should be mutually decided in advance. In making these decisions, a manager and his subordinates should consider output and intervening variables, short- and long-range goals. This process has two advantages. First, it will permit subordinates to participate in determining the basis on which their efforts will be judged. Second, involving subordinates in the planning process will increase their commitment to the goals and objectives established. Research evidence seems to support this contention.

One of the classic studies in this area was done by Coch and French in an American factory.[13] They found that when managers and employees discussed proposed technological changes, productivity increased and resistance to change decreased once these procedures were initiated. Other studies have shown similar results.[14] These studies suggest that involving employees in decision making tends to be effective in our society. Once again, though, we must remember that the success of using participative management depends on the situation. While this approach tends to be effective in some industrial settings in America, it may not be appropriate in other countries.

This argument was illustrated clearly when French, Israel, and Ās attempted to replicate the original Coch and French experiment in a Norwegian factory.[15] In this setting, they found no significant difference in productivity between work groups in which participative management was used and those in which it was *not* used. In other words, increased participation in decision making did not have the same positive influence on factory workers in Norway as it did in America. Similar to Hersey's replication of one of Likert's studies in Nigeria, this Norwegian study suggests that cultural differences in the followers and the situation may be important in determining the appropriate leadership style.

management by objectives

We realize that it is not an easy task to integrate the goals and objectives of all individuals with the goals of the organization. Yet it is not an impossible task. A participative approach to this problem which has been used successfully in some organizations in our culture is a process called *management by objectives.*

Management by objectives is basically:

> A process whereby the superior and the subordinate managers of an enterprise jointly, identify its common goals, define each individual's major areas of responsibility in terms of the results expected of him, and use these measures as guides for operating the unit and assessing the contribution of each of its members.[16]

This process in some cases has been successfully carried beyond the managerial level to include hourly employees. A number of companies, including Non-Linear Systems and Union Carbide, have had significant success in broadening individual responsibility and involvement in work planning at the lowest organizational levels.[17] The concept rests on a philosophy of management which emphasizes an integration between external control (by managers) and self-control (by subordinates). It can apply to any manager or individual no matter what his level or function, and to any organization, regardless of size.

The smooth functioning of this system is an agreement between a manager and his subordinate about his own or his group's performance goals during a stated time period. These goals can emphasize either output variables or intervening variables, or some combination of both. The important thing is that goals are jointly established and agreed upon in advance. This is then followed by a review of the subordinate's performance in relation to accepted goals at the end of the time period. Both superior and subordinate participate in this review and in any other evaluation that takes place. It has been found that objectives that are formulated with each person participating seem to gain more acceptance than those imposed by an authority figure in the organization. Consultation and participation in this area tends to establish personal risk for the attainment of the formulated objective by those who actually perform the task.

Prior to setting individual objectives, the common goals of the entire organization should be clarified, and, at this time, any appropriate changes in the organizational structure should be made: changes in titles, duties, relationships, authority, responsibility, span of control, and so forth.

Throughout the time period what is to be accomplished by the entire organization should be compared with what is being accomplished; necessary adjustments should be made and inappropriate goals discarded. At the end of the time period, a final mutual review of objectives and performance takes place. If there is a discrepancy between the two, efforts are initiated to determine what steps can be taken to overcome these problems. This sets the stage for the determination of objectives for the next time period.

The entire cycle of management by objectives is represented graphically in Figure 5.9 on page 106.[18]

Management by objectives may become a powerful tool in gaining mutual commitment and high productivity for an organization where management realizes this type of involvement of subordinates is appropriate in its situation.

STYLE AND EFFECTIVENESS

Examples of research that support the argument that all the basic leader behavior styles may be effective or ineffective depending on the situation are readily available.

A. K. Korman gathered some of the most convincing evidence that dispels the idea of a single best style of leader behavior.[19] Korman attempted to review all studies that examined the relationships between the Ohio State behavior dimensions of Initiating Structure (task) and Consideration (relationships) and various measures of effectiveness, in-

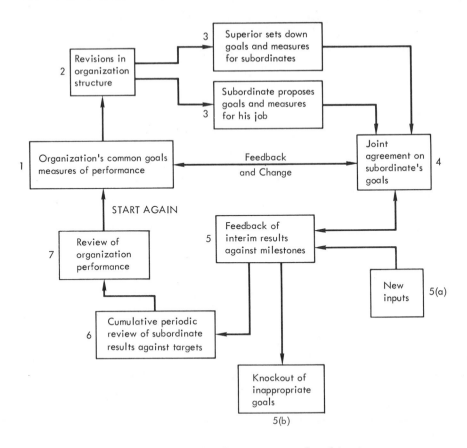

FIGURE 5.9   The cycle of management by objectives.

cluding group productivity, salary, performance under stress, administrative reputation, work group grievances, absenteeism, and turnover. In all, over twenty-five studies were reviewed. In every case the two dimensions were measured by either the Leadership Opinion Questionnaire or the Leader Behavior Description Questionnaire. The former is used to assess how a leader thinks he should behave in a given situation, while the latter measures follower perceptions of leader behavior. Korman concluded that

> Despite the fact that "Consideration" and "Initiating Structure" have become almost bywords in American industrial psychology, it seems apparent that very little is now known as to how these variables may predict work group performance and the conditions which affect

such predictions. At the current time, we cannot even say whether they have any predictive significance at all.[20]

Thus, Korman found that Consideration and Initiating Structure had no significant predictive value in terms of effectiveness. This suggests that since situations differ, so must leader style.

Fred Fiedler, in testing his contingency model of leadership in over fifty studies covering a span of sixteen years (1951–67), concluded that both directive, task-oriented leaders and nondirective, human relations-oriented leaders are successful under some conditions. As Fiedler argues:

> While one can never say that something is impossible, and while someone may well discover the all-purpose leadership style or behavior at some future time, our own data and those which have come out of sound research by other investigators do not promise such miraculous cures.[21]

A number of other investigators besides Likert, Korman, and Fiedler have also shown that *different leadership situations require different leader styles.*[22] In summary, the evidence is clear that there is no single, all-purpose leader behavior style that is effective in all situations.

While our basic conclusion in this chapter is that the type of leader behavior needed depends on the situation, this conclusion leaves many questions unanswered for a specific individual in a leadership role. Such an individual may be personally interested in how leadership depends on the situation and how he can find some practical value in theory. To accommodate this type of concern, in Chapter 6 we will discuss the environmental variables that may help a leader or a manager to make effective decisions in problematic leadership situations.

NOTES

1. Amitai Etzioni, *A Comparative Analysis of Complex Organizations* (New York: The Free Press, 1961).
2. Niccolò Machiavelli, "Of Cruelty and Clemency, Whether It Is Better to Be Loved or Feared," *The Prince and the Discourses* (New York: Random House, Inc., 1950), Chap. XVII.
3. Suggested by Bernard M. Bass in *Leadership, Psychology, and Organizational Behavior* (New York: Harper & Brothers, 1960).
4. Rensis Likert, *The Human Organization* (New York: McGraw-Hill Book Company, 1967), pp. 26–29.

5. Rensis Likert, *New Patterns of Management* (New York: McGraw-Hill Book Company, 1961), p. 2.

6. Fred E. Fiedler, *A Theory of Leadership Effectiveness* (New York: McGraw-Hill Book Company, 1967), p. 9.

7. William J. Reddin, "The 3-D Management Style Theory," *Training and Development Journal*, April 1967. This is one of the critical differences between Reddin's 3-D Management Style Theory and the Tri-Dimensional Leader Effectiveness Model. Reddin in his model seems to consider only output variables in determining effectiveness, while in the Tri-Dimensional Leader Effectiveness Model both intervening variables and output variables are considered.

8. Adapted from Likert, *The Human Organization*, pp. 47–77.

9. *Ibid.*, p. 77.

10. Kurt Lewin, "Frontiers in Group Dynamics: Concept, Method, and Reality in Social Science; Social Equilibria and Social Change," *Human Relations*, I, No. 1 (June 1947), 5–41.

11. Douglas McGregor, *The Human Side of Enterprise* (New York: McGraw-Hill Book Company, 1960). See also McGregor, *Leadership and Motivation* (Boston: MIT Press, 1966).

12. Saul W. Gellerman, *Motivation and Productivity* (New York: American Management Association, 1963), p. 265. See also Gellerman, *Management by Motivation* (New York: American Management Association, 1968).

13. L. Coch and J. R. P. French, "Overcoming Resistance to Change," in Dorwin Cartwright and Alvin Zander, eds., *Group Dynamics: Research and Theory*, 2nd ed. (Evanston, Ill.: Row, Peterson & Company, 1960).

14. See Kurt Lewin "Group Decision and Social Change," in G. Swanson, T. Newcomb, and E. Hartley, eds., *Readings in Social Psychology* (New York: Henry Holt, 1952), pp. 459–73; K. Lewin, R. Lippitt, and R. White, "Leader Behavior and Member Reaction in Three 'Social Climates,'" in Cartwright and Zander, *Group Dynamics: Research and Theory;* and N. Morse and E. Reimer, "The Experimental Change of a Major Organizatioanl Variable," *Journal of Abnormal Social Psychology*, 52 (1956), 120–29.

15. John R. P. French, Jr., Joachim Israel, and Dagfinn Ās, "An Experiment on Participation in a Norwegian Factory," *Human Relations*, 13 (1960), 3–19.

16. George S. Odiorne, *Management by Objectives* (New York: Pitman Publishing Corp., 1965).

17. Chris Argyris, *Integrating the Individual and the Organization* (New York: John Wiley & Sons, Inc., 1964); Abraham Maslow, *Eupsychian Management* (Homewood, Ill.: Richard D. Irwin, Inc., and Dorsey Press, 1965).

18. Odiorne, *Management by Objectives*, p. 78.

19. A. K. Korman, "'Consideration,' 'Initiating Structure,' and Organizational Criteria —A Review," *Personnel Psychology: A Journal of Applied Research*, XIX, No. 4 (Winter 1966), 349–61.

20. *Ibid.*, p. 360.

21. Fiedler, *A Theory of Leadership Effectiveness*, p. 247.

22. See C. A. Gibb, "Leadership," in *Handbook of Social Psychology*, Gardner Lindzey, ed. (Cambridge, Mass.: Addison-Wesley Publishing Company, Inc., 1964); A. P. Hare, *Handbook of Small Group Research* (New York: John Wiley & Sons, Inc., 1965); and D. C. Pelz, "Leadership within a Hierarchial Organization," *Journal of Social Issues*, 7 (1961), 49–55.

diagnosing

the environment

6

The Tri-Dimensional Leader Effectiveness Model is built on the concept that effectiveness results from a leader using a behavioral style that is appropriate to the demands of the environment. The key for a manager is learning how to diagnose his environment.

ENVIRONMENTAL VARIABLES

The environment consists of the leader himself and his followers, superiors, associates, organization, and job demands.[1] This list is not all-inclusive, but it contains some of the interacting components that tend to be important to a manager, as illustrated in Figure 6.1.

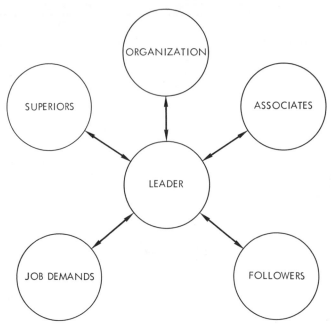

FIGURE 6.1 Interacting components of an organizational setting.

Except for job demands, each of these environmental variables can be viewed as having two major components—personality and expectations. Thus our list of variables is expanded to include the following:

Leader's personality	Leader's expectations
Followers' personalities	Followers' expectations
Superiors' personalities	Superiors' expectations
Associates' personalities	Associates' expectations
Organization's personality	Organization's expectations

Job Demands

personality defined

As previously discussed, we are using the terms *personality* and *style* interchangeably. Personality is defined as consistent behavior patterns of an individual as perceived by others. These patterns emerge as an individual begins to respond in the same fashion under similar conditions; he develops habits of action which become somewhat predictable to those who work with him.

expectations defined

Expectations are the perceptions of appropriate behavior for one's own role or position or one's perceptions of the roles of others within the organization. In other words, the expectations of an individual define for him what he should do under various circumstances in his particular job and how he thinks others—his superiors, peers, and subordinates—should behave in relation to his position. To say that a person has *shared expectations* with another person means that each of the individuals involved perceives accurately and accepts his role and the role of the other. If expectations are to be compatible it is important to share common goals and objectives. While two people may have differing personalities because their roles require different styles of behavior, it is imperative for an organization's effectiveness that they perceive and accept the institution's goals and objectives as their own.

The task of diagnosing a leader environment is very complex when we realize that the leader is the pivotal point around which all of the other environmental variables interact, as shown in Figure 6.1. In a sense, all these variables are communicating role expectations to him.

PERSONALITY AND EXPECTATIONS

Behavior of an individual in an organization, according to Jacob W. Getzels, results from the interaction of personality and expectations.[2] Some positions or roles are structured greatly by expectations; that is, they allow the person occupying that position very little room to express his individual personality. The behavior of an army private, for example, may be said to conform almost completely to role expectations.[3] Little innovative behavior is tolerated. In highly structured, routine jobs based on Theory X assumptions about human nature, the behavior required by an individual is predetermined.

On the other hand, some positions have fewer formal expectations, allowing for more individual latitude in expressing one's personality. The behavior of a research chemist, for example, is derived extensively from his personality, and innovation and creativity are encouraged. It seems that as an individual moves to a more responsible job, personality becomes more important and expectations become less structured.

The difference between these two positions in terms of personality and expectations is illustrated in Figure 6.2.[3]

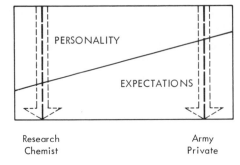

Research
Chemist

Army
Private

FIGURE 6.2   Personality and expectations as related to two different positions or roles.

While the mix varies from job to job, behavior in an organization remains a function of both personality and expectations and involves some combination of task and relationships orientation.

leader's personality and expectations

One of the most important elements of a leadership situation is the personality of the leader himself. The leader develops this *style* over a period of time from experience, education, and training. This style is not how the leader thinks he behaves in his situation but how others (most importantly, his followers) perceive his behavior. This is often a difficult concept for a leader to understand. If a leader's followers think he is a hard-nosed, task-oriented leader, this is very valuable information for him to know. In fact, it makes little difference whether he thinks he is a relationships-oriented, democratic leader, because his followers will behave according to how *they* perceive his behavior. In this case, the followers will treat the leader as if he were a hard-nosed, task-oriented leader. Thus, a leader has to learn how he is coming across to others. Yet this kind of information is difficult to obtain. People are often reluctant to be honest with one another on this subject, especially if they are in a superior-subordinate relationship.

One method that has been developed to help individuals learn how others perceive their behavior is "sensitivity or T-group training." This method of training was developed at Bethel, Maine, in 1947, by Leland P. Bradford, Kenneth D. Benne, and Ronald Lippitt.[4] It is based on the assumption that a number of individuals meeting in an unstructured situation with an open climate will develop working relations with each other and learn a great deal about themselves as perceived by the other group members.

The training process relies primarily and almost exclusively on the behavior experienced by the participants; i.e., the *group itself* becomes the focus of inquiry ... In short, the participants learn to analyze and become more sensitive to the processes of human interaction and acquire concepts to order and control these phenomena.[5]

An example follows of one of Chris Argyris's experiences with a T-group where the president and nine vice-presidents of a large industrial organization went into a retreat for a week to discuss their problems.

At the outset, after defining the objectives of this educational experience, the seminar leader said, in effect, "O.K. Let's go." There was a very loud silence and someone said, "What do you want us to do?"

(Silence.)

"Where's the agenda?"

(Silence.)

"Look, here, what's going on? Aren't you going to lead this?"

(Silence.)

"I didn't come up here to feel my stomach move. What's up?"

(Silence.)

"Fellows, if he doesn't speak in five minutes, I'm getting out of here."

"Gentlemen," said the treasurer, "We've paid for the day, so let's remain at least till five."

"You know, there's something funny going on here."

"What's funny about it?"

"Well, up until a few minutes ago we trusted this man enough that all of us were willing to leave the company for a week. Now we dislike him. Why? He hasn't done anything."

"That's right. And it's his job to do something. He's the leader and he ought to lead."

"But I'm learning something already about how we react under these conditions. I honestly feel uncomfortable and somewhat fearful. Does anybody else?"

"That's interesting that you mention fear, because I think that we run the company by fear."

The president turned slightly red and became annoyed: "I don't think that we run this company by fear and I don't think you should have said that."

A loud silence followed. The vice president thought for a moment, took a breath, looked the president straight in the eye and said, "I still think we run this company by fear and I agree with you. I should not have said it."

The group laughed and the tension was broken.

"I'm sorry," the president said. "I wanted all you fellows with me here so that we can try to develop a higher sense of openness and trust. The first one that really levels with us, I let him have it. I'm sorry—but it isn't easy to hear about management by fear . . ."

"And it's not easy to tell you."

"Why not? Haven't I told you that my door is open?"

And the group plunged into the issue of how they judge the openness of a person—by the way he speaks or by the way he behaves? [6]

Argyris reported that

The group explored their views about each other—the way each individual tended unintentionally to inhibit the other (the vice presidents learned that they inhibited each other as much as the president did, but for years had felt it was his fault); their levels of aspiration, their goals in their company life and in their total life; their ways of getting around each other, ranging from not being honest with one another to creating organizational fires which had to be put out by someone else; their skill at polarizing issues when deep disagreements occurred so that the decisions could be bucked right up to the president, who would have to take the responsibility and the blame; their techniques in the game of one-upmanship, etc. [7]

The result was highly satisfying. Once these top executives returned home, they found that they could reduce the number of meetings, the time spent at meetings, the defensive politicking, and the windmilling at the lower levels. In time they also found that they could truly delegate more responsibility, get more valid information up from the ranks, and make the decisions more freely.

Although the main objective of T-group training was originally personal growth or self-insight, the process is now being used extensively to implement organization improvement or change. [8] It should be remembered, though, that this approach is relatively new and is still being developed. It has some critics as well as advocates among organizations that have experimented with these techniques.

A central problem according to some is that sensitivity training is designed to change an individual, not necessarily to change the environment he works. in. When the individual attempts to use what he has learned, he often finds his co-workers unwilling to accept it or, even worse, what he has learned may not be appropriate for his "back home" situation. In an article from the *Wall Street Journal* entitled "The Truth Hurts," an example was cited where this very thing happened:

> A division manager at one big company was described by a source familiar with his case as "a ferocious guy—brilliant but a thoroughgoing autocrat—who everyone agreed was just what the division needed, because it was a tough, competitive business." Deciding to smooth over his rough edges, the company sent him to sensitivity training—where he found out exactly what people thought of him. "So he stopped being a beast," says the source, "and his effectiveness fell apart." The reason he'd been so good was that he didn't realize what a beast he was. Eventually, they put in a new manager.

All leaders have expectations about the way they should behave in a certain situation. How they actually behave often depends on these expectations. The resulting behavior, though, is sometimes modified by the impact of how they interpret the expectations of other persons in their environment, that is, how they feel their boss expects them to operate.

followers' personalities and expectations

The personalities or styles of his followers (subordinates) are an important consideration for a leader in appraising his situation. In fact, as Fillmore Sanford has indicated, there is some justification for regarding the followers "as the most crucial factor in any leadership event." [9] Followers in any situation are vital, not only because individually they accept or reject the leader but because as a group they actually determine whatever personal power he may have.

This element is important at all levels of management. Victor H. Vroom has uncovered evidence that the effectiveness of a leader is dependent to a great extent on the personality or style of the individual workers.[10]

> Place a group with strong independence drives under a supervisor who needs to keep his men under his thumb, and the result is very likely to be trouble. Similarly, if you take docile men who are accustomed to obedience and respect for their supervisors and place them under a supervisor who tries to make them manage their own work, they are likely to wonder uneasily whether he really knows what he is doing.[11]

Therefore, even though a manager would prefer to change his followers' styles, he may find that he must adapt, at least temporarily, to their present behavior. For example, a supervisor who wants his subordinates to take more responsibility and to operate under general rather than close supervision cannot expect this kind of change to take place overnight. His current behavior, at least to some extent, must be compatible with the present expectations of the group, with planned change taking place over a long-term period.

A leader should know the expectations followers have about the way he should behave in certain situations. This is especially important if a leader is new in his position. His predecessor's leader behavior style is then a powerful influence. If this style is different from the one the leader plans to use, this may create an immediate problem.[12] The leader must either change his style to coincide with followers' expectations or change their expectations. Since the leader's style has often been developed over a long period of time, it can be difficult for him to make any drastic changes in the short run. It may, therefore, be more effective if he concentrates on changing the expectations of his followers. In other words, in some cases he may be able to convince his followers that his style, while not what they would normally expect, if accepted, will be adequate.

superiors' personalities and expectations

Another element of the environment is the leader personality of one's boss. Everyone has a boss of one kind or another. While most managers give considerable attention to supervising subordinates, some do not pay enough attention to being a subordinate themselves, and yet meeting the superior's expectations is often an important factor affecting one's style. If a boss is very task-oriented, for example, he might expect his subordinate to operate in the same manner. Relationships-oriented behavior might be evaluated as inappropriate, without even considering results. This has become evident when first-line supervisors are sent to training programs to improve their "human relations skills." Upon returning to the plant, they try to implement some of these new ideas in working with their people. Yet, because their superior has not accepted these concepts, he becomes impatient with the first-line supervisor's new-found concern for people. "Joe, cut out all that talking with the men and get the work out." With such reactions, it would not take the supervisor long to revert to his old style, and in the future, it will be much more difficult to implement any change in his behavior.

It is important for a manager to know his boss's expectations, particularly if he wants to advance in the organization. If he is predisposed toward promotion, he may tend to adhere to the customs and mores (styles and expectations) of the group to which he aspires to join rather than those of his peer group.[13] Consequently, his superiors' expectations have become more important to him than those of the other groups with which he interacts—his followers or associates.

The importance of the expectations of one's boss and the effect it can have on leadership style was vividly illustrated by Robert H. Guest in a case analysis of organizational change.[14] He examined a large assembly plant of an automobile company, Plant Y, and contrasted the situation under two different leaders.

Under Mr. Stewart, the plant manager, working relationships at Plant Y were dominated by hostility and mistrust. His high task style was characterized by a continual attempt to increase the driving forces pushing for productivity. As a result, the prevailing atmosphere was that of one emergency following on the heels of another, and the governing motivation for employee activity was fear—fear of being "chewed out" right on the assembly line, fear of being held responsible for happenings in which one had no clear authority, fear of losing one's job. Consequently, of the six plants in this division of the corporation, Plant Y had the poorest performance record, and it was getting worse.

Stewart was replaced by Cooley, who seemed like an extremely effective leader. Three years later, dramatic changes had occurred. In various cost and performance measures used to rate the six plants, Plant Y was now truly the leader; and the atmosphere of interpersonal cooperation and personal satisfaction had improved impressively over the situation under Stewart. These changes, moreover, were effected through an insignificant number of dismissals and reassignments. Using a much higher relationships style, Cooley succeeded in "turning Plant Y around."

On the surface, the big difference was style of leadership. Cooley was a good leader. Stewart was not. But Guest points out clearly in his analysis that leadership style was only one of two important factors. "The other was that while Stewart received daily orders from division headquarters to correct specific situations, Cooley was left alone. Cooley was allowed to lead; Stewart was told how to lead." [15] In other words, when productivity in Plant Y began to decline during changeover from wartime to peacetime operations, Stewart's superiors expected him to get productivity back on the upswing by taking control of the reins, and they put tremendous pressure on him to do just that. Guest suggests that these expectations forced Stewart to operate in a very crisis-oriented, autocratic way. However, when Cooley was given charge as plant manager, a "hands-off" policy was initiated by his superiors. The fact that the expectations of top management had changed enough to put a moratorium on random, troublesome outside stimuli from headquarters gave Cooley an opportunity to operate in a completely different style.

associates' personalities and expectations

A leader's associates or peers are those individuals who have similar positions within the organization. For example, the associates of a vice-president for production are the other vice-presidents in his company. Yet not all associates are significant for a leader; only those he interacts with regularly are going to have impact on his style and effectiveness.

The styles and expectations of one's associates are important when a leader has frequent interaction with them, for example, a situation that involves trading and bargaining for resources, such as budget money.[16]

In discussing superiors we mentioned the manager who has a strong drive to advance in an organization. Some people, however, are satisfied with their present position. For these people, the expectations of their associates may be more important in influencing their behavior than those of their superiors. College professors tend to be good examples. Often they are more concerned about their peer group, other professors or colleagues in their area of expertise, than they are in being promoted to administrative positions. As a result, college presidents and deans often have little position power with professors.

organization's personality and expectations

The personality and expectations of an organization are determined by the history and tradition of the organization as well as by the organizational goals and objectives which reflect the style and expectations of present top management.

Over a period of time, an organization, much like an individual, becomes characterized by certain modes of behavior which are perceived as *its* personality or style. The development of an organizational personality, or "corporate image," has been referred to as the process of institutionalization.[17] In this process, the organization is infused with a system of values that reflect its history and the people who have played vital roles in its formation and growth. Thus, it is difficult to understand Ford Motor Company without knowing the impact that Henry Ford had on its formation.

Members of the organization soon become conscious of the value system operating within the institution and guide their actions from many expectations derived from these values. The organization's expectations are most often expressed in forms of policy, operating procedures, and controls, as well as in informal customs and mores developed over time.

ORGANIZATIONAL GOALS. The goals of an organization usually consist of some combination of output and intervening variables. As we have discussed earlier, output variables are those short-run goals that can easily be measured, such as net profits, annual earnings, and won-lost record. On the other hand, intervening variables consist of those long-run goals reflecting the internal condition of the organization that *cannot* easily be measured, such as its capacity for effective interaction, communication, and decision making. These organizational goals can be expressed in terms of task and relationships, as illustrated in Figure 6.3.

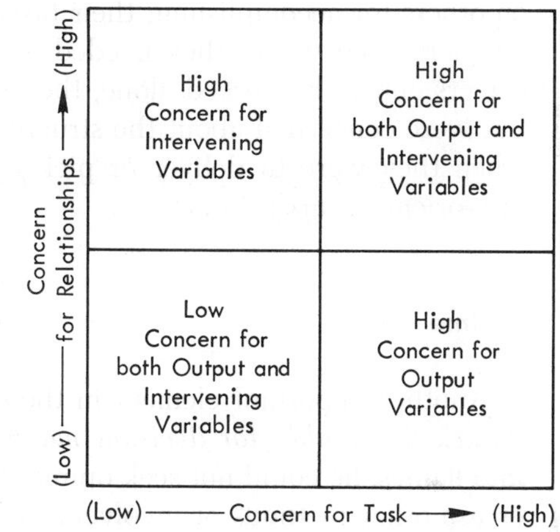

FIGURE 6.3 Organizational goals as expressed in terms of task and relationships.

OTHER SITUATIONAL VARIABLES

job demands

Another important element of a leadership situation is the demands of the job that the leader's group has been assigned to perform. Fiedler called this situational variable *task structure*.[18] He found that a task that has specific instructions on what the leader and his followers should do requires a different leadership style than an unstructured task that has no prescribed operating procedures. Research findings indicate that highly *structured* jobs which need directions seem to require high task behavior, while *unstructured* jobs which do not need directions seem to favor relationships-oriented behavior.

The *amount of interaction* the job requires of subordinates is another important consideration for a manager in analyzing his work environment. Vroom and Floyd C. Mann studied this aspect of a job in a large trucking company.[19] They investigated two groups of workers: One group was involved in the package and handling operation and the other consisted of truck drivers and their dispatchers. The nature of the work in the package and handling operation required that the men work closely together in small groups. Cooperation and teamwork was required not only among the workers but between the workers and their superiors. In this situation, the workers preferred and worked better under employee-centered supervisors. The truck drivers, on the other hand, usually worked alone, having little contact with other people. These men did not depend on others for accomplishing their task. The only exceptions were the dispatchers from whom they needed accurate information. Since the truck drivers generally worked alone, they were not concerned about harmony but were concerned about the structure of the job in terms of where and when they were to deliver or pick up. In this situation, they preferred task-oriented supervisors.

time

Another important element in the environment of a leader is the *time duration available for decision making*. If a manager's work area burst into flames, he could not seek opinions and suggestions from his followers or use other methods of involvement to determine the best way to leave the building. The leader must make an immediate decision and point the way. Therefore, short time demands, such as in an emergency, tend to require task-oriented behavior. On the other hand, if time is not a major factor in the situation, there is more opportunity for the leader to select from a broader range of leadership style, depending on the other situational variables.

One could probably enumerate many more variables. For example, even the physical stature of a leader can have effect on the kind of style he can use. Take the example of the foreman in the steel mill who is six feet six inches tall and weighs over 250 pounds. He may be able to use a different style than a foreman five feet four inches tall weighing 98 pounds, since their subordinates' expectations about their behavior will probably be influenced by their physical appearance.

The kinds of environmental variables we have been discussing tend to be important whether one is concerned about an educational, a business, or an informal organization. But specific organizations may have additional variables that are unique to themselves which must be evaluated before determining effectiveness.

STYLE ADAPTABILITY

Adaptability is the range of behavior within which a leader can vary his style. If the variation is appropriate to the situation, the leader will be effective; if it is inappropriate, the leader tends to be ineffective.

Leaders differ in their ability to vary their style to different situations. Some leaders seem to be limited to one basic style. As a result, rigid leaders tend to be effective only in situations where their styles are compatible with the environment. Other leaders are able to modify their behavior to fit any of the four basic styles, while others can utilize two or three styles. Adaptive leaders have the *potential* to be effective in a number of situations.

determining style range

The style range of a leader can be illustrated in terms of task and relationships,[20] as shown in Figure 6.4. The shape of the circle indicates the range of style. If the shape has a small area as in A, then the range of behavior of the leader is limited; whereas if it has a large area, as in B, the leader has a wide range of behavior.

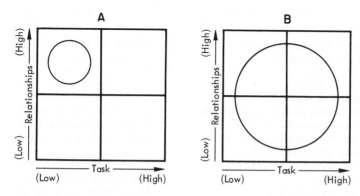

FIGURE 6.4   Style range in terms of task and relationships.

In A, the leader has basically a relationships-oriented style with little flexibility; in B, however, the leader has a broad range of leader behavior and is able to use, to some extent, any of the four basic styles. In this example, A may be effective in situations that demand a relationships-oriented style, such as in coaching or counseling situations. B, however, has the potential to be effective in a wide variety of instances. It should be remembered, though, that his style flexibility will not guarantee effectiveness. B will be effective only if he changes his style appropriately to fit the situation. For example, when his group needs some socioemotional support, he may be unavailable; when his work group needs some goal setting, B may be supportive but nondirective; and when his followers have their objectives clearly in line, he may exert undue pressure for productivity. These examples demonstrate that B has a wide range of flexibility, but in each case the behavior he used was inappropriate to the environment. This fact emphasizes the importance of a leader's *diagnostic* ability: his ability to understand the nature and impact of the environmental variables discussed earlier and to evaluate them in terms of task and relationship demands.

low and high adaptability demands

Leadership situations vary in the extent to which they make demands on adaptability. Reddin has cited some of the conditions that demand, in his terms, low and high flexibility. These conditions are listed in Table 6.1.[21]

TABLE 6.1 Low and high flexibility demands.

Low Flexibility Demands	*High Flexibility Demands*
Low-level managerial jobs	High-level managerial jobs
Simple managerial jobs	Complex managerial jobs
Established goals	Emerging goals
Tight procedures	Fluid procedures
Established tasks	Unstructured tasks
Routine, automated, decision-making	Nonroutine decision-making
Little environmental change	Rapid environmental change
Manager has complete power	Manager does not have complete power
Following plans essential	Using initiative essential
Manager accepted or rejected by subordinates	Subordinates neutral to manager
Few interconnecting jobs	Many interconnecting jobs

Some jobs require a high degree of adaptability, other jobs have low demands on adaptability.

HIGH ADAPTABILITY JOB. The president of a college or a university must continually deal with numerous groups, including his board of trustees, administrative staff, faculty, and students. With his board of trustees, he might have to "talk softly but carry a big stick"; with his administrative staff, he might have to be task-oriented and stress planning, organizing, and controlling; with his faculty, he might have to act like a salesman and push for his ideas; with his student body, he might want to appear relationships-oriented, emphasizing morale and school spirit; while with an individual problem student, he might want to take a firm stand. In dealing with each of these groups, a different leadership style might be appropriate.

LOW ADAPTABILITY JOB. A sergeant supervising a large group of draftees in an army boot camp might be able to use the same style with all his men. He may act toward everyone in a cold manner. Since he is training these men for possible battle, he must emphasize and demand strict discipline. Therefore, he might effectively be task-oriented in almost everything he does.

DEVELOPING STRATEGIES

changing style

One of the most difficult changes to make is a complete change in the personality of a person, and yet industry invests many millions of dollars annually for training and development programs that concentrate on changing the style of its leaders. As Fiedler suggests:

> A person's leadership style reflects the individual's basic motivational and need structure. At best it takes one, two, or three years of intensive psychotherapy to effect lasting changes in personality structure. It is difficult to see how we can change in more than a few cases an equally important set of core values in a few hours of lectures and role playing or even in the course of a more intensive training program of one or two weeks.[22]

Fiedler's point is well taken. It is indeed difficult to effect changes in the styles of managers overnight. However, it is not completely hopeless.

But, at best, it is a slow and expensive process that requires creative planning and patience. In fact, Likert found that it takes from three to to seven years, depending on the size and complexity of the organization, to effectively implement a new management theory.

> Haste is self-defeating because of the anxieties and stresses it creates. There is no substitute for ample time to enable the members of an organization to reach the level of skillful and easy, habitual use of the new leadership.[23]

What generally happens in present training and development programs is that managers are encouraged to adopt certain normative behavior styles. In our culture, these styles are usually high relationships or high task and relationships styles. While we agree that there is a growing tendency for these two styles to be more effective than the high task or low task and relationships styles, we recognize that this is not universally the case, even in our own culture. In fact, it is often not the case, even within a single work group. While most workers might respond favorably to the high relationships-oriented styles a few might react to these styles in a negative manner, taking advantage of what they consider a "soft touch." As a result, certain individuals will have to be handled in a different way. Perhaps they will only respond to the proverbial "kick in the pants" (a high task-oriented style). Thus, it is unrealistic to think that any of these styles can be successfully applied everywhere. In addition to considering application, it is questionable whether every leader can adapt to one "normative" style.

Most training and development programs do not recognize these two considerations. Consequently, a foreman who has been operating as a task-oriented, authoritarian leader for many years is encouraged to change his style—"get in step with the times." Upon returning from the training program, the foreman will probably try to utilize some of the new relationships-oriented techniques he has recently been taught. The problem is that his personality is not compatible with the new concepts. As long as things are running smoothly, he has no difficulty using them. However, the minute an important issue or a crisis develops he tends to revert to his old basic style and becomes inconsistent, vacillating between the new relationships-oriented style he has been taught and his old task-oriented style which has the force of habit behind it.

This idea was supported in a study the General Electric Company conducted at one of its turbine and generator plants.[24] In this study the leadership styles of about ninety foremen were analyzed and rated as "democratic," "authoritarian," or "mixed." In discussing the findings, Saul W. Gellerman reported that

The lowest morale in the plant was found among those men whose foremen were rated *between* the democratic and authoritarian extremes. The GE research team felt that these foremen may have varied inconsistently in their tactics, permissive at one moment and hardfisted the next, in a way that left their men frustrated and unable to anticipate how they would be treated. The naturally autocratic supervisor who is exposed to human relations training may behave in exactly such a manner . . . a pattern which will probably make him even harder to work for than he was before being "enlightened." [25]

In summary, changing the style of managers is a difficult process, and one that takes considerable time. Expecting miracles overnight will only lead to frustration and uneasiness for both managers and their subordinates. Consequently, we recommend that change in overall management style in an organization should be planned and implemented on a long-term basis so that expectations can be realistic for all involved.

changes in expectations versus changes in style

Using the feedback model appearing in Chapter 2, we can begin to explain why it is so difficult to make changes in leader personality in the short run.

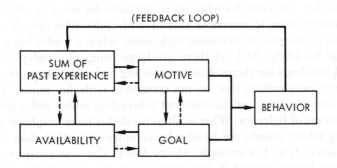

FIGURE 6.5 Feedback model.

As discussed earlier, when a person behaves in a motivating situation, his behavior becomes a new input to his inventory of past experience. The earlier in life that this input occurs, the greater its potential effect on future behavior. At that time, this behavior represents a larger portion of the individual's total past experience than the same behavior input will later in life. In addition, the longer a behavior is reinforced, the more patterned it becomes and the more difficult it is to change. That is why it is easier to make personality changes early in life. As a person gets older, more time and new experiences are necessary to effect a change in behavior.

As was discussed in Chapter 1, changes in behavior are much more difficult and time consuming than changes in knowledge and attitudes. Since changes in expectations, in reality, are changes in knowledge and attitudes, these can be implemented more rapidly than changes in personality. In fact, changes in expectations may be accomplished merely by having the leader sit down and clarify what his behavior will be with the individuals involved. Once they understand his style they can more easily adjust their expectations to it. This is easier than attempting the tedious task of changing his basic personality.

selection of key subordinates

It may be important to point out that it is not always necessary for superiors and subordinates within an organization to have similar styles. People do not have to have the same personalities to be compatible. What is necessary is that they share perceptions of each other's roles and have common goals and objectives. It is often more appropriate for a manager to recruit key subordinates who can compensate for areas in which he has shortcomings than to surround himself with aides who are all alike. In fact, this is one way of increasing style range when a leader has a limited range of flexibility. And yet there are large companies today who have created problems for themselves by a testing and selection process which eliminates personalities that are not congruent with the "norm." This can lead to organizational or management inbreeding which stifles new ideas and patterns of behavior. What is often needed is more emphasis on team building where people are hired who complement rather than replicate a manager's style. For example, Henry Ford, who was considered a paternalistic leader, placed in key positions in the organization men who supplemented him rather than duplicated his style. Henry Bennett, for one, acted as a "hatchet man," clearing deadwood from the organization (high task). Another subordinate acted as a confidant to Henry (high relationships). While these styles differed considerably, Ford's success during that time was based on compatibility of expectations; each understood the other's role and was committed to common goals and objectives.

Other examples could be cited. This kind of team building is common in sports like football. Assistant coaches not only may have differential task roles, that is, line coach, backfield coach, and so forth, but may have different behavioral roles with the players.

changing situational variables

Recognizing some of the limitations of training and development programs that concentrate only on changing leadership styles, Fiedler has suggested that "it would seem more promising at this time to teach the individual to recognize the conditions under which he can perform best and to modify the situation to suit his leadership style." [26] This philosophy, which he calls "organizational engineering," is based on the assumption: "It is almost always easier to change a man's work environment than it is to change his personality or his style of relating to others." [27] While we basically agree with Fiedler's assumption, we want to make it clear that we feel changes in both are difficult, but possible. In many cases, the best strategy might be to attempt to make some changes in his style and expectations and some changes in the other variables of his situation rather than concentrate on one or the other.

Fiedler is helpful, though, in suggesting ways in which a leadership situation can be modified to fit the leader's style. These suggestions are based on his Leadership Contingency Model which we discussed in Chapter 4. As you will recall, Fiedler feels there are three major situational variables which seem to determine whether a given situation is favorable or unfavorable to a leader: (1) *leader-member relations* —his personal relations with the members of his group, (2) *position power*—the power and authority that his position provides and (3) *task structure*—the degree of structure (routine vs. challenging) in the task that the group has been assigned to perform. The changes in each of these variables that Fiedler recommends can be expressed in task or relationship terms; each change tends to favor either a task-oriented or a relationships-oriented leader, as illustrated in Table 6.2 on page 128.[28]

With changes like these, Fiedler suggests that the situational variables confronting a leader can be modified to fit his style. He recognized, though, as we have been arguing, that the success of organizational engineering depends on training an individual to be able to diagnose his own leader personality or style and the other situational variables. Only when he has accurately interpreted these variables can he determine whether any changes are necessary. If changes are needed, the leader does not necessarily have to initiate any in his own particular situation. He might prefer to transfer to a situation that better fits his style. In this new environment no immediate changes may be necessary.

TABLE 6.2   Changes in the leadership situation expressed in terms of task and relationships.

VARIABLE BEING CHANGED	CHANGE MADE	
	STYLE FAVORS	
	Task	*Relationships*
LEADER-MEMBER RELATIONS	The leader could be given: 1. Followers who are quite different from him in a number of ways. 2. Followers who are notorious for their conflict.	The leader could be given: 1. Followers who are very similar to him in attitude, opinion, technical background, race, etc. 2. Followers who generally get along well with their superiors.
POSITION POWER OF THE LEADER	The leader could be given: 1. High rank and corresponding recognition, i.e., a vice-presidency. 2. Followers who are two or three ranks below him. 3. Followers who are dependent upon their leader for guidance and instruction. 4. Final authority in making all the decisions for the group. 5. All information about organizational plans, thus making him an expert in his group.	The leader could be given: 1. Little rank (office) or official recognition. 2. Followers who are equal to him in rank. 3. Followers who are experts in their field and are independent of their leader. 4. No authority in making decisions for the group. 5. No more information about organizational plans than his followers get, placing him on an equal "footing" with them.
TASK STRUCTURE	The leader could be given: 1. A structured production task which has specific instructions on what he and his followers should do.	The leader could be given: 1. An unstructured policy-making task which has no prescribed operating procedures.

DIAGNOSING THE ENVIRONMENT—A CASE

Any of the situational elements we have discussed may be analyzed in terms of task and relationships. Let us take the case of Steve, a general foreman who has been offered a promotion to superintendent in another plant. In his present position, which he has held for fifteen years, Steve has been extremely effective as a task-oriented manager responsible for the operation of several assembly-line processes.

The first impulse is for Steve to immediately accept this promotion in status and salary and move his family to the new location. But instead, he feels it is important first to visit the plant and to talk with some of the people with whom he will be working. In talking with these people, Steve may gain some insight into some of the important dimensions of this new position. An analysis of all these variables in terms of task and relationships could be summarized together as illustrated in Figure 6.6.[29]

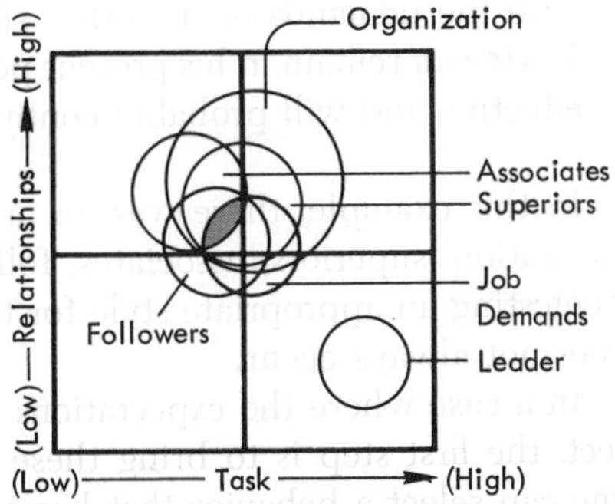

FIGURE 6.6 An example of all the environmental variables being analyzed together in terms of task and relationships.

If Steve, using diagnostic skills, makes this type of analysis, he has gone a long way toward gathering the necessary information he needs for effectively determining his appropriate actions.

The circle designated for the leader represents Steve's leadership style or personality which has been reinforced over the past fifteen years. The other circles represent the expectations of all the other environmental variables in terms of what is considered appropriate behavior for a foreman. The shaded area indicates where the expectations of these variables intersect. If Steve took the superintendent's job, he would probably have to behave within this area to maximize his effectiveness. In this plant, the situation seems to demand a moderately high task and relationships-oriented superintendent. Unfortunately, Steve's style and expectations do not intersect any of the other variables, and his personality tends to be limited to task-oriented behavior. Thus, if he accepts the job and makes no changes, there is a high probability that Steve will be ineffective. At this point, he has to make a decision. Several other alternatives are available to him.

1. He can attempt to expand his range of behavior, thus bringing himself into the area of effectiveness.
2. He can attempt to change some or all of the situational elements. For example, he can attempt to change the behavior and the expectations of his followers through training and development programs and/or coaching and counseling.
3. He can attempt to make *some* changes in both his own range of behavior and some or all of the situational elements, thus attempting in the long run to have the two move toward each other rather than concentrating only on changing one or the other.
4. He can reject the job and seek another superintendent's position in an environment where his range of behavior is more compatible with the demands of the other situational elements.
5. He can remain in his present position where he knows he has been effective and will probably continue to be.

In this example, there was an area where the expectations of the organization, superiors, associates, followers, and job demands intersected, suggesting an appropriate style for the demands of the environment. This does not always occur.

In a case where the expectations of various key variables do not intersect, the first step is to bring these various expectations into line before one can select a behavior that has a high probability of success. If, however, only one of the variables in the environment is important, it may not be necessary to realign the others. For example, the followers may be crucial, while top management may not be as important because they may be located five hundred miles away in the central office. In this case as long as performance is satisfactory, top management may not be concerned about what style is used.

While these examples have been written from the point of view of an individual, this type of analysis is just as important from an organization's point of view. It is vital that the men placed in key positions throughout the organization have the prerequisites for carrying out the organizational goals effectively. Management must realize that it does not follow that a man will be effective in one position merely because he has been effective in another situation. It is assumptions like these about which Laurence J. Peter writes. The Peter principle is stated as follows: "In a hierarchy every employee tends to rise to his level of incompetence." [30]

anti–Peter Principle vaccine

The dilemma expressed by Peter is not necessarily a self-fulfilling prophecy or principle. There are several ways an organization can develop an immunity to the problem. One method is appropriate training and development before upward mobility takes place. This training may often include, prior to movement, the delegation of some responsibility, so the person has had an opportunity for some real experience that approximates the new position. Another part of the solution is careful selection of people whose personality and expectations are appropriate for the new job, instead of having upward mobility depend only on good performance at the preceding level.

NOTES

1. These environmental variables have been adapted from a list of situational elements discussed by William J. Reddin in *The 3-D Management Style Theory,* Theory Paper #5—Diagnostic Skill (Fredericton, N.B., Canada: Social Science Systems, 1967), p. 2.
2. Jacob W. Getzels and Egon G. Guba, "Social Behavior and the Administrative Process," *The School Review,* LXV, No. 4 (Winter 1957), 423–41. See also Getzels, "Administration as a Social Process," in Andrew W. Halpin, ed., *Administrative Theory in Education* (Chicago: Midwest Administration Center, University of Chicago, 1958).
3. Adapted from Getzels, p. 158.
4. Leland P. Bradford, Jack R. Gibb, and Kenneth D. Benne, *T-Group Theory and Laboratory Method* (New York: John Wiley & Sons, Inc., 1964).
5. Warren G. Bennis, *Changing Organizations* (New York: McGraw-Hill Book Company, 1966), p. 120.
6. Chris Argyris, "We Must Make Work Worthwhile," *Life,* May 5, 1967, p. 66.
7. *Ibid.*
8. See Chris Argyris, "T-Groups for Organization Effectiveness," *Harvard Business Review,* 42 (1964), 60–74; Edgar H. Schein and Warren G. Bennis, *Personal and Organizational Change through Group Methods* (New York: John Wiley & Sons, Inc., 1965); Robert R. Blake *et al.,* "Breakthrough in Organization Development," *Harvard Business Review,* November-December 1964; and Chris Argyris, *Interpersonal Competence and Organizatioanl Effectiveness* (Homewood, Ill.: Dorsey Press, 1962).
9. Fillmore H. Sanford, *Authoritarianism and Leadership* (Philadelphia: Institute for Research in Human Relations, 1950).
10. Victor H. Vroom, *Some Personality Determinants of the Effects of Participation* (Englewood Cliffs, N.J.: Prentice-Hall, Inc., 1960).
11. Saul W. Gellerman, *Motivation and Productivity* (New York: American Management Association, 1963).
12. Reddin, *The 3-D Management Style Theory,* Theory Paper #5—Diagnostic Skill, p. 4.

13. William E. Henry, "The Business Executive: The Psychodynamics of a Social Role," *The American Journal of Sociology*, LIV, No. 4 (January 1949), 286–91.
14. Robert H. Guest, *Organizational Change: The Effect of Successful Leadership* (Homewood, Ill.: Dorsey Press and Richard D. Irwin, Inc., 1964).
15. Charles Perrow, *Organizational Analysis: A Sociological View* (Belmont, Calif: Wadsworth Publishing Co., Inc., 1970), p. 12.
16. Reddin, Theory Paper #5—Diagnostic Skill, p. 4.
17. Waino W. Suojanen, *The Dynamics of Management* (New York: Holt, Rinehart & Winston, Inc., 1966).
18. Fred E. Fiedler, *A Theory of Leadership Effectiveness* (New York: McGraw-Hill Book Company, 1967).
19. Victor H. Vroom and Floyd C. Mann, "Leader Authoritarianism and Employee Attitudes," *Personnel Psychology*, XIII, No. 2 (1960).
20. Reddin, *The 3-D Management Style Theory, Theory Paper #6*—Style Flex (Fredericton, N.B., Canada: Social Science Systems, 1967), p. 6.
21. *Ibid.*, p. 4.
22. Fiedler, *A Theory of Leadership Effectiveness*, p. 248.
23. Rensis Likert, *New Patterns of Management* (New York: McGraw-Hill Book Company, 1961), p. 248.
24. *Leadership Style and Employee Morale* (New York: General Electric Company, Public and Employee Relations Services, 1959).
25. Gellerman, *Motivation and Productivity*, p. 43.
26. Fiedler, *A Theory of Leadership Effectiveness*, p. 255.
27. *Ibid.*
28. This table was adapted from Fiedler's discussion in *A Theory of Leadership Effectiveness*, pp. 255–56.
29. Adapted from Reddin, Theory Paper #6—Style Flex, p. 6.
30. Laurence J. Peter and Raymond Hull, *The Peter Principle: Why Things Always Go Wrong* (New York: William Morrow & Co., Inc., 1969).

managing
for organizational
effectiveness

7

The importance of a leader's *diagnostic ability* cannot be overemphasized. Edgar H. Schein expresses it well when he contends that *"the successful manager must be a good diagnostician and must value a spirit of inquiry. If the abilities and motives of the people under him are so variable, he must have the sensitivity and diagnostic ability to be able to sense and appreciate the differences."* [1] In other words, a manager must be able to identify clues in an environment. Yet even with good diagnostic skills, a leader may still not be effective unless he can *adapt* his leader personality to meet the demands of his environment. "He must have the personal flexibility and range of skills necessary to vary his own behavior. If the needs and motives of his subordinates are different, they must be treated differently." [2]

In this chapter a leadership theory that is an outgrowth of the Tri-Dimensional Leader Effectiveness Model will be presented in an attempt to provide a conceptual framework that may help a manager develop strategies for adapting his style in working with the many individuals and groups within his environment.

LIFE CYCLE THEORY OF LEADERSHIP

Korman, in his extensive review of studies examining the Ohio State concepts of Initiating Structure and Consideration, concluded that

What is needed . . . in future concurrent (and predictive) studies is not just recognition of this factor of "situational determinants" but, rather, a systematic conceptualization of situational variance as it might relate to leadership behavior [Initiating Structure and Consideration].[3]

In discussing this conclusion, Korman suggests the possibility of a curvilinear relationship rather than a simple linear relationship between Initiating Structure and Consideration and other variables. The Life Cycle Theory, which is an outgrowth of the Tri-Dimensional Leader Effectiveness Model, is based on a curvilinear relationship between task behavior and relationships behavior and maturity.[4] This theory will attempt to provide a leader with some understanding of the relationships between an effective style of leadership and the level of maturity of his followers.

Thus, the emphasis in the Life Cycle Theory of Leadership will be on the behavior of a leader in relationship to his followers. As Filmore H. Sanford has indicated, there is some justification for regarding the followers "as the most crucial factor in any leadership event."[5] Followers in any situation are vital, not only because individually they accept or reject the leader but because as a group they actually determine whatever personal power he may have.

maturity

According to Life Cycle Theory, as the level of maturity of one's followers continues to increase, appropriate leader behavior not only requires less and less structure (task) while increasing consideration but should eventually entail decreases in socioemotional support (relationships). This cycle can be illustrated in the four quadrants of the basic styles portion of the 3–D Leader Effectiveness Model, as shown in Figure 7.1 on page 135.

Maturity is defined in Life Cycle Theory by achievement-motivation,[6] the willingness and ability to take responsibility, and task relevant education and experience of an individual or a group. These components of maturity are consistent with Chris Argyris's Immaturity-Maturity continuum where he contends that as a person matures over time he moves from a passive state to a state of increasing activity, from dependency

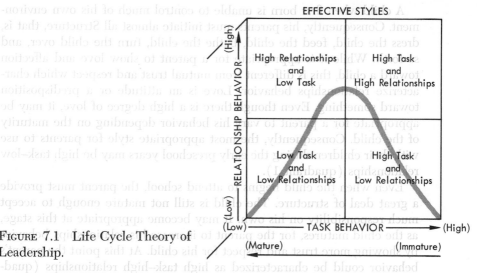

FIGURE 7.1 Life Cycle Theory of Leadership.

on others to relative independence, and the like.[7] While age may be a factor, it is not directly related to maturity as used in the Life Cycle. Our concern is for psychological age, not chronological age. Beginning with structured task behavior, which is appropriate for working with immature people, Life Cycle Theory suggests that leader behavior should move through (1) high task–low relationships behavior to (2) high task–high relationships and (3) high relationships–low task behavior to (4) low task–low relationships behavior, if one's followers progress from immaturity to maturity.

parent-child relationship

An illustration of this Life Cycle Theory familiar to everyone is the parent-child relationship.[8] As a child begins to mature, it is appropriate for the parent to provide less structure, giving the child an opportunity to increase his own responsibility. As the child increases his ability, this is reinforced by an increase in socioemotional support. Experience shows us that if the parent provides too much relationships before a child is somewhat mature, this behavior is often misinterpreted by the child as permissiveness. Thus, it is appropriate to decrease Structure as the child becomes able to increase his maturity or capacity to take responsibility and respond to mutual trust. Eventually, as the child moves toward adulthood, he will need less socioemotional support too as he begins to mature psychologically.

A child when first born is unable to control much of his own environment. Consequently, his parents must initiate almost all Structure, that is, dress the child, feed the child, bathe the child, turn the child over, and so forth. While it is appropriate for a parent to show love and affection toward a child, this is different from mutual trust and respect which characterize relationships behavior. Love is an attitude or a predisposition toward something. Even though there is a high degree of love, it may be appropriate for a parent to vary his behavior depending on the maturity of the child. Consequently, the most appropriate style for parents to use with their children during the early preschool years may be high task–low relationships (quadrant 1).

Even when the child begins to attend school, the parent must provide a great deal of structure. The child is still not mature enough to accept much responsibility on his own. It may become appropriate at this stage, as the child matures, for the parent to increase his relationships behavior by showing more trust and respect for his child. At this point the parent's behavior could be characterized as high task–high relationships (quadrant 2).

Gradually, as the child moves into high school and/or college, he begins to seek and accept more and more responsibility for his own behavior. At this time, a parent should begin to engage in less structured behavior and continue a relatively high level of socioemotional support (quadrant 3). This does not mean that the child's life will have less Structure, but it will now be internally imposed by the "young man" rather than externally imposed by the parent. When this happens in the cycle, not only is structure decreasing, but it also becomes appropriate to begin to cut the psychological umbilical cord as shown in Figure 7.1 with behavior heading toward quadrant 4. The child is now not only able to structure many of the activities in which he engages but also able to provide self-control in terms of his interpersonal and emotional needs.

As the child begins to make his own living, start his own family, and take full responsibility for his actions, a decrease in structure and socioemotional support by the parents becomes appropriate. In reality, the umbilical cord has been severed and the child is now "on his own." At this stage of the parent-child relationship, a low task–low relationships style seems to be most appropriate (quadrant 4).

In meeting specific contingencies that develop because of changes in maturity, it may be necessary to vary one's style anywhere within the four quadrants to deal appropriately with a particular event. For example, when a young man is away at college, his parents' behavior would normally be considered high relationships. But if they discover that their son is not behaving in as mature a way as expected (he is a discipline problem for the university), it may be appropriate for them temporarily to change their behavior and initiate more Structure with their son (spell out the behavior they expect and the consequences for nonperformance) while decreasing their socioemotional support. Too much relationships behavior at this time may be interpreted by the young man as approval or support for his actions. However, once he begins to display more maturity again, it will be appropriate for his parents' behavior to move back through the cycle to high relationships behavior.

The attempt in Life Cycle Theory is to discuss *appropriate* leadership styles according to the maturity of one's followers. Thus the curvilinear function of the cycle would be portrayed on the effective side of the Tri-Dimensional Leader Effectiveness Model. In the 3–D Model we might also examine some of the consequences that could result from using an inappropriate style in terms of the level of maturity of the child. We can take four examples of parents who tend to use a single leadership style during the entire developmental years of the child, as illustrated in Figure 7.2 on page 137.

First, let us look at some of the potential consequences of a parent using a high structure–low consideration style (quadrant 1) with his child throughout the developmental years, for example, "As long as you're living in this house, you'll be home at ten o'clock and abide by the rules I've set." Two predictions might be made. The first one is that the child will tend to pack his bag and leave home at the earliest opportunity. If this does not occur, the child may succumb to his parents' authority and become a very passive, dependent person throughout his life, always needing someone to tell him "what to do" and "when to do it."

A high probability result of a parent using exclusively a style of extremely High Structure and socioemotional support (quadrant 2) might be called the "Mama's boy syndrome." Even when the child gets older, he may chronologically be an adult, but he is still psychologically dependent upon the parent to make decisions for him.

What happens when a parent only engages in high Consideration behavior but never structures any of his child's activities? The response to this style may be a "spoiled brat" as a child and a person who has little regard for rules and regulations or consideration for the rights of others as an adult.

A style of Low Structure and low socioemotional support (quadrant 4) seems to be characteristic of two of the socioeconomic classifications described by Lloyd Warner, the *upper-upper* level and the *lower-lower* level.[9] In both cases the child may become a product of his environment rather than a product of the parent's style itself. In the case of the upper-upper level, this responsibility may be delegated to a private school, while in the case of the lower-lower level, the child is often left on his own and learns to cope with the day-to-day contingencies of his environment.

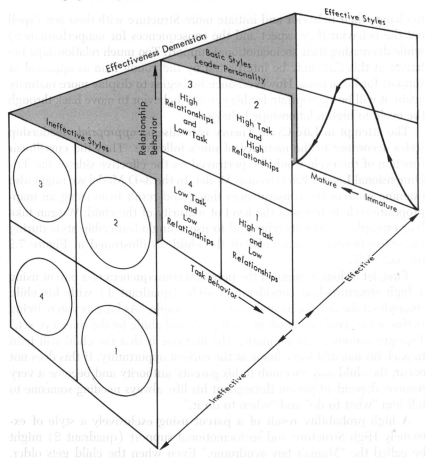

FIGURE 7.2   Consequences of using a *single*
parent/child style over time.

The parent-child relationship is only one example of the Life Cycle Theory of Leadership. This cycle is also discernible in other organizations in the interaction between superiors and subordinates.

management of research and development personnel

In working with highly trained and emotionally mature personnel, an effective leader behavior style in many cases is low task–low relationships.[10] This was dramatically demonstrated in a military setting. Normally, in basically crisis-oriented organizations like the military or the police, the most appropriate style tends to be high task; since under combat or riot conditions success often depends upon immediate response to orders. Time demands do not permit talking things over or explaining decisions. For success, behavior must be automatic. While a high task style may be effective for a combat officer, it is often ineffective in working with research and development personnel within the military. This was pointed out when line officers trained at West Point were sent to command outposts in the DEW line, which was part of an advanced-warning system. The scientific and technical personnel involved, living in close quarters in an Arctic region, did not respond favorably to the task-oriented behavior of these combat-trained officers. The level of education, research experience, and maturity of these people was such that they did not need their commanding officer to initiate a great deal of structure in their work. In fact, they tended to resent it. Other experiences with scientific and research-oriented personnel indicate that many of these people desire, or need, a limited amount of socioemotional support.

PROJECT CYCLE. Even research and development managers using low task–low relationships styles appropriately with their groups may on occasion deviate from this style. For instance, during the early stages of a particular project, a certain amount of structure as to the requirements and limitations of the project must be established. Once these boundaries are understood by the project group, the research and development manager may move rapidly through the "project cycle" back to low task–low relationships style appropriate for working with mature, responsible, self-motivated personnel.

An example can be cited: At the outset of a project in an organization whose major function is the development of weapons systems for the armed forces, the weapons development group will meet with representatives from the various services. Each service will specify certain performance capabilities or operating conditions of the system or components being developed, such as the specification of the variety of environmental conditions that the weapon will have to withstand. In spelling out these requirements, a certain amount of structure is being imposed, particularly with regard to the range in which creativity and development are concentrated. Once this structure has been initiated, the project manager turns his staff "loose" to carry on their respective roles with a minimum of close supervision.

Other deviations from the low task–low relationships may be necessary. The case of a researcher who works well on his own but is facing an emotional crisis at home which begins to affect his performance on the job is an example. Under this situation, it might be appropriate for the manager to increase his socioemotional support during this crisis period and to some extent increase his initiation of structure until the researcher regains his composure. In summary, the effective research and development manager must know his staff well enough to meet the ever-changing demands upon the people or the group for which he is responsible.

educational setting and life cycle theory

Educational settings provide us with numerous examples of Life Cycle Theory in operation.[11]

TEACHER-STUDENT RELATIONSHIP.   In a college setting the Life Cycle Theory is being used in studying the teacher-student relationship. Effective teaching of lower-division students (freshmen and sophomores) has been characterized by structured behavior on the part of the teacher as he reinforces appropriate patterns in attendance and study habits, while more relationships behavior seems to be appropriate for working with upper-division undergraduates and master's degree candidates. And finally the cycle seems to be completed as a teacher begins to work with mature doctoral candidates, who need less guidance or socioemotional support.

Life Cycle Theory may provide some insights into problems that have developed in the innovative self-paced learning curricula that have sprung up across the country at many educational levels, particularly in elementary and secondary schools.[12] These programs have been developed in an attempt to individualize instruction and are premised on maximum freedom for the student. For example, in learning basic chemistry, students are given a detailed outline of what they must know and must do to pass a proficiency exam in chemistry. Once this initial structure has been provided, the teacher quickly moves through the cycle to a high Consideration–Low Structure style. The intention now is for the student to initiate Structure for himself. The teacher becomes involved only at the student's request. Students can often take the exam any time they are ready.

Problems sometimes develop when this unstructured program is used universally for all students in a school. For the intellectually and emotionally mature student with clear goals and objectives, such a curriculum has numerous advantages. These include "a savings of time which can be devoted to other areas of interest, a genuine and personal recognition of his ability, and the opportunity to be treated and behave as an adult."[13] For the immature student who lacks direction and ability to structure his own work schedule, such a low structure–low consideration teaching style can be detrimental. It can even encourage immaturity if the student perceives the lack of structure as permissiveness. In the case of students who look at the educational system as something that must be tolerated but is not well integrated with their own personal goals, a more highly structured and a somewhat lower consideration style would seem more appropriate until the students begin to show signs of maturing and the teacher can vary his style accordingly.

ADMINISTRATOR–GOVERNING BOARD RELATIONSHIP.   An important area for the top administrator (college president or superintendent) in an educational institution is his relationship with his governing board. Since these boards have the ultimate power to remove college presidents or superintendents when they lose confidence in their leadership, these administrators often tend to use a high consideration style, providing only a limited amount of structure for these decision-making groups.[14] In fact, they sometimes seem to shy away from directing the activities of their board for fear of arousing their criticism. Life Cycle Theory questions this behavior.

While the members of the governing board are often responsible, well-educated individuals, they tend to have little work experience in an educational setting. For example, in a survey of college trustees in New York State, it was found that less than 10 percent of the trustees serving on these boards had any teaching or administrative experience in an educational institution.[15] In fact, the large majority of the 1,269 trustees sampled were occupied primarily in industry, insurance and banking, merchandising and transportation, and medicine and law. Virtually half acted as corporation officials with the rank of treasurer, director, or above. In addition to their involvement in other than educational institutions, these trustees tended to be overcommitted and were probably unable to give the time to university problems that they would have liked to give. In fact, the most frequent dissatisfaction expressed by trustees was the "lack of time to devote to the board."

This relative inexperience of trustees and heavy commitment elsewhere suggests that it may be appropriate for college presidents to combine with their high Consideration behavior an increase of Initiating Structure behavior in working with their trustees. In fact, the responsibility for structuring the work of trustees should fall on the college president. Henry Wriston, former president of Brown University, has said it well:

It may seem strange, at first thought, that this should be a president's duty. A moment's reflection makes it clear that it can evolve on no other person. Trustees are unpaid; they have no method of analyzing talents and making assignments. The president is in a position to do so.[16]

ADMINISTRATOR-FACULTY RELATIONSHIP.   In working with experienced faculty, the low Structure–low Consideration style characterized by a decentralized organization structure and delegation of responsibility to individuals may be an appropriate style. The level of education and maturity of these people is often such that they do not need their principal or department chairman to initiate much structure. Sometimes they tend to resent it. In addition, some teachers desire or need only a limited amount of socioemotional support (Consideration).

While often an effective leader style in working with faculty tends to be low Structure–low Consideration, certain deviations from this may be necessary. For example, during the early stages of a school year or curriculum change, a certain amount of structure as to the specific areas to be taught, by whom, when, and where must be established. Once these requirements and limitations are understood by the faculty, the administrator may move rapidly through this "project" cycle back to low Structure–low Consideration style appropriate for working with mature, responsible, self-motivated personnel.

Other deviations may be necessary. For example, a new inexperienced teacher might need more Structure and Consideration until he gains experience in the classroom.

DIFFERING LEVELS OF MATURITY.   By dividing the maturity continuum of the Life Cycle into three levels—below average, average, and above average—some bench marks or degrees of maturity, as illustrated in Figure 7.3, can be provided for determining appropriate leadership style.

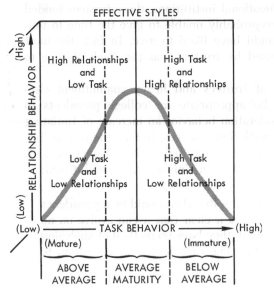

FIGURE 7.3   Maturity levels.

Life Cycle Theory of Leadership postulates that when working with people of below average maturity, a high task style (quadrant 1) has the best probability of success; whereas in dealing with people of average maturity, the style of quadrants 2 and 3 appear to be most appropriate; and quadrant 4 has the highest probability of success with people of above average maturity.

THE INFLUENCE OF CULTURAL CHANGE

The scientific and technical advancements in society since the turn of the century almost stagger the imagination.[17] As a result we have become a dynamic, industrial society with a higher level of education and standard of living than ever thought possible. This phenomenon is beginning to have a pronounced effect on much of the work force utilized by organizations.

Today many employees enjoy a higher standard of living and tend to be better educated and more sophisticated than ever before. As a result, these workers have increased potential for self-direction and self-control. Consistent with these changes in maturity, a large majority of our population, in Maslow's terms, now have their basic physiological and safety-security needs fairly satisfied. Management can no longer depend on the satisfaction of these needs, through pay, incentive plans, hospitalization, and so forth, as primary motivating factors which influence industrial employees. In our society today, there is almost a built-in expectation in people that physiological and safety needs will be fulfilled. In fact, in our society people do not generally have to worry about where their next meal will come from or whether they will be protected from the elements or physical danger. They are now more susceptible to motivation from other needs: People want to belong, be recognized as "somebody," and have a chance to develop to their fullest potential. As William H. Haney has said:

> The managerial practice, therefore, should be geared to the subordinate's *current level of maturity with the overall goal of helping him to develop, to require progressively less external control, and to gain more and more self-control.* And why would a man want this? Because under these conditions he achieves satisfaction on the job at the levels, primarily the ego and self-fulfillment levels, at which he is the most *motivatable.*[18]

This concept is illustrated in Figure 7.4.

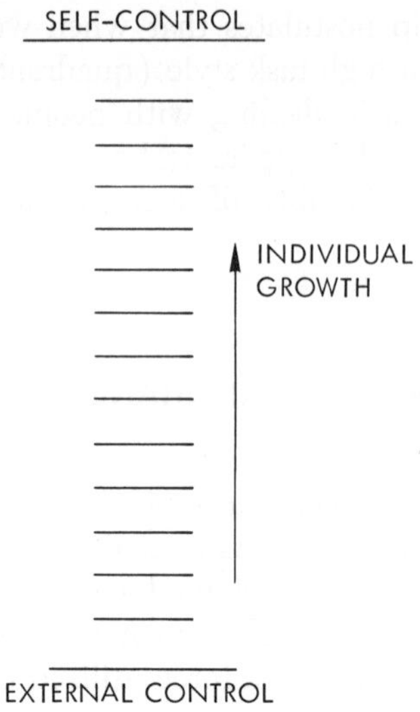

SELF–CONTROL

FIGURE 7.4.   Balance of external control and self-control.

This shift in the maturity level and need disposition of our general population helps us to understand why the findings of many of the studies in our society of the relationship between leadership styles and productivity, like those conducted by Likert and Halpin, seem to cluster around quadrants 2 and 3, but not at the extremes (quadrants 1 and 4). See Figure 7.3.

If one accepts the theory that the level of maturity and responsibility and need satisfaction of much of our work force has indeed increased, this has an impact on many of our traditional principles of management, such as span of control and the role of the manager in planning, organizing, motivating, and controlling.

span of control

For years it has been argued by many management writers that one man can supervise only a relatively few people; therefore, all managers should have a limited span of control. For example, Harold Koontz and Cyril O'Donnell state that

In every organization it must be decided how many subordinates a superior can manage. Students of management have found that this number is usually four to eight subordinates at the upper levels of organization and eight to fifteen or more at the lower levels.[19]

While the suggested number of subordinates that one can supervise varies anywhere from three to thirty, the principle usually states that the number should decrease as one moves higher in the organization. Top management should have fewer subordinates to supervise than lower-level managers. This principle has resulted in the traditional pyramidal organization and hierarchy of authority.

This traditional hierarchy may not be as applicable today in light of the educational and cultural progress of much of the work force. Instead, it might be suggested that span of control, should be a function of the maturity and self-control of the individuals being supervised. It would seem that the more mature and better educated one's subordinates are, the more people a manager could supervise. It is theoretically possible to supervise an infinite number of subordinates if everyone is completely mature and able to be responsible for his own job. This does not mean that there is less control, but these subordinates are self-controlled rather than externally controlled by their superiors. Since people occupying higher-level jobs in an organization tend to be more "mature" and therefore need less close supervision than people occupying lower-level jobs, it seems reasonable to assume that top managers should be able to supervise more subordinates than their counterparts at lower levels.[20]

narrow span at bottom

If any difference in span of control is necessary because of varying educational and maturity levels, it follows that some organizations should be structured to have a narrower span of control at the bottom than at the top. An example of this might involve dealing with an unskilled labor force of culturally deprived persons from ghetto areas or second- and third-generation unemployed. Such inexperienced employees often have not had the educational opportunities enjoyed by most of our society and need much more personal interaction with their supervisors. Since a manager can realistically work closely in a coaching and counseling relationship with only a few workers, the span of control should be very small at this lower entry level under these conditions. Once these workers acquire the skills and training to be responsible for their own work, they can move into organizational units that are characterized by more general supervision and less close control and wider spans of control.

If larger numbers of our work force are capable of self-direction and being responsible for their own work and if others can develop this maturity through appropriate coaching and counseling, what are the implication for management behavior?

the role of the manager—a linking pin

Traditionally, the role of the manager was characterized by planning, organizing, motivating, and controlling. In essence, the manager told his subordinates what to do and how to do it. Managers tended to use financial incentives and the manipulation of rewards and punishments to motivate workers. Management behavior was characterized by highly structured, close supervision.

While this management style may sometimes be appropriate with less-educated, unskilled workers at lower organizational levels, management by direction and control seems questionable as a method for motivating people with a higher level of education who tend to be capable of more mature behavior. It becomes increasingly apparent that the role of the manager should change as his subordinates become more responsible.

In dealing with these mature, better-educated workers, the emphasis of a manager's role shifts from formal supervision and strict control of his work group to more general supervision and loose control. With this change in management behavior, the supervisor is now free to devote more of his energies to serving as his group's representative in the next higher level of the organizational hierarchy.

Rensis Likert is helpful in explaining this role in his discussion of the "linking pin concept." *"The capacity to exert influence upward is essential if a supervisor (or manager) is to perform his supervisory functions successfully.* To be effective in leading his own work group, a superior must be able to influence his own boss, that is, he needs to be skilled both as a supervisor and as a subordinate." [21]

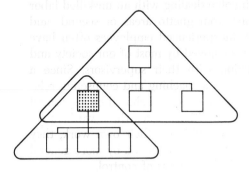

FIGURE 7.5 Supervisor as group's representative in next level of the organization.

two responsibilities

In essence, every superior is a member of two work groups—the one he is responsible *for* and the one he is responsible *to*. When his subordinates are immature, that is, when they are very dependent on him and are not willing and able to take responsibility, he must use his position power and close supervision to insure a minimum level of productivity. However, when his subordinates are mature enough to handle their own work with little supervision, it is possible for a manager to use personal power and general supervision. In this situation, he can spend more time in his "linking pin" role. Specifically, his activities can move from an emphasis on organizing, directing, motivating, and controlling his group to a stressing of long-range planning, interdepartmental coordination, and acquisition of resources at the next level of the organizational hierarchy. The time spent in these "linking pin" activities can often increase the productivity of a mature group much more than close supervision of their work.

SUMMARY

Organizational structures and management behavior are going to have to respond to cultural and educational differences apparent in the work force. Mature, responsible workers need a loosely controlled, flexible organization with general supervision to utilize their full potential. Immature, untrained workers need a structured organization with more individual attention and personal interaction with supervision to develop their talents. Perhaps increased awareness of cultural changes by management could make organizational structures and management behavior relevant to more workers, thus helping organizations to maximize their potential for productivity and increasing their impact on emerging problems in our society.

NOTES

1. Edgar H. Schein, *Organizational Psychology* (Englewood Cliffs, N.J.: Prentice-Hall, Inc., 1965), p. 61.
2. *Ibid.*
3. A. K. Korman, " 'Consideration,' 'Initiating Structure,' and Organizational Criteria —A Review," *Personnel Psychology: A Journal of Applied Research*, XIX, No. 4 (Winter 1966), 349–61.
4. Life Cycle Theory of Leadership was developed at the Center for Leadership Studies, Ohio University, Athens, Ohio. It was first published in Paul Hersey and Kenneth H. Blanchard, "Life Cycle Theory of Leadership," *Training and Development Journal,* May 1969.
5. Fillmore H. Sanford, *Authoritarianism and Leadership* (Philadelphia: Institute for Research in Human Relations, 1950).

6. David C. McClelland, J. W. Atkinson, R. A. Clark, and E. L. Lowell, *The Achievement Motive* (New York: Appleton-Century-Crofts, 1953); and *The Achieving Society* (Princeton, N.J.: D. Van Nostrand Co., Inc., 1961).

7. Chris Argyris, *Personality and Organization* (New York: Harper & Row, Publishers, 1957); *Interpersonal Competence and Organizational Effectiveness* (Homewood, Ill.: Dorsey Press, 1962); and *Integrating the Individual and the Organization* (New York: John Wiley & Sons, Inc., 1964).

8. W. Lloyd Warner, *Social Class in America* (New York: Harper & Row, Publishers. 1960).

9. *Ibid.*

10. See Paul Hersey and Kenneth H. Blanchard, "Managing Research and Development Personnel: An Application of Leadership Theory," *Research Management,* September 1969.

11. See Kenneth H. Blanchard and Paul Hersey, "A Leadership Theory for Educational Administrators," *Education,* Spring 1970.

12. Examples of self-paced learning curricula can be found at the Nova Educational Complex, Fort Lauderdale, Florida, where they are being used from elementary school through graduate study; Valley High School, Las Vegas, Nevada; and Brigham Young University and Ohio University in some undergraduate courses.

13. Jesse H. Day and Clifford Houk, "Student-Paced Learning: A Proposal for an Experiment in the Improvement of Learning in General Chemistry," unpublished proposal (Athens: Ohio University, 1968), p. 10.

14. Kenneth H. Blanchard, "College Boards of Trustees: A Need for Directive Leadership," *Academy of Management Journal,* December 1967.

15. F. H. Stutz, R. G. Morrow and K. H. Blanchard, "Report of a Survey," in *College and University Trustees and Trusteeship, Recommendations and Report of a Survey* (Ithaca, N. Y.: New York State Regents Advisory Committee on Educational Leadership, 1966).

16. Henry M. Wriston, *Academic Procession* (New York: Columbia University Press, 1959), p. 78.

17. See Paul Hersey and Kenneth H. Blanchard, "Cultural Changes: Their Influence on Organizational Structure and Management Behavior," *Training and Development Journal,* October 1970.

18. William H. Haney, *Communication and Organizational Behavior: Text and Cases,* rev. ed. (Homewood, Ill.: Richard D. Irwin, Inc., 1967), p. 20.

19. Harold Koontz and Cyril O'Donnell, *Principles of Management,* 4th ed. (New York: McGraw-Hill Book Company, 1968), p. 242.

20. Support for this discussion is provided by Peter F. Drucker, *The Practice of Management* (New York: Harper & Brothers, 1954), pp. 139–40.

21. Rensis Likert, *New Patterns of Management* (New York: McGraw-Hill Book Company, 1961), p. 14.

planning
for change

8

An effective leader must not only have good *diagnostic skills*. Once he has analyzed the demands of his environment, he must then be able to *adapt* his leadership personality to fit these demands and develop the means to *change* some or all of the other variables. Recognizing that sometimes the only avenue to effectiveness is through change, we will concentrate in this chapter on the processes and strategies for planning and implementing change.

INCREASING EFFECTIVENESS

Likert found that employee-centered supervisors who use general supervision *tend* to have higher producing sections than job-centered supervisors who use close supervision.[1] We emphasize the word *tend* because this seems to be increasingly the case in our society, yet we must also realize that there are exceptions to this tendency which are even evident in Likert's data. What Likert found was that a subordinate generally responds well to a superior's high expectations and genuine confidence in him and tries to justify his boss's expectations of him. His resulting high performance will reinforce his superior's high trust for him, for it is easy to trust and respect the man who meets or exceeds your expectations. This occurrence could be called the effective cycle.

FIGURE 8.1   Effective cycle.

Yet, as we have pointed out earlier, the concentration on output variables, as a means of evaluating effectiveness, tends to lead to short-run, task-oriented leader behavior. This style, in some cases, does not allow much room for a trusting relationship with employees. Instead, subordinates are told what to do and how to do it, with little consideration expressed for their ideas or feelings. After a while, the subordinates respond with minimal effort and resentment; low performance results in these instances. Reinforced by low expectations, it becomes a vicious cycle. Many other examples could be given which result in this all-too-common problem in organizations, as shown in Figure 8.2.

FIGURE 8.2   Ineffective cycle.

These cycles are depicted as static, but in reality they are very dynamic. The situation tends to get better or worse. For example, high expectations result in high performance, which reinforces the high expectations and produces even higher productivity. It almost becomes a spiral effect, as illustrated in Figure 8.3.

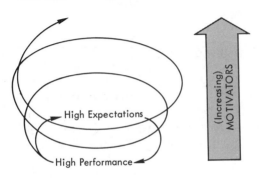

FIGURE 8.3   Spiraling effect of effective cycle.

In many cases, this spiraling effect is caused by an increase in leverage created through the use of the motivators. As people perform they are given more responsibility and opportunities for achievement and growth and development.

This spiraling effect can also occur in a downward direction. Low expectations result in low performance, which reinforces the low expectations and produces even lower productivity. It becomes a spiral effect like a whirlpool, as shown in Figure 8.4.

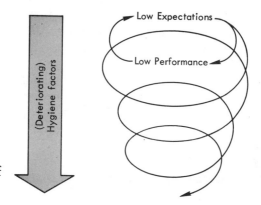

FIGURE 8.4 Spiraling effect of ineffective cycle.

If this downward spiraling continues long enough, the cycle may reach a point where it cannot be turned around in a short period of time because of the large reservoir of negative past experience that has built up in the organization. Much of the focus and energy is directed toward perceived problems in the environment such as interpersonal relations and respect for supervision rather than toward the work itself. Reaction to deteriorating hygiene factors takes such form as hostility, undermining, and slowdown in work performance. When this happens, even if a manager actually changes his behavior, the credibility gap based on long-term experience is such that the response is still distrust and skepticism rather than change.

One alternative that is sometimes necessary at this juncture is to bring in a new manager from the outside. The reason this has a higher probability of success is that the sum of the past experience of the people involved with the new manager is likened to a "clean slate," and thus different behaviors are on a much more believable basis. This was evident in the case of Plant Y described by Guest, which was discussed on pages 117–18. The ineffective cycle had been in a downward spiral far past the point where Stewart would have a good opportunity to make significant change. But with the introduction of a new manager, Cooley, significant changes were now possible.

breaking the ineffective cycle

The question is, How do we break this ineffective cycle and make it effective? At least two alternatives are available to both the subordinate and the superior.

The subordinate can either leave this job and seek a situation in which his superior will have higher expectations of his performance, or he can respond to low expectations and trust with high performance, thus hoping eventually to gain the respect of his superior and change his expectations.

The latter choice is difficult for both the subordinate and the superior. In effect, the problem is to change the expectations or behavior of one or another or both. Because the subordinate is not likely to be in a position of potential control, the superior must be the change agent. This is particularly difficult for a superior if the subordinate has shown no indication that he deserves to be trusted. The key, then, is to accomplish change appropriately, and this is where the practice of behavior modification may be helpful.

CHANGING MATURITY THROUGH BEHAVIOR MODIFICATION

In the normal work environment, managers often feel that either pressure (high task) or permissiveness (high relationships) is the only way to focus a subordinate on his task or change patterns of behavior. Even when these methods prove unsuccessful, managers use them because they are unaware of better techniques. At one time, managers were too structured, rigid, and punishing. Now there seems to be a swing to the overly permissive, unstructured manager. Both these strategies when inappropriate have created problems. Another alternative is Behavior Modification, which can accomplish the shifting of a leadership style according to Life Cycle Theory to stimulate changes in maturity.[2] To illustrate the difference between these three strategies—high task, high relationships and behavior modification—we can compare how a manager using each might handle a potential problem-worker.

Tony, a new employee right out of high school, is a very aggressive, competitive individual. During his first day on the job, he argues over tools with another young employee. Table 8.1 attempts to illustrate the possible reactions of a high task manager, a high relationships manager and a manager using behavior modification techniques.

Behavior modification (derived from studies of operant behavior conditioning through the use of reinforcement operations) is based on *observed* behavior and not internal unobserved feelings or attitudes.[3] Its basic premise is that *behavior is controlled by its immediate consequences.*

TABLE 8.1 Different approaches used in dealing with a disruptive worker

	High Task Manager	High Relationships Manager	Behavior Modification Manager
Manager reaction	"This worker is going to be a troublemaker. This behavior must be stopped!"	"I hope I can get them interacting and working together."	Feels Tony needs to learn to cope in positive ways to replace aggressive behavior! Separates conflicting workers without hostility or comment.
Supervisor subordinate interaction	"Hey, you, Knock it off! We don't allow fighting around here," said with coldness or anger.	"How would you both like to give me a hand on a job over here?"	Interaction between Tony and his supervisor is generally pleasant as manager watches for any positive behavior he can *immediately* reinforce. Follows this up with specific strategies. 1. Decides which new behaviors Tony needs to learn first. 2. Plans strategy to get desired behavior. 3. Attempts to understand Tony better in an effort to use incentives appropriate for his need structure. 4. Uses the incentives to reinforce behavior Tony needs to learn. 5. Continues to evaluate to make sure these incentives are still appropriate, since these tend to change with time.
Worker reaction	Tony builds resentment and hostility. Next few days, behavior becomes more aggressive. Gets in more trouble. Refuses to cooperate. Spends much time being reprimanded.	Tony finds he can get attention of supervisor by being disruptive because the supervisor wants to be "understanding." He causes trouble and watches supervisor's reaction. Supervisor pays more and more attention as his behavior gets worse. Disruptive behavior is reinforced.	Tony finds the supervisor appreciates good things about him. Wants to gain his respect; begins to behave in positive ways.

	High Task Manager	High Relationships Manager	Behavior Modification Manager
Outcome	Tony feels disliked by supervisor. Self-image deteriorates as he attempts to defend ego from assaults. Becomes more hostile and aggressive or withdrawn. Avoids supervisor and learning tasks.	Aggressiveness remains. Becomes more obnoxious as other workers withdraw. Creates incidents to get attention and assigned to those jobs he wants. Does not learn. No friends. Low self-image covered by bravado.	*Outcome in two or three weeks.* Tony's work and acceptance by other members of his work group continue to improve. Builds new self-image on basis of new behavior he has learned. Hostile and aggressive behavior toward other employees stops. Begins to have a sense of accomplishment. Inner needs and feelings start to change. Aggressiveness used in constructive ways. Has friends and becomes a positive rather than a disruptive influence on his work group.

Behavior can be increased, suppressed, or decreased by what happens immediately after it occurs. If the consequence is positive, the probability of that behavior occurring again is increased. Because probabilities are difficult to work with, we use observations of the future frequency of the behavior as a measure of the effectiveness of a consequence.

Reinforcement depends on the individual. What is reinforcing to one person may not be reinforcing to another. Money may motivate some people to work harder, but to others money is not a positive reinforcer; the challenge of the job might be the most rewarding aspect of the situation. Managers must look for unique differences in their people and recognize the dangers of over-generalizing.

Positive reinforcement is anything that is rewarding to the individual whose behavior is being reinforced. For a desirable behavior to be obtained, the slightest appropriate behavior exhibited by the individual in that direction must be rewarded as soon as possible. This is called *reinforcing positively successive approximations* of a certain response. For example, when an individual's performance is low, one cannot expect drastic changes overnight, regardless of changes in expectations or reinforcers.

Similar to the child learning some new behavior, we do not expect polished performance at the outset. So, as a parent, teacher, or supervisor we use positive reinforcement as the behavior approaches the desired level of performance. The manager must be aware of any progress of his subordinate, so that he will be in a position to reinforce this change appropriately.

This strategy is compatible with the concept of setting interim rather than final performance criteria and then reinforcing appropriate progress toward the final goal as interim goals are accomplished. In setting these goals it is important that they be programmed to be difficult but obtainable so that the individual proceeds along a path of gradual and systematic development. Eventually he reaches the point of a polished performance.

The type of consequence an individual experiences as a result of his behavior will determine the speed with which he approaches the final desired performance. Behavior consequences can be either positive (money, praise, award, promotion), negative (scolding, fines, layoffs, embarrassment), or neutral.

Another important aspect of the consequence, when viewing behavior modification, is the manner in which it is made known to the behaver. That is, a positive consequence can be presented or removed. A negative consequence can be presented or removed. And both positive and negative consequences can be withheld or suspended. Each of these operations or contingencies for behavior has a label as well as a description for how behavior is influenced, as illustrated in Table 8.2.[4]

TABLE 8.2 Contingency table showing how behavior is influenced depending on the type of consequence and the manner in which it is presented.

Type of Consequence	*Manner in Which Reinforcement Is Presented*		
	Presentation	*Removal*	*Withholding*
	Positive Reinforcement	Negative Punishment	NO LABEL
Positive Consequence	Behavior increases in rate	Behavior is suppressed or disrupted	Behavior extinguishes
	Positive Punishment	Negative reinforcement	NO LABEL
Negative Consequence	Behavior is suppressed or disrupted	Behavior increases in rate	Behavior extinguishes

An example of Behavior Modification in a hypothetical situation may be helpful. Suppose, for instance, a manager reprimands Al, one of his subordinates, for sloppy work, rather than giving him his usual praise. If Al becomes just anxious enough to find out what he did wrong, and then he does it right to get his boss' praise, the unpleasantness of the reprimand can be seen to have operated as Positive Punishment. In this case, when the boss punished him, Al immediately stopped his sloppy work and began to work more carefully. The disruption of an activity is produced by punishment such as a reprimand. When Al responded to this reprimand by working carefully, the manager was given a chance to use positive reinforcement once again. By praising Al he now increased the probability of Al's working carefully in the future.

Let us imagine that Al's supervisor is less understanding. Suppose that instead of giving a reprimand to Al for sloppy work, he fines him $100 for such behavior. Immediately Al settles down, figures out what is wrong, and begins working carefully. The boss notices this and says, "If you don't continue working carefully, you will be fired." Now Al is nervous. He doesn't want to be fired, so he is very careful. When the boss fined Al, he used negative punishment by removing something positive ($100) from Al. Notice that Al's sloppy performance was disrupted—sloppiness became suppressed. Then, the supervisor instituted negative reinforcement in the fear of a threat. The threat of job loss is removed only so long as Al works neatly; therefore, Al's neat working behavior increases in frequency.

The important thing to notice is the basic difference between reinforcement and punishment. Reinforcement as a behavioral consequence results in an increase in the rewarded behavior in the future. Punishment merely disrupts or suppresses ongoing behavior. It has neither a lasting nor a sure effect on future behavior.

Finally, let us consider the role of withholding an expected consequence after behavior occurs. (This is sometimes called *Extinction* because it gets rid of a behavior.) Imagine that Al has adjusted pretty well to his setting. He works carefully and neatly, because that is what pays off. But suddenly, the boss stops rewarding him for neat work. Al goes for maybe a week, maybe two weeks working neatly with no reward. He may not be able to tell us what is different, but gradually his behavior gives us a clue. He soon begins to try other behaviors. He becomes less careful and neat. If the former consequences of punishment are also withheld, we see that within days he has reverted to his earlier behavior pattern. In essence, neatness and carefulness have extinguished. People seldom continue to do things that do not provide positive reinforcement. This is even true sometimes when they are behaving well as in Al's case. Parents often get into this bind when they tend to pay attention to their kids only when they are behaving poorly. When the children are behaving appropriately, they may pay little or no attention to them, which in a sense puts that behavior on extinction. If a child wants attention from his parents (it is rewarding to him), he may be willing to endure what the parent thinks is punishment for that attention. So, in the long run, the parents might be reinforcing the very behavior they do not want and extinguishing more appropriate behavior.

An additional aspect of extinction, which illustrates its impact on stable behavior, is emotional in nature. We could predict with an excellent chance of being correct, that Al will likely become surly, he may complain more than before, or he may have problems getting along with his co-workers. Emotional behavior usually accompanies extinction in performance when expected reinforcement or former consequences of punishment are withheld.

As we discussed in Chapter 2, a leader or manager has to be careful in using punishment. He does not always know what a person will do when he is punished. One person, like Al, may shape up. Another may become completely incompetent. Furthermore, the use of withholding is uncertain. Among the thousands of potentially dangerous emotional behaviors a person can engage in, it would be just your luck to touch off an extremely disruptive episode. Lying, manipulation, and other kinds of undesirable behavior may be resorted to by a person seeking to avoid punishment. If the supervisor is unobservant, he could actually be reinforcing these rather than behaviors he considers important.

Behavior modification is a useful tool for supervisors because it can be applied in most environments. Although it may involve a reassessment of traditionally used methods for obtaining compliance and cooperation, it has relevance for persons interested in accomplishing objectives through other people. This is not the case with psychotherapy.

Psychotherapy is based on an assumption that to change behavior one has first to start with the feelings and attitudes within an individual. The problem with psychotherapy from a practitioner's viewpoint is that it is too expensive and is appropriate for use only by professionals. One way of illustrating the main difference between these two approaches is to go back to a portion of the basic motivation situation model as illustrated in Figure 8.5.

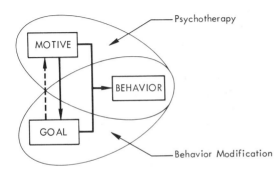

FIGURE 8.5 Comparison between psychotherapy and behavior modification.

Figure 8.5 shows that both psychotherapy and behavior modification are interested in affecting behavior. The emphasis in psychotherapy is on analyzing the reasons underlying behavior that is often the result of early experiences in life. On the other hand, behavior modification concentrates on observed behavior, using goals or rewards outside the individual to modify and shape behavior toward a desired performance.

LEVELS OF CHANGE

In Chapter 1 we talked about four levels of change: (1) knowledge changes, (2) attitudinal changes, (3) individual behavior changes, and (4) group or organizational performance changes.

Changes in knowledge tend to be the easiest to make; all one has to do is give a person a book or an article to read, or have someone whom he respects tell him something new. Attitude structures differ from knowledge structures in that they are emotionally charged in a positive or a negative way. The addition of emotion often makes attitudes more difficult to change than knowledge.

Changes in individual behavior seem to be significantly more difficult and time consuming than either of the two preceding levels. For example, a person may have knowledge about the potential dangers of smoking, may even actually feel that smoking is a bad habit he would like to change, and may still be unable to stop smoking because a habit pattern has been reinforced over a long period of time. It is important to point out that we are talking about change in patterned behavior and not a single event. In our example, anyone can quit smoking for a short period of time; the real test comes months later to see if a new long-term pattern has evolved.

While individual behavior is difficult enough, when we get to the implementation of group or organizational performance, it is compounded because at this level we are concerned with changing customs, mores, and traditions. Being a group it tends to be a self-reinforcing unit, and therefore a person's behavior as a member of a group is more difficult to modify without first changing the group norms.[5]

THE CHANGE CYCLES

The levels of change become very significant when we examine two different change cycles—the participative change cycle and the coerced change cycle.

participative change

A participative change cycle is implemented when new knowledge is made available to the individual or the group. It is hoped that the group will accept the data and will develop a positive attitude and commitment in the direction of the desired change. At this level the strategy may be direct participation by the individual or the group in helping to select or formalize the goals or the new methods for obtaining the goals. This is group participation in problem solving. The next step is to attempt to translate this commitment into actual behavior. This tends to be the most difficult barrier to overcome. For example, it is one thing to be concerned (attitude) about a social problem but another thing to be willing to actually get involved in doing something (behavior) about the problem. One strategy that is often useful is to attempt to identify informal as well as formal leaders within the group and concentrate on gaining their acceptance and behavior. Once this is accomplished we have moved a long way in getting others in the group to begin to pattern their behavior after those persons whom they respect and perceive in leadership roles. This participative change cycle is illustrated in Figure 8.6.

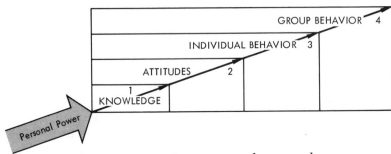

FIGURE 8.6   Participative change cycle.

coerced change

We have all probably been faced with a situation similar to the one in which there is an announcement on Monday morning that "as of today all members of this organization shall begin to operate in accordance with Form 10125." This is an example of a coerced change cycle. This cycle begins by imposing change on the total organization. This will tend to affect the interaction-influence system at the individual level. The new contacts and modes of behavior create new knowledge which tends to develop predispositions toward or against the change. This coerced change cycle is illustrated in Figure 8.7.

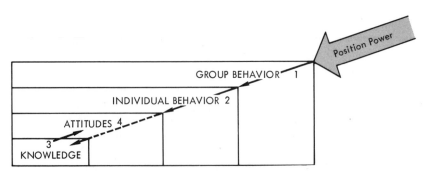

FIGURE 8.7   Coerced change cycle.

In some cases, where change is forced, the new behavior which is engaged in creates the kind of knowledge that develops commitment to the change and therefore begins to approximate a participative change cycle as it reinforces the individual and the group behavior.

DIFFERENCES BETWEEN THE TWO CHANGE CYCLES

In terms of the Life Cycle Theory of Leadership, the participative change cycle tends to be more appropriate for working with mature groups, since they are achievement-motivated and have a degree of knowledge and experience that may be useful in developing new strategies for accomplishing goals. Once the change starts, mature people are much more capable of assuming responsibilities for implementation. On the other hand, with immature people the coerced change cycle may be more productive because they are often dependent and not willing to take new responsibilities unless forced to do so. In fact, by their very nature, these people might prefer direction and structure to being faced with decisions that might be frightening to them.

There are some other significant differences between these two change cycles. The participative change cycle tends to be effective when induced by leaders with personal power, while the coerced cycle necessitates significant position power—rewards, punishments, and sanctions.

With the participative cycle, the main advantage is that once accepted it tends to be long lasting, since the people are highly committed to the change. Its disadvantage is that it tends to be slow and evolutionary. On the other hand, the advantage of the coerced cycle is speed. Using his position power, the leader can often impose change immediately. The disadvantage of this cycle is that it tends to be volatile. It can only be maintained as long as the leader has position power to make it stick. Even it often results in animosity, hostility, and in some cases overt and covert behavior to undermine and overthrow.

These cycles have been described as if they were either/or positions. In reality it is more a question of the proper blend of each, depending upon the situation.

CHANGE PROCESS

In examining change, Kurt Lewin identified three phases of the change process.[6]

unfreezing

The aim of unfreezing is to motivate and make the individual or the group ready to change. It is a "thawing out" process where the forces acting on an individual are rearranged so that now he sees the need for change. According to Edgar H. Schein, some elements that unfreezing situations seem to have in common are (1) the physical removal of the individual being changed from his accustomed routines, sources of information, and social relationships; (2) the undermining and destruction of all social supports; (3) demeaning and humiliating experience to help the individual being changed to see his old self as unworthy and thus to be motivated to change; (4) the consistent linking of reward with willingness to change and of punishment with unwillingness to change.[7]

In brief, unfreezing is the breaking down of the mores, customs, and traditions of an individual—the old ways of doing things—so that he is ready to accept new alternatives. In terms of force field analysis, unfreezing may occur when either the driving forces are increased or the restraining forces that are resisting change are reduced.

changing

Once the individual has become motivated to change, he is ready to be provided with new patterns of behavior. This process is most likely to occur by one of two mechanisms: identification and internalization.[8] *Identification* occurs when one or more models are provided in the environment, models from whom an individual can learn new behavior patterns by identifying with them and trying to become like them. *Internalization* occurs when an individual is placed in a situation where new behaviors are demanded of him if he is to operate successfully in that situation. He learns these new behavior patterns not only because they are necessary to survive but because of new high strength needs induced by coping behavior.

> Internalization is a more common outcome in those influence settings where the direction of change is left more to the individual. The influence which occurs in programs such as Alcoholics Anonymous, in psychotherapy or counseling for hospitalized or incarcerated populations, in religious retreats, in human relations training of the kind pursued by the National Training Laboratories (1953), and in certain kinds of progressive education programs is more likely to occur through internalization or, at least, to lead ultimately to more internalization.[9]

Identification and internalization are not either/or courses of action, but effective change is often the result of combining the two into a strategy for change.

Force or compliance is sometimes discussed as another mechanism for inducing change.[10] It occurs when an individual is forced to change by the direct manipulation of rewards and punishment by someone in a power position. In this case, behavior appears to have changed when the change agent is present but is often dropped when supervision is removed. Thus, rather than discuss force as a mechanism of changing, we should think of it as a tool for unfreezing.

refreezing

The process by which the newly acquired behavior comes to be integrated as patterned behavior into the individual's personality and/or ongoing significant emotional relationships is referred to as *refreezing*. As Schein contends, if the new behavior has been internalized while being learned, "this has automatically facilitated refreezing because it has been fitted naturally into the individual's personality. If it has been learned through identification, it will persist only so long as the target's relationship with the original influence model persists unless new surrogate models are found or social support and reinforcement is obtained for expressions of the new attitudes." [11]

This highlights how important it is for an individual engaged in a change process to be in an environment that is continually reinforcing the desired change. The effect of many a training program has been short-lived when the person returns to an environment that does not reinforce the new patterns or, even worse, is hostile toward them.

What we are concerned about in refreezing is that the new behavior does not get extinguished over time. To insure this not happening, reinforcement must be scheduled in an effective way. There seem to be two main reinforcement schedules: continuous and intermittent.[12] Continuous reinforcement means that the individual being changed is reinforced every time he engages in the desired new pattern. With intermittent reinforcement, on the other hand, not every desired response is reinforced. Reinforcement either can be completely random or can be scheduled according to a prescribed number of responses occurring or a particular interval of time elapsing before reinforcement is given. With continuous reinforcement, the individual learns the new behavior quickly, but if his environment changes to one of nonreinforcement, extinction can be expected to take place relatively soon. With intermittent reinforcement, extinction is much slower because the individual has been conditioned to go for periods of time without any reinforcement. Thus, for fast learning a continuous reinforcement schedule should be used. But once the individual has learned the new pattern, a switch to intermittent reinforcement should insure a long-lasting change.

change process—some examples

To see the change process in operation, several examples can be cited.

A college basketball coach recruited for his team Bob Anderson, a center six feet four inches tall from a small town in a rural area. In his district, six feet four inches was good height for a center. This fact, combined with his deadly turnaround jump shot, made Anderson the rage of his league and enabled him to average close to thirty points a game.

Recognizing that six feet four inches is small for a college center, the coach hoped that he could make Anderson a forward, moving him inside only when they were playing a double pivot. One of the things the coach was concerned about, though, was how Anderson, when used in the pivot, could get his jump shot off when he came up against other players ranging in height from six feet eight inches to seven feet. He felt that Anderson would have to learn to shoot a hook shot, which is much harder to block, if he was going to have scoring potential against this kind of competition. The approach that many coaches use to solve this problem would probably be as follows: The first day of practice when Anderson arrived, the coach would welcome Anderson and would then explain the problem to him as he had analyzed it. As a solution he would probably ask Anderson to start to work with the varsity center, Steve Cram, who was six feet ten inches tall and had an excellent hook. "Steve can help you start working on that new shot, Bob," the coach would say. Anderson's reaction to this interchange might be one of resentment, and he would go over and work with Cram only because of the coach's position power. After all, he might think to himself, "Who does he think he is? I've been averaging close to thirty points a game for three years now and the first day I show up here the coach wants me to learn a new shot." So he may start to work with Cram reluctantly, concentrating on the hook shot only when the coach is looking but taking his favorite jump shot when he is not observing him. Anderson is by no means unfrozen or ready to learn to shoot another way. Let us look at another approach the Coach could have used to solve this problem.

Suppose that on the first day of practice he sets up a scrimmage between the varsity and the freshmen. Before he starts the scrimmage he gets big Steve Cram, the varsity center, aside and tells him, "Steve, we have this new freshman named Anderson who has real potential to be a fine ball player. What I'd like you to do today, though, is not to worry about scoring or rebounding—just make sure every time Anderson goes up for a shot you make him eat it. I want him to see that he will have to learn to shoot some other shots if he is to survive against guys like you." So when the scrimmage starts, the first time Anderson gets the ball and turns around to shoot, Cram leaps up and "stuffs the ball right down his throat." Time after time this occurs. Soon Anderson starts to engage in some coping behavior, trying to fall away from the basket, shooting from the side of his head rather than from the front in an attempt to get his shot off. After the scrimmage, Anderson comes off the court dejected. The coach says, "What's wrong, Bob?" Bob replies, "I don't know coach, I just can't seem to get my shot off against a man as big as Cram. What do you think I should do, coach?" he asks. "Well, Bob, why don't you go over and start working with Steve on a hook shot. I think you'll find it much harder to block. And with your shooting eye I don't think it will take long for you to learn." How do you think Anderson feels about working with Cram now? He is enthusiastic and ready to learn. Having been placed in a situation where he learns for himself that he has a problem has gone a long way in unfreezing Anderson from his past patterns of behavior and preparing him for making the attempt at identification. Now he is ready for identification. He has had an opportunity to internalize his problem and is ready to work with Steve Cram.

So often the leader who has knowledge of an existing problem forgets that until the people involved recognize the problem as their own, it is going to be much more difficult to produce change in their behavior. Internalization and identification are not either/or alternatives but can be parts of developing specific change strategies appropriate to the situation.

Another example of the change processes in operation can be seen in the military, particularly in the induction phase. There are probably few organizations that have entering their ranks people who are less motivated and committed to the organization than the recruits the military gets. And yet in a few short months they are able to mold these men into a relatively effective combat team. This is not an accident. Let us look at some of the processes that help accomplish this.

The most dramatic and harsh aspects of the training are the unfreezing phase. All four of the elements that Schein claims unfreezing situations have in common are present. Let us look at some specific examples of these elements in operation.

1. The recruits are *physically removed from their accustomed routines, sources of information, and social relationships* in the isolation of Parris Island.

During this first week of training at Parris Island, the recruit is . . . hermetically sealed in a hostile environment, required to rise at 4:55 A.M., do exhausting exercises, attend classes on strange subjects, drill for hours in the hot sun, eat meals in silence and stand at rigid attention the rest of the time; he has no television, no radio, no candy, no coke, no beer, no telephone—and can write letters only during one hour of free time a day.[13]

2. *The undermining and destruction of social supports* is one of the DI's (drill instructor's) tasks. "Using their voices and the threat of extra PT (physical training), the DI . . . must shock the recruit out of the emotional stability of home, pool hall, street corner, girl friend or school." [14]

3. *Demeaning and humiliating experiences* are commonplace during the first two weeks of the training as the DIs help the recruits *see themselves as unworthy and thus motivated to change* into what they want a marine to be. "It's a total shock . . . Carrying full seabags, 80 terrified privates are herded into their "barn," a barracks floor with 40 double-decker bunks. Sixteen hours a day, for two weeks, they will do nothing right.[15]

4. Throughout the training there is *consistent linking of reward with willingness to change and of punishment with unwillingness to change.*

Rebels or laggards are sent to the Motivation Platoon to get "squared away." A day at Motivation combines constant harassment and PT (physical training), ending the day with the infiltration course. This hot, 225 yard ordeal of crawling, jumping and screaming through ditches and obstacles is climaxed by the recruit dragging two 30 pound ammo boxes 60 yards in mud and water. If he falters he starts again. At the end, the privates are lined up and asked if they are ready to go back to their home platoons . . . almost all go back for good.[16]

While the recruits go through a severe unfreezing process, they quickly move to the changing phase, first identifying with the DI and then emulating informal leaders as they develop. "Toward the end of the third week a break occurs. What one DI calls 'that five per cent—the slow, fat, dumb, or difficult' have been dropped. The remaining recruits have emerged from their first week vacuum with one passionate desire—to stay with their platoon at all costs." [17]

Internalization takes place when the recruits through their forced interactions develop different high strength needs. "Fear of the DI gives way to respect, and survival evolves into achievement toward the end of training. 'I learned I had more guts than I imagined' is a typical comment." [18]

Since the group tends to stay together throughout the entire program, it serves as a positive reinforcer which can help refreeze the new behavior.

MANAGING INTERGROUP CONFLICT

A total organization is really a composite of its various working units or groups. The important thing for organizational accomplishment, whether these groups be formal or informal, is that these groups either perceive their goals as being the same as the goals of the organization or, although different, see their own goals being satisfied as a direct result of working for the goals of the organization.

On occasion groups or parts of an organization come into conflict. The atmosphere *between* groups can affect the total productivity of the organization. According to Schein,

> this problem exists because as groups become more committed to their own goals and norms, they are likely to become competitive with one another and seek to undermine their rivals' activities, thereby becoming a liability to the organization as a whole. The overall problem, then, is how to establish high-productive, *collaborative* intergroup relations.[19]

consequences of group competition

Sherif was the first to study systematically the consequences of intergroup conflict.[20] His original studies and more recent replications have found the effects of competition on individuals quite consistent to the extent that they can readily be described.[21] As Schein reports, some interesting phenomena occur both *within* and *between* each competing group.[22]

During competition, each group becomes more cohesive; internal differences are forgotten for the moment as increased loyalty takes over. The group atmosphere becomes more task-oriented as group accomplishment becomes paramount. The leadership shifts more toward an autocratic style as the group becomes more tolerant of someone taking the lead. The group becomes more organized and highly structured, and with this demands more loyalty and conformity from its members in order to present a "solid front."

At the same time that these phenomena are occurring *within* the group, the relationship *between* the groups has some common characteristic. Each group starts to see the other as the enemy and distorts perceptions of reality—recognizing only their own strengths and the weaknesses of the other group. Hostility toward the other group increases, while communication decreases. This makes it easier to maintain negative feelings and more difficult to correct false perceptions. If the groups are forced to interact, as at a bargaining table, neither one really listens to the other but only listens for cues that support its arguments.

Schein stresses that while competition and the responses it generates may be very useful to a group in making it more effective and achievement-motivated, "the same factors which improve intragroup effectiveness may have negative consequences for intergroup effectiveness." [23] Labor-management disputes are cases in point because the more these parties perceive themselves as competitors, the more difficult they find it to resolve their differences.

When win-lose confrontations occur between two groups or teams, even though there eventually is a winner, the loser (if it is not a clear-cut win) is not convinced that he lost, and intergroup tension is higher than before the competition began. If the win is clear-cut, the winner often loses his edge, becomes complacent, and is less interested in goal accomplishment. The loser in this case often develops internal conflict while trying to discover the cause of the loss or someone to blame. If reevaluation takes place, however, the group may reorganize and become more cohesive and effective. [24]

When the negative consequences of intergroup conflict outweigh the gains, management seeks ways to reduce this intergroup tension. As Schein suggests, "the basic strategy of reducing conflict, therefore, is to find goals upon which groups can agree and to re-establish valid communication between the group." [25] He contends that this strategy can be implemented by any combination of the following: *locating a common enemy, inventing a negotiation strategy which brings subgroups of the competing groups into interaction with each other*, and *locating a superordinate goal*.

preventing intergroup conflict

Since it is difficult to reduce intergroup conflict once it has developed, it may be desirable to prevent its occurrence in the first place. This might be done in several ways. First of all, management should emphasize the contributions to total goals rather than the accomplishment of subgroup goals. Second, an attempt should be made to increase the frequency of communication and interaction between groups and develop a reward system for groups who help each other. Third, where possible individuals should be given experiences in a wide range of departments to broaden their base for empathy and understanding of intergroup problems. [26]

Collaborative organizations often appear to have an abundance of task relevant conflict which improves overall effectiveness. This may occur because under these conditions individuals trust each other and are frank and open in sharing information and ideas. In competitive situations characterized by win-lose confrontations, observations may suggest lower levels of open conflict, since total interaction is significantly less and each group is committed to withholding its resources and information from the other groups, thus lowering the potential for overall organizational effectiveness.

IMPACT OF CHANGE ON TOTAL SYSTEM

The importance of combining the social and the technical into a unified social systems concept is stressed by Robert Guest.

On his part the social scientist often makes the error of concentrating on human motivation and group behavior without fully accounting for the technical environment which circumscribes, even determines, the roles which the actors play. Motivation, group structure, interaction processes, authority—none of these abstractions of behavior takes place in a technological vacuum.[27]

A dramatic example of the consequences of introducing technical change and ignoring its consequences on the social system is the case of the introduction of the steel axe to a group of Australian aboriginals.[28]

This tribe remained considerably isolated, both geographically and socially, from the influence of Western cultures. In fact, their only contact was an Anglican mission established in the adjacent territory.

The polished stone axe was traditionally a basic part of the tribe's technology. Used by men, women, and children, the stone axe was vital to the subsistence economy. But more than that, it was actually a key to the smooth running of the social system; it defined interpersonal relationships and was a symbol of masculinity and male superiority. "Only an adult male could make and own a stone axe; a woman or a child had to ask his permission to obtain one."[29]

The Anglican mission, in an effort to help improve the situation of the aboriginals, introduced the steel axe, a product of European technology. It was given indiscriminately to men, women, and children. Because the tool was more efficient than the stone axe it was readily accepted, but it produced severe repercussions unforeseen by the missionaries or the tribe. As Stephen R. Cain reports:

The adult male was unable to make the steel axe and no longer had to make the stone axe. Consequently, his exclusive axe-making ability was no longer a necessary or desirable skill, and his status as sole possessor and dispensor of a vital element of technology was lost. The most drastic overall result was that traditional values, beliefs, and attitudes were unintentionally undermined.[30]

The focus in this book has been on the management of human resources, and as a result we have spent little time on how technical change can have an impact on the total system. Our attempt in this example was to show that an organization is an "open social system," that is, all aspects of an organization are interrelated; a change in any part of an organization may have an impact on other parts or on the organization itself. Thus a proposed change in one part of an organization must be carefully assessed in terms of its likely impact on the rest of the organization.

NOTES

1. Rensis Likert, *New Patterns of Management* (New York: McGraw-Hill Book Company, 1961), p. 7.
2. Considerable help in developing this section on behavior modification was provided by review comments made by Patrick D. Slattery and Glenna G. Holsinger in *Motivating the Reluctant Learner* (Lexington, Mass.: Motivity, Inc., 1970).
3. The most classic discussions of behavior modification, or operant conditioning, have been done by B. F. Skinner. See Skinner, *Science and Human Behavior* (New York: The Macmillan Company, 1953). See also A. Bandura, *Principles of Behavior Modification* (New York: Holt, Rinehart & Winston, 1969) and C. M. Franks, *Behavior Therapy: Appraisal & Status* (New York: McGraw-Hill, 1969).
4. Adapted from Table developed by P. D. Slattery.
5. J. A. C. Brown, *The Social Psychology of Industry* (Baltimore: Penguin Books, Inc., 1954), p. 249.
6. Kurt Lewin, "Frontiers in Group Dynamics: Concept, Method, and Reality in Social Science; Social Equilibria and Social Change," *Human Relations,* I, No. 1 (June 1947), 5–41.
7. Edgar H. Schein, "Management Development as a Process of Influence," in David R. Hampton, *Behavioral Concepts in Management* (Belmont, Calif.: Dickinson Publishing Co., Inc., 1968), p. 110. Reprinted from *Industrial Management Review,* II, No. 2 (May 1961), 59–77.
8. The mechanisms are taken from H. C. Kelman, "Compliance, Indentification and Internalization: Three Processes of Attitude Change," *Conflict Resolution,* II (1958), 51–60.
9. Schein, "Management Development," p. 112.
10. Kelman discussed compliance as a third mechanism for attitude change.
11. Schein, "Management Development," p. 112.
12. See C. B. Ferster and B. F. Skinner, *Schedules of Reinforcement* (New York: Appleton-Century-Crofts, 1957).

13. "Marine Machine," *Look Magazine,* August 12, 1969.

14. *Ibid.*

15. *Ibid.*

16. *Ibid.*

17. *Ibid.*

18. *Ibid.*

19. Edgar H. Schein, *Organizational Psychology* (Englewood Cliffs, N.J.: Prentice-Hall, Inc., 1965), p. 80.

20. M. Sherif, O. J. Harvey, B. J. White, W. R. Hood, and Carolyn Sherif, *Intergroup Conflict and Cooperation: The Robbers Cave Experiment* (Norman, Okla.: Book Exchange, 1961).

21. Robert R. Blake and Jane S. Mouton, "Reactions to Intergroup Competition under Win-Lose Conditions," *Management Science,* 7 (1961), 420–35.

22. Schein, *Organizational Psychology,* p. 81.

23. *Ibid.*

24. *Ibid.,* p. 82.

25. *Ibid.,* p. 83.

26. *Ibid.,* p. 85.

27. Robert H. Guest, *Organizational Change: The Effect of Successful Leadership* (Homewood, Ill.: Dorsey Press and Richard D. Irwin, Inc., 1964), p. 4.

28. Lauriston Sharp, "Steel Axes for Stone Age Australians," in *Human Problems in Technology Changes,* ed. Edward H. Spicer (New York: Russell Sage Foundation, 1952), pp. 69–94.

29. Stephen R. Cain, "Anthropology and Change," taken from *Growth and Change,* University of Kentucky, I, No. 3 (July 1970).

30. *Ibid.*

management:

a synthesis

of theory

9

All the theories, concepts, and empirical research presented in earlier chapters have made a contribution to the field of management and seem to have some relevance in diagnosing an environment, in making some predictions, and in planning for changes in behavior. These viewpoints have often appeared to us to be like threads, each thread being unique to itself.

Our attempt in this book has been to take these independent viewpoints and weave them into a fabric, and in the attempt to increase significantly the usefulness of each in diagnosis and prediction. In this last chapter we will make one final attempt to integrate these theories, using the Life Cycle Theory of Leadership (discussed in Chapter 7) as a synthesizing framework to portray their compatibilities rather than their differences.

LIFE CYCLE THEORY OF LEADERSHIP AND MOTIVATION

In developing the model of the motivating situation (Chapter 2), it was contended that motives directed toward goals result in behavior. One way of classifying high strength motives is Maslow's hierarchy of needs (Chapter 2), while goals or incentives that tend to satisfy these needs can be described by Herzberg's hygiene factors and motivators (Chapter 3). Both these frameworks can be illustrated in Life Cycle Theory in terms of those leadership styles that have a high probability of satisfying these needs or providing the corresponding incentives, as illustrated in Figure 9.1. It should be stressed that in relating Maslow's or Herzberg's theories to styles in the Life Cycle, these are not absolutes but only bench marks for the practitioner to use in analysis. While styles associated with a certain quadrant may be "heavy" on one concept, they are not exclusively; other styles may also satisfy them to some degree. This caution will hold true throughout our discussions in this chapter.

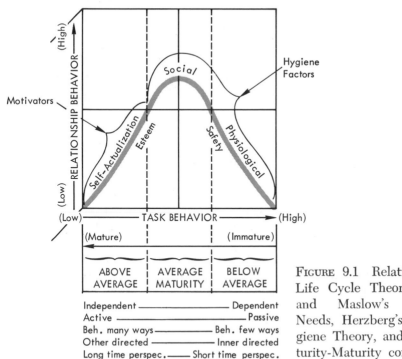

FIGURE 9.1 Relationship between Life Cycle Theory of leadership and Maslow's Hierarchy of Needs, Herzberg's Motivation-Hygiene Theory, and Argyris' Immaturity-Maturity continuum.

Upon examining the curvilinear function of the cycle, one can begin to plot the styles that tend to correspond with the various high strength needs described by Maslow. At the same time, it is leadership styles in the first three quadrants of the cycle that tend to provide incentives consistent with hygiene factors, whereas it is in quadrant 4 that behaviors that facilitates motivators occur.

As can also be noted in Figure 9.1, maturity in Life Cycle Theory is consistent with Argyris's Immaturity-Maturity continuum (Chapter 3).

LIFE CYCLE THEORY OF LEADERSHIP, MANAGEMENT STYLES, AND THE NATURE OF MAN

McGregor's Theory X and Theory Y and Likert's Management Systems (Chapter 3) blend easily into Life Cycle Theory, as illustrated in Figure 9.2.

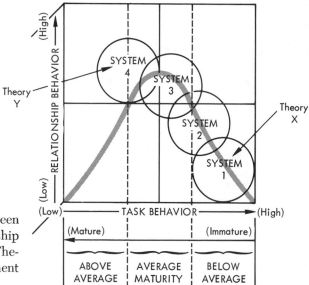

FIGURE 9.2 Relationship between Life Cycle Theory of Leadership and McGregor's Theory X and Theory Y and Likert's Management Systems.

In essence, Likert's System 1 describes behaviors that have a high probability of being evoked by Theory X assumptions. According to these assumptions, most people prefer to be directed, are not interested in assuming responsibility, and want security above all. On the other hand, System 4 illustrates behaviors that tend to be elicited by Theory Y assumptions. A Theory Y manager assumes that people are *not*, by nature, lazy and unreliable and thus can be self-directed and creative at work if properly motivated. System 1 is a task-oriented, highly structured authoritarian management style while System 4 is based on teamwork, mutual trust, and confidence. Systems 2 and 3 are intermediate stages between these two extremes.

In his book *Organizational Psychology*, Schein discusses four assumptions about people: (1) rational-economic man, (2) social man, (3) self-actualizing man, and (4) complex man, and he describes their implied managerial styles.[1] These styles seem to be relevant to Life Cycle Theory, as illustrated in Figure 9.3.

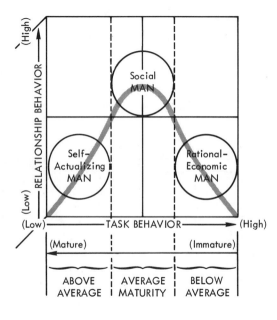

FIGURE 9.3   Relationship between Life Cycle Theory of Leadership and Schein's four assumptions about people and their implied managerial strategies.

The assumptions underlying *rational-economic man* are very similar to those depicted by McGregor's Theory X. In essence, man is seen as primarily motivated by economic incentives; a passive being to be manipulated, motivated, and controlled by the organization; an irrational being whose feelings must be neutralized and controlled. These assumptions imply a managerial strategy that places prime emphasis on efficient task performance and would thus be consistent with quadrant 1 (high task–low relationships).

With *social man* come the assumptions that man is basically motivated by social needs; he seeks meaning in the social relationships on the job and is more responsive to these than to the incentives and the controls of the organization. The managerial strategy implied for the social man suggests that a manager should not limit his attention to the task to be performed but should give more attention to the needs of the people. The manager should be concerned with the feelings of his subordinates, and in doing so, must often act as the communication link between the employees and higher management. In this situation the initiative for work begins to shift from management to the worker, with the leader tending to engage in behaviors related to quadrant 2 (high task–high relationships) and quadrant 3 (high relationships–low task).

Self-actualizing man is seen as seeking meaning and accomplishment in his work as his other needs become fairly well satisfied, being primarily self-motivated and capable of being mature on the job, and being willing to integrate his own goals with those of the organization. With a self-actualizing man, the manager will worry less about being considerate to employees and more about how he can enrich their jobs and make them more challenging and meaningful. The manager attempts to determine what will challenge a particular worker—he becomes a catalyst and a facilitator rather than a motivator and a controller. He delegates as much responsibility as he feels workers can handle. The manager now is able to leave him alone to structure his own job and to provide his own socio-emotional support through task accomplishment. This strategy is consistent with a low task–low relationships style appropriate for working with people of above average maturity (quadrant 4).

According to Schein, man is really more complex than rational-economic, social, or self-actualizing. In fact, man is highly viable, is capable of learning new motives, is motivated on the basis of many different kinds of needs, and can respond to numerous different kinds of leadership styles. *Complex man* taxes the diagnostic skills of a manager, and as Life Cycle Theory implies, it requires that he change his style appropriately to meet various contingencies.

LIFE CYCLE THEORY
OF LEADERSHIP AND CHANGE

Whenever you talk about initiating a change cycle (Chapter 8), the first step is determining the maturity level of the people with whom you are working. If they are below average in maturity—dependent and unwilling to take responsibility—they will tend to require more unfreezing than if you are working with people who are average or above average in maturity. As illustrated in Figure 9.4, the leadership styles in quadrants

1 and 2 tend to be heavy in terms of unfreezing, while the emphasis in quadrants 2 and 3 is on the change process, with quadrants 3 and 4 stressing the refreezing process.

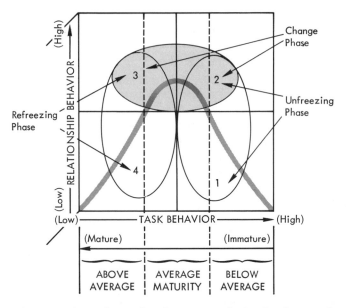

FIGURE 9.4   Relationship between Life Cycle Theory of Leadership and the process of change.

One of the techniques used to move through the curvilinear function is behavior modification (Chapter 8). When working with immature people, at first you tend to cut back on the structure, giving the individuals an opportunity to take some responsibility. When the leader gets the smallest approximation of mature behavior, he immediately increases the socio-emotional support as positive reinforcement. This stairlike process (cut back on structure, then increase socioemotional support) continues until the change or changes start to become a habit as the people mature. At that point, the leader tends to cut back also on reinforcement as he moves toward quadrant 4 and a low structure–low consideration style. If done earlier, this cutback on socioemotional support would have appeared as punishment to the below average or average mature person. But now to the person of above average maturity, the fact that his boss tends to leave him alone not only in terms of the task but also in terms of socioemotional support is positive reinforcement.

The styles representing quadrants 1 and 2 seem to be consistent with the behaviors associated with a coerced change cycle, while quadrants 3 and 4 are more representative of a participative change cycle (Chapter 8). In a participative change cycle, the change begins at the knowledge level and moves eventually to the organization, while the coercive change cycle starts with changes in the organization and moves gradually toward changes in knowledge and attitudes.

Quadrants 1 and 2 tend to be styles that have a high probability of being interpreted as driving forces; quadrants 3 and 4 seem to approximate behaviors directed toward eliminating restraining forces (Chapter 5). In increasing the driving forces the emphasis seems to be on short-term output, while when attempting to eliminate restraining forces the concern is more with building intervening variables and concentrating on long-term goals. It should be emphasized again that these are only tendencies and bench marks, and it should be recognized that under certain conditions other styles might be appropriate.

CONCLUSIONS

There is still much unknown about human behavior. Unanswered questions remain and further research is necessary. Knowledge about motivation and leader behavior will continue to be of great concern to practitioners of management for several reasons: It can help improve the effective utilization of human resources; it can help in preventing resistance to change, restriction of output, and labor disputes; and often it can lead to a more profitable organization.

Our intention has been to provide a conceptual framework that may be useful to the reader in applying the conclusions of the behavioral sciences. The value a framework of this kind has is *not* in changing one's knowledge but comes when it is applied in changing one's behavior in working with people.

NOTE

1. Edgar H. Schein, *Organizational Psychology* (Englewood Cliffs, N.J.: Prentice-Hall, Inc., 1965), pp. 47–63.

recommended

supplementary

reading

APPLEWHITE, PHILLIP, *Organizational Behavior*. Englewood Cliffs, N.J.: Prentice-Hall, Inc., 1965.

ARGYRIS, CHRIS, *Integrating the Individual and the Organization*. New York: John Wiley & Sons, Inc., 1964.

BENNIS, WARREN G., *Changing Organizations*. New York: McGraw-Hill Book Company, 1966.

BERELSON, BERNARD, AND GARY A. STEINER, *Human Behavior: An Inventory of Scientific Findings*. New York: Harcourt, Brace & World, Inc., 1964.

CARTWRIGHT, DORWIN, AND ALVIN ZANDER, eds., *Group Dynamics: Research and Theory* (2nd ed.). Evanston, Ill.: Row, Peterson & Company, 1960.

DRUCKER, PETER F., *Managing for Results*. New York: Harper & Row, Publishers, 1964.

FILLEY, ALAN C., AND ROBERT J. HOUSE, *Managerial Process and Organizational Behavior*. Glenview, Ill.: Scott, Foresman & Company, 1969.

GUEST, ROBERT H., *Organizational Change: The Effect of Successful Leadership*. Homewood, Ill.: Dorsey Press and Richard D. Irwin, Inc., 1964.

HERZBERG, FREDERICK, *Work and the Nature of Man*. New York: World Publishing Co., 1966.

KEPNER, C. H., AND B. B. TREGOE, *The Rational Manager*. New York: McGraw-Hill Book Company, 1965.

KOBB, DAVID A., IRWIN M. RUBIN, AND JAMES M. McINTYRE, *Organizational Psychology: A Book of Readings*. Englewood Cliffs, N.J.: Prentice-Hall, Inc., 1971.

LIKERT, RENSIS, *New Patterns of Management*. New York: McGraw-Hill Book Company, 1961.

MACHIAVELLI, NICCOLÒ, *The Prince*. New York: Mentor Classic—New American Library, 1952.

MARROW, ALFRED J., *Practical Theorist: The Life and Work of Kurt Lewin*. New York: Basic Books, Inc., Publishers, 1969.

MASLOW, ABRAHAM H., *Motivation and Personality*. New York: Harper & Row, Publishers, 1954.

MAYO, ELTON, *The Social Problems of an Industrial Civilization*. Boston: Harvard Business School, 1945.

McCLELLAND, DAVID C., *et al.*, *The Achieving Society*. Princeton, N.J.: D. Van Nostrand Co., Inc., 1961.

McGREGOR, DOUGLAS, *The Human Side of Enterprise*. New York: McGraw-Hill Book Company, 1960.

SCHEIN, EDGAR H., *Organizational Psychology*. Englewood Cliffs, N.J.: Prentice-Hall, Inc., 1965.

WARNER, W. LLOYD, AND NORMAN H. MARTIN, eds., *Industrial Man*. New York: Harper & Brothers, 1959.

selected

bibliography

ANSBACHER, K. L., AND R. R. ANSBACHER, eds., *The Individual Psychology of Alfred Adler*. New York: Basic Books, Inc., Publishers, 1956.

APPLEWHITE, PHILLIP, *Organizational Behavior*. Englewood Cliffs, N.J.: Prentice-Hall, Inc., 1965.

ARENDT, HANNAH, *The Human Condition*. Chicago: University of Chicago Press, 1958.

ARENSBURG, C. M., AND D. McGREGOR, "Determination of Morale in an Industrial Company," *Applied Anthropology*, I, No. 2 (1942), 12–34.

ARGYLE, MICHAEL, GODFREY GARDNER, AND FRANK CIOFFI, "Supervisory Methods Related to Productivity and Absenteeism, and Labor Turnover," *Human Relations*, 11 (1958), 23–40.

ARGYRIS, CHRIS, *Executive Leadership: An Appraisal of a Manager in Action*. Hamden, Conn.: Shoe String Press, Inc., 1953.

———, *Integrating the Individual and the Organization*. New York: John Wiley & Sons, Inc., 1964.

———, *Interpersonal Competence and Organizational Effectiveness*. Homewood, Ill.: Dorsey Press and Richard D. Irwin, Inc., 1962.

————, *Organization and Innovation.* Homewood, Ill.: Dorsey Press and Richard D. Irwin, Inc., 1965.

————, *Personality and Organization.* New York: Harper & Row, Publishers, 1957.

————, "T-Groups for Organization Effectiveness," *Harvard Business Review,* 42, 1964.

ASCH, S. E., "Effects of Group Pressure upon the Modification and Distortion of Judgements," in *Group Dynamics* (2nd ed.), Dorwin Cartwright and Alvin Zander, eds., pp. 189–200. Evanston, Ill.: Row, Peterson & Company, 1960.

————, *Social Psychology.* Englewood Cliffs, N.J.: Prentice-Hall, Inc., 1952.

ATHOS, ANTHONY G., AND ROBERT E. COFFEY, *Behavior in Organizations: A Multidimensional View.* Englewood Cliffs, N.J.: Prentice-Hall, Inc., 1968.

BARKER, H., T. DEMBO, AND K. LEWIN, *Frustration and Aggression.* Iowa City: University of Iowa Press, 1942.

BARNARD, CHESTER I., *The Functions of the Executive.* Cambridge: Harvard University Press, 1938.

BASS, BERNARD M., *Leadership, Psychology, and Organizational Behavior.* New York: Harper & Row Publishers, 1960.

————, *Organization and Management.* Cambridge: Harvard University Press, 1948.

————, MARGARET W. PRYER, EUGENE L. GAIER, AND AUSTIN W. FLINT, "Interacting Effects of Control, Motivation, Group Practice, and Problem Difficulty on Attempted Leadership," *Journal of Abnormal and Social Psychology,* 56 (1958), 352–58.

BAUMGARTEL, H. J., JR., "Leadership Motivation and Attitudes in Research Laboratories," *Journal of Social Issues,* XII, No. 2 (1956), 24–31.

BAVELAS, A., "Communication Patterns in Task-Oriented Groups," in *Group Dynamics,* D. Cartwright and A. Zander eds. Evanston, Ill.: Row, Peterson & Company, 1953.

BEER, MICHAEL, ROBERT BUCKHOUT, MILTON W. HOROWITZ, AND SEYMOUR LEVY, "Some Perceived Properties of the Difference between Leaders and Non-Leaders," *The Journal of Psychology,* 47 (1959), 49–56.

BELL, GRAHAM B., AND ROBERT L. FRENCH, "Consistency of Individual Leadership Position in Small Groups of Varying Membership," *Journal of Abnormal and Social Psychology,* 45 (1950), 764–67.

BENDIX, R., *Work and Authority in Industry.* New York: John Wiley & Sons, Inc., 1956.

BENNE, KENNETH D., AND PAUL SHEATS, "Functional Roles of Group Members," *Journal of Social Issues,* IV, No. 2 (1948), 41–49.

BENNIS, WARREN G., *Changing Organizations.* New York: McGraw-Hill Book Company, 1966.

————, "Leadership Theory and Administrative Behavior: The Problem of Authority," *Administrative Science Quarterly,* IV, No. 3 (December 1959), 259–301.

BERELSON, BERNARD, AND GARY A. STEINER, *Human Behavior: An Inventory of Scientific Findings.* New York: Harcourt, Brace & World, Inc., 1964.

BERGEN, GARRET L., AND WILLIAM V. HANEY, *Organizational Relations and Management Action*. New York: McGraw-Hill Book Company, 1966.

BLAKE, ROBERT R., *et al.*, "Breakthrough in Organizational Development," *Harvard Business Review*, November–December 1964.

BLAKE, ROBERT R., AND JANE S. MOUTON, *The Managerial Grid*. Houston, Tex.: Gulf Publishing, 1964.

————, "Reactions to Intergroup Competition under Win-Lose Conditions," *Management Science*, 7 (1961), 420–35.

BLANCHARD, KENNETH H., "College Boards of Trustees: A Need for Directive Leadership," *Academy of Management Journal*, December 1967.

BLAU, PETER M., *The Dynamics of Bureaucracy*. Chicago: University of Chicago Press, 1955.

BLUM, F. H., *Toward a Democratic Work Process*. New York: Harper & Row, Publishers, 1953.

BORG, WALTER R., "The Behavior of Emergent and Designated Leaders in Situational Tests," *Sociometry*, 20 (1957), 95–104.

———— AND ERNST C. TUPES, "Personality Characteristics Related to Leadership Behavior in Two Types of Small Group Situational Problems," *Journal of Applied Psychology*, 42 (1958), 252–56.

BORGATTA, EDGAR F., ROBERT F. BALES, AND ARTHUR S. COUCH, "Some Findings Relevant to the Great Man Theory of Leadership," *American Sociological Review*, 19 (1954), 755–59.

BOWERS, D. G., AND S. E. SEASHORE, "Predicting Organizational Effectiveness with a Four-Factor Theory of Leadership," *Administrative Science Quarterly*, XI, No. 2 (1966), 238–63.

BRADFORD, LELAND P., JACK R. GIBB, AND KENNETH D. BENNE, *T-Group Theory and Laboratory Method*. New York: John Wiley & Sons, Inc., 1964.

BREMAN, N., *The Making of a Moron*. New York: Sheed & Ward, 1953.

BROOKS, E., "What Successful Executives Do," *Personnel*, XXXII, No. 3 (1955), 210–25.

BROWN, J. A. C., *The Social Psychology of Industry*. London: Penguin Books, 1954.

BROWNE, C. G., AND B. J. NEITZEL, "Communication, Supervision and Morale," *Journal of Applied Psychology*, 36 (1952), 86–91.

BROWNE, C. G., AND RICHARD P. SHORE, "Leadership and Predictive Abstracting," *Journal of Applied Psychology*, 40 (1956), 112–16.

CARLSON, RICHARD O., *Executive Succession and Organizational Change*. Chicago: Midwest Administration Center, University of Chicago, 1962.

CARP, FRANCIS M., BART M. VITOLA, AND FRANK L. MCLANATHAN, "Human Relations Knowledge and Social Distance Set in Supervisors," *Journal of Applied Psychology*, 47 (1963), 78–90.

CARTER, LAUHOR, WILLIAM HAYTHORN, AND MARGARET HOWELL, "A Further Investigation of The Criteria of Leadership," *Journal of Abnormal and Social Psychology*, 45 (1950), 350–58.

CARTWRIGHT, D., "Achieving Change in People: Some Applications of Group Dynamics Theory," *Human Relations*, 4 (1951), 381–92.

————, "The Potential Contribution of Graph Theory to Organization Theory," in *Modern Organization Theory*, M. Haire, ed. New York: John Wiley & Sons, Inc., 1959.

————, AND R. LIPPITT, "Group Dynamics and the Individual," *International Journal of Group Psychotherapy*, VII, No. 1 (1957), 86–102.

————, AND A. ZANDER, eds., *Group Dynamics: Research and Theory* (2nd ed.). Evanston, Ill.: Row, Peterson & Company, 1960.

CATTELL, RAYMOND B., "New Concepts for Measuring Leadership in Terms of Group Syntality," *Human Relations*, 4 (1951), 161–84.

CHOWDHRY, KAMLA, AND THEODORE M. NEWCOMB, "The Relative Abilities of Leaders and Non-Leaders to Estimate Opinions of Their Own Groups," *Journal of Abnormal and Social Psychology*, 47 (1952), 51–57.

CHRISTNER, CHARLOTTE A., AND JOHN K. HEMPHILL, "Leader Behavior of B–29 Commanders and Changes in Crew Members' Attitudes toward the Crew," *Sociometry*, 18 (1955), 82–87.

COATES, CHARLES H., AND ROLAND J. PELLEGRIN, "Executives and Supervisors: Informal Factors in Differential Bureaucratic Promotion," *Administrative Science Quarterly*, 2 (1957), 200–215.

————, "Executives and Supervisors: Contrasting Self-Conceptions of Each Other," *American Sociological Review*, 22, 1957, 217–20.

COCH, L., AND J. R. P. FRENCH, JR., "Overcoming Resistance to Change," *Human Relations*, I, No. 4 (1948), 512–32.

COMREY, A. L., W. S. HIGH, AND R. C. WILSON, "Factors Influencing Organizational Effectiveness," VII. *Personnel Psychology*, VIII, No. 2 (1955), 245–57.

COOLEY, C. H., *Social Organization*. New York: Scribner, 1909.

COOPER, WILLIAM W., HAROLD J. LEAVITT, AND MAYNARD W. SHELLY II, eds. *New Perspectives in Organization Research*. New York: John Wiley & Sons, Inc., 1964.

COWLEY, W. H., "The Traits of Face-to-Face Leaders," *Journal of Abnormal and Social Psychology*, 26 (1931), 304–13.

CROCKETT, WALTER H., "Emergent Leadership in Small Decision-Making Groups," *Journal of Abnormal and Social Psychology*, 51 (1955), 378–83.

CROZIER, MICHAEL, *The Bureaucratic Phenomenon*. Chicago: University of Chicago Press, 1964.

CYERT, RICHARD M., W. R. DILL, AND JAMES G. MARCH, "The Role of Expectations in Business Decision Making," *Administrative Science Quarterly*, 3 (December 1958), 307–40.

CYERT, RICHARD M., AND JAMES G. MARCH, *A Behavioral Theory of the Firm*. Englewood Cliffs, N.J.: Prentice-Hall, Inc., 1963.

DALE, ERNEST, *The Great Organizers*. New York: McGraw-Hill Book Company, 1960.

DALTON, M., *Men Who Manage*. New York: John Wiley & Sons, Inc., 1959.

DAY, ROBERT C., AND ROBERT L. HAMBLIN, "Some Effects of Close and Punitive Styles of Supervision," *The American Journal of Sociology*, 69 (1964), 499–510.

DENT, J. K., "Managerial Leadership Styles: Some Dimensions, Determinants, and Behavioral Correlates." Unpublished doctoral dissertation, University of of Michigan, 1957.

DEUTSCH, MORTON, "An Experimental Study of the Effects of Cooperation and Competition upon Group Process," *Human Relations,* 2 (1949), 199–231.

DILL, WILLIAM R., "Environment as an Influence of Managerial Autonomy," *Administrative Science Quarterly,* 2 (March 1958), 409–43.

————, THOMAS L. HINTON, AND WALTER R. REITMAN, *The New Managers.* Englewood Cliffs, N.J.: Prentice-Hall, Inc., 1962.

DITTES, JAMES E., "Attractiveness of Group as Function of Self-Esteem and Acceptance by Group," *Journal of Abnormal and Social Psychology,* 59 (1959), 77–82.

DRUCKER, PETER F., *Effective Executive.* New York: Harper & Row, Publishers, 1967.

————, *Landmarks of Tomorrow.* New York: Harper & Row, Publishers, 1959.

————, *Managing for Results.* New York: Harper & Row, Publishers, 1964.

————, *The Practice of Management.* New York: Harper & Row, Publishers, 1954.

DUBIN, R., *Human Relations in Administration.* Englewood Cliffs, N.J.: Prentice-Hall, Inc., 1951.

————, *et al., Leadership and Productivity.* San Francisco, Calif.: Chandler Publishing Co., 1965.

ETZIONI, AMITAI, *A Comparative Analysis of Complex Organizations on Power, Involvement and Their Correlates.* New York: The Free Press, 1961.

EVAN, WILLIAM M., "The Organization-Set: Toward a Theory of Inter-Organizational Relations," *Approaches to Organizational Design,* James D. Thompson, ed. Pittsburgh, Pa.: The University of Pittsburgh Press, 1966.

EVANS, C. E., "Supervisory Responsibility and Authority," *American Management Association, Reserve Report,* 30 (1957).

FERSTER, C. B. AND B. F. SKINNER, *Schedules of Reinforcement.* New York: Appleton-Century-Crofts, 1957.

FESTINGER, LEON, *A Theory of Cognitive Dissonance.* Stanford, Calif.: Stanford University Press, 1957.

————, STANLEY SCHACHTER, AND KURT BACK, *Social Pressures in Informal Groups.* New York: Harper & Row, Publishers, 1950.

FIEDLER, FRED E., *Leader Attitudes and Group Effectiveness.* Urbana: University of Illinois Press, 1958.

————, "Leadership and Leadership Effectiveness Traits: A Reconceptualization of the Leadership Trait Problem," *Leadership and Interpersonal Behavior,* Luigi Petrullo and Bernard M. Bass, eds. New York: Holt, Rinehart & Winston, Inc., 1961.

————, *A Theory of Leadership Effectiveness.* New York: McGraw-Hill Book Company, 1967.

FILLEY, ALAN C., AND ROBERT J. HOUSE, *Managerial Process and Organizational Behavior.* Glenview, Ill.: Scott, Foresman & Company, 1969.

FLEISHMAN, EDWIN A., "Leadership Climate, Human Relations Training, and Supervisory Behavior," *Personnel Psychology,* 6 (1953), 205–22.

————, "The Measurement of Leadership Attitudes in Industry," *Journal of Applied Psychology,* 37 (1953), 153–58.

————, E. F. HARRIS AND H. E. BURTT, "Leadership and Supervision in Industry," *Ohio State Business Education Reserve Monograph,* 33 (1955).

FLEISHMAN, EDWIN A., AND EDWIN HARRIS, "Patterns of Leadership Behavior Related to Employee Grievances and Turnover," *Personnel Psychology,* 15 (1962), 43–56.

————, AND DAVID R. PETERS, "Interpersonal Values, Leadership Attitudes, and Managerial 'Success'," *Personnel Psychology,* 15 (1962), 127–43.

FOA, URIEL G., "Relation of Worker's Expectations to Satisfaction with the Supervisor," *Personnel Psychology,* 10 (1957), 161–68.

Foundation for Research on Human Behavior, *Assessing Managerial Potential.* Ann Arbor, Mich.: author, 1958.

————, *Creativity and Conformity: A Problem for Organizations.* Ann Arbor, Mich.: author, 1958.

————, *Communication Problems in Superior-Subordinate Relationships.* Ann Arbor, Mich.: author, 1960.

————, *An Action Research Program for Organization Improvement.* Ann Arbor, Mich.: author, 1960.

————, *Managing Major Change in Organizations.* Ann Arbor, Mich.: 1960.

FRANK, ANDREW G., "Goal Ambiguity and Conflicting Standards," *Human Organization,* 17 (Winter 1958), 8–13.

FRENCH, J. R. P., JR., "A Formal Theory of Social Power," *Psychological Review,* LXIII, No. 3 (1956), 181–94.

————, JOACHIM ISRAEL, AND DAGFINN ĀS, "An Experiment on Participation in a Norwegian Factory," *Human Relations,* XIII, No. 1 (1960), 3–19.

FRENCH, J. R. P., JR., J. C. ROSS, S. KIRBY, J. R. NELSON AND P. SMYTH, "Employee Participation in a Program of Industrial Change," *Personnel,* November–December 1958, 16–29.

FREUD, SIGMUND, *The Ego and the Id.* London: Hogarth Press, 1927.

————, *New Introductory Lectures on Psychoanalysis.* New York: W. W. Norton & Company, Inc., 1933.

FRIEDMANN, G., *Industrial Society: The Emergency of Human Problems of Automation.* Glencoe, Ill.: The Free Press, 1948.

FROMM, ERIC, *The Sane Society.* New York: Rinehart, 1955.

GARDNER, JOHN W., "The Antileadership Vaccine." (Reprinted from the 1965 *Annual Report,* Carnegie Corporation of New York.) See also "Executive Trends Beat the Management Shortage," *Nation's Business,* LII, No. 9 (September 1964).

GAUDET, FREDERICK J., AND A. RALPH CARLI, "Why Executives Fail," *Personnel Psychology,* 10 (1957), 7–21.

GELLERMAN, SAUL W., *Leadership Style and Employee Morale.* New York: General Electric Company, Public and Employee Relations Services, 1959.

————, *Motivation and Productivity.* New York: American Management Association, 1963.

GETZELS, JACOB W., AND EGON E. GUBA, "Social Behavior and the Administrative Process," *The School Review,* LXV, No. 4 (Winter 1957), 423–41.

GHISELLI, EDWIN E., "Individuality as a Factor in the Success of Management Personnel," *Personnel Psychology,* 13 (1960), 1–10.

————, AND R. BARTHOL, "Role Perceptions of Successful and Unsuccessful Supervisors," *Journal of Applied Psychology,* 40 (1956), 241–44.

GIBB, CECIL A., "Leadership," in *Handbook of Social Psychology,* Gardner Lindzey, ed. Cambridge, Mass.: Addison-Wesley Publishing Company, Inc., 1954.

————, "The Principles and Traits of Leadership," *Journal of Abnormal and Social Psychology,* 42 (1947), 267–84.

————, "The Sociometry of Leaderhip in Temporary Groups," *Sociometry,* 13 (1950), 226–43.

GOODACRE, D. M., "Group Characteristics of Good and Poor Performing Combat Units," *Sociometry,* XVI, No. 2 (1953), 168–79.

————, "Stimulating Improved Man Management," *Personnel Psychology,* 16 (1963), 133–43.

GORDON, OAKLEY J., "A Factor Analysis of Human Needs and Industrial Morale," *Personnel Psychology,* 8 (1955), 1–18.

GORDON, T., *Group-centered Leadership.* Boston: Houghton Mifflin Company, 1955.

GORE, WILLIAM J., *Administrative Decision-making.* New York: John Wiley & Sons, Inc., 1964.

GREEN, B., "Attitude Measurement," in *Handbook of Social Psychology,* G. Lindzey, ed. Cambridge, Mass.: Addison-Wesley Publishing Company, Inc., 1954.

GREER, F. LOYAL, "Leader Indulgence and Group Performance," *Psychological Monographs,* 75, No. 12, Whole No. 516 (1961).

GROSS, N., W. S. MASON, AND A. MCEACHERN, *Explorations in Role Analysis.* New York: John Wiley & Sons, Inc., 1958.

GROSS, NEAL, AND WILLIAM E. MARTIN, "On Group Cohesiveness," *American Journal of Sociology,* 57 (1952), 546–54.

GUEST, ROBERT H., *Organizational Change: The Effect of Successful Leadership.* Homewood, Ill.: Dorsey Press and Richard D. Irwin, Inc., 1964.

GULICK, LUTHER, AND L. URWICK, eds., *Papers on the Science of Administration.* New York: Institute of Public Administration, 1937.

HAIRE, M., *Psychology in Management.* New York: McGraw-Hill Book Company, 1956.

HALPIN, ANDREW W., *The Leadership Behavior of School Superintendents.* Chicago: Midwest Administration Center, The University of Chicago, 1959.

HAMBLIN, ROBERT L., "Leadership and Crises," in *Group Dynamics: Research and Theory* (2nd ed.), Dorwin Cartwright and Alvin Zander, eds. Evanston, Ill.: Row, Peterson & Company, 1960. Also in *Sociometry,* 21 (1958), 322–35.

HAMMOND, LEO K., AND MORTON GOLDMAN, "Competition and Non-competition and Its Relationship to Individual and Group Productivity," *Sociometry,* 24 (1961), 46–60.

HAMPTON, DAVID R., *Behavioral Concepts in Management.* Belmont, Calif.: Dickinson Publishing Co., Inc., 1968.

HANEY, WILLIAM H., *Communication and Organizational Behavior: Text and Cases* (rev. ed.). Homewood, Ill.: Richard D. Irwin, Inc., 1967.

HARARY, F., AND R. NORMAN, *Graph Theory as a Mathematical Model in the Social Sciences.* Ann Arbor, Mich.: Institute for Social Research, 1953.

HARE, A. PAUL, *Handbook of Small Group Research.* New York: The Free Press, 1962.

———, E. F. BORGATTA, AND R. F. BALES, *Small Group.* New York: Alfred A. Knopf, Inc., 1955.

HEALY, JAMES H., "Coordination and Control of Executive Functions," *Personnel,* 33 (1956), 106–17.

HEMPHILL, JOHN K., "Relations between the Size of the Group and the Behavior of 'Superior' Leaders," *The Journal of Social Psychology,* 32 (1950), 11–32.

———, *Situational Factors in Leadership,* Monograph No. 32. Columbus: Bureau of Educational Research, Ohio State University, 1949.

———, "Why People Attempt to Lead," in *Leadership and Interpersonal Behavior,* Luigi Petrullo and Bernard M. Bass, eds. New York: Holt, Rinehart & Winston, Inc., 1961.

———, AND ALVIN E. COONS, "Development of the Leader Behavior Description and Questionnaire," in *Leader Behavior: Its Description and Measurement,* Monograph No. 88, Ralph M. Stogdill and Alvin E. Coons, eds. Columbus: Bureau of Business Research, Ohio State University, 1957.

HERSEY, PAUL, AND KENNETH H. BLANCHARD, "Cultural Changes: Their Influence on Organizational Structure and Management Behavior," *Training and Development Journal,* October 1970.

———, "Life Cycle Theory of Leadership," *Training and Development Journal,* May 1969.

HERZBERG, FREDERICK, *Work and the Nature of Man.* New York: World Publishing Co., 1966.

———, B. MAUSNER, AND BARBARA SNYDERMAN, *The Motivation to Work* (2nd ed.). New York: John Wiley & Sons, Inc., 1959.

HOLLANDER, E. P., "Emergent Leadership and Social Influence," in *Leadership and Interpersonal Behavior,* Luigi Petrullo and Barnard M. Bass, eds. New York: Holt, Rinehart & Winston, Inc., 1961.

HOLSINGER, GLENNA G., *Motivating the Reluctant Learner.* Lexington, Mass.: Motivity, Inc., 1970.

HOMANS, G. C., *The Human Group.* New York: Harcourt, Brace & World, Inc., 1950.

HOPPOCK, R., *Job Satisfaction.* New York: Harper & Brothers, Publishers, 1935.

HORSFALL, A. B., AND C. M. ARENSBERG, "Teamwork and Productivity in a Shoe Factory," *Human Organization,* 8 (1949), 13–25.

HOUSE, ROBERT J., *Management Development: Design, Implementation and Evaluation.* Ann Arbor: Bureau of Industrial Relations, University of Michigan, 1967.

HOUSER, J. D., *What People Want from Business.* New York: McGraw-Hill Book Company, 1938.

HOVLAND, C. I., I. L. JANIS, AND H. H. KELLEY, *Communication and Persuasion.* New Haven, Conn.: Yale University Press, 1953.

HOVLAND, C. I., AND I. L. JANIS, eds., *Personality and Persuasibility,* 2, Yale Studies in Attitude and Communication. New Haven, Conn.: Yale University Press, 1959.

HOVLAND, C. I., AND M.J. ROSEBERG, *Attitude, Organization and Change,* 3,

Yale Studies in Attitude and Communication. New Haven, Conn.: Yale University Press, 1960.

HUGHES, EVERETT C., *Men and their Work*. New York: The Free Press, 1958.

HYMAN, HERBERT H., "The Psychology of Status," *Archives of Psychology*, 269 (1942).

INDIK, BERNARD P., BASIL S. GEORGOPOULOS, AND STANLEY E. SEASHORE, "Superior Subordinate Relationships and Performance," *Personnel Psychology*, 14 (1961), 357–74.

Institute for Social Research, *Factors Related to Productivity*. Ann Arbor, Mich.: author, 1951.

JACKSON, J. M., "The Effect of Changing the Leadership of Small Work Groups," *Human Relations*, VI, No. 1 (1953), 25–44.

———, AND H. D. SALTZSTEIN, *Group Membership and Group Conformity Processes*. Ann Arbor, Mich.: Institute for Social Research, 1956.

JAMES, WILLIAM, *The Principles of Psychology*, Vol. 1. London: Macmillan & Co. Ltd., 1890.

JANOWITZ, MORRIS, "Changing Patterns of Organizational Authority: The Military Establishment," *Administrative Science Quarterly*, 3 (March 1959), 473–93.

JAQUES, E., *The Changing Culture of a Factory*. London: Tavistock Publications, 1951.

———, *Measurement of Responsibility*. London: Tavistock Publications, 1956.

JENKINS, W. O., "A Review of Leadership Studies with Particular Reference to Military Problems," *Psychological Bulletin*, XLIV, No. 1 (1947), 54–79.

JENNINGS, EUGENE E., "The Anatomy of Leadership," *Management of Personnel Quarterly*, I, No. 1 (Autumn 1961).

JOHNSON, DEWEY E., *Concepts of Air Force Leadership*. Washington, D.C.: Air Force ROTC, 1970.

KAHN, R. L., "Human Relations on the Shop Floor," *Human Relations and Modern Management*, E. M. Hugh-Jones, ed., pp. 43–74. Amsterdam: North-Holland Publishing Co., 1958.

———, "The Prediction of Productivity," *Journal of Social Issues*, XII, No. 2 (1956), 41–49.

———, "Productivity and Job Satisfaction," *Personnel Psychology*, XIII, No. 3 (1960), 275–78.

———, AND D. KATZ, "Leadership Practices in Relation to Productivity and Morale," *Group Dynamics: Research and Theory* (2nd ed.), D. Cartwright and A. Zander, eds., pp. 554–71. Evanston, Ill.: Row, Peterson & Company, 1960.

KATZ, D., "Morale and Motivation in Industry," in *Current Trends in Industrial Psychology*, W. Dennis, ed., pp. 145–71. Pittsburgh: University of Pittsburgh, 1949.

———, N. MACCOBY, G. GURIN, AND L. G. FLOOR, *Productivity, Supervision and Morale among Railroad Workers*. Ann Arbor, Mich.: Institute for Social Research, 1951.

KATZ, D., N. MACCOBY, AND NANCY C. MORSE, *Productivity, Supervision, and Morale in an Office Situation*. Ann Arbor, Mich.: Institute for Social Research, 1950.

KATZ, ROBERT L., "Skills of an Effective Administrator," *Harvard Business Review*, January–February 1955, pp. 33–42.

KELMAN, H. C., "Compliance, Identification and Internalization: Three Processes of Attitude Change," *Conflict Resolution*, II (1958), 51–60.

KEPNER, C. H., AND B. B. TREGOE, *The Rational Manager*. New York: McGraw-Hill Book Company, 1965.

KNICKERBOCKER, IRVING, "Leadership: A Conception and Some Implications," *The Journal of Social Issues*, IV, No. 3 (1948), 23–40.

KNOWLES, HENRY P., AND BORJE O. SAXBERG, *Personality and Leadership Behavior*. Reading, Mass.: Addison-Wesley Publishing Company, Inc., 1970.

KOBB, DAVID A., IRWIN M. RUBIN, AND JAMES M. MCINTYRE, *Organizational Psychology: A Book of Readings*. Englewood Cliffs, N.J.: Prentice-Hall, Inc., 1971.

KOONTZ, HAROLD, AND CYRIL O'DONNELL, *Principles of Management* (4th ed.). New York: McGraw-Hill Book Company, 1968.

KORMAN, A. K., "'Consideration,' 'Initiating Structure,' and Organizational Criteria—A Review," *Personnel Psychology: A Journal of Applied Research*, XIX, No. 4 (1966), 349–61.

KRULEE, G. K., "The Scanlon Plan: Co-operation through Participation," *Journal of Business*, University of Chicago, XXVIII, No. 2 (1955), 100–13.

LEAVITT, H. J., *Managerial Psychology*. Chicago: University of Chicago Press, 1958.

LEWIN, K., *Field Theory in Social Science*, D. Cartwright, ed. New York: Harper & Brothers, 1951.

———, "Frontiers in Group Dynamics," *Human Relations*, 1 (1947), 5–41.

———, "Group Decision and Social Change," *Readings in Social Psychology* (3rd ed.), E. E. Maccoby, T. M. Newcomb, and E. L. Hartley, eds., pp. 197–211. New York: Holt, Rinehart & Winston, Inc., 1958.

———, *Resolving Social Conflict*, Gertrude Lewin, ed. New York: Harper & Brothers, 1948.

———, R. LIPPITT, AND R. WHITE, "Leader Behavior and Member Reaction in Three 'Social Climates,'" in *Group Dynamics: Research and Theory* (2nd ed.), Cartwright and Zander, eds. Evanston, Ill.: Row, Peterson & Company, 1960.

LIEBERMAN, S., "The Effects of Changes in Roles on the Attitudes of Role Occupants," *Human Relations*, IX, No. 4 (1956), 385–402.

LIKERT, RENSIS, "Effective Supervision: An Adaptive and Relative Process," *Personnel Psychology*, II, No. 3 (1958), 317–52.

———, *The Human Organization*. New York: McGraw-Hill Book Company, 1967.

———, "Measuring Organizational Performance," *Harvard Business Review*, XXXVI, No. 2 (1958), 41–50.

———, "Motivational Approach to Management Development," *Harvard Business Review*, XXXVII, No. 4, (1959), 75–82.

———, "Motivation: The Core of Management," American Management Association, *Personnel Series* (155), 3–21.

———, *New Patterns of Management*. New York: McGraw-Hill Book Company, 1961.

————, AND D. KATZ, "Supervisory Practices and Organizational Structures as They Affect Employee Productivity and Morale," American Management Association, *Personnel Series* (120), 1948, 14–24.

LIPPITT, GORDON, *Organizational Renewal*. New York: Appleton-Century-Crofts, 1969.

————, JEANNE WATSON, AND B. WESTLEY, *The Dynamics of Planned Change: A Comparative Study of Principles and Techniques*. New York: Harcourt, Brace & World, Inc., 1958.

LITTERER, J. A., *Analysis of Organizations*. New York: John Wiley & Sons, Inc., 1965.

MACHIAVELLI, NICCOLÒ, *The Prince*. New York: Mentor Classic—New American Library, 1952.

MAIER, NORMAN R. F., *Frustration*. Ann Arbor: The University of Michigan Press, 1961.

————, *Psychology in Industry* (2nd ed.). New York: Houghton Mifflin Company, 1955.

MAILICK, SIDNEY, AND EDWARD H. VAN NESS, *Concepts and Issues in Administrative Behavior*. Englewood Cliffs, N.J.: Prentice-Hall, Inc., 1962.

MANN, F. C., "Changing Superior-Subordinate Relationships," *Journal of Social Issues*, VII, No. 3 (1951), 56–63.

————, "Putting Human Relations Research Findings to Work," *Michigan Business Review*, II, No. 2 (1950), 16–20.

————, "Studying and Creating Change: A Means of Understanding Social Organization," *Research in Industrial Human Relations*, pp. 146–67. Madison, Wis.: Industrial Relations Research Association, 1957.

————, AND L. R. HOFFMAN, *Automation and the Worker: A Study of Social Change in Power Plants*. New York: Holt, Rinehart & Winston, Inc., 1960.

MARCH, J. G., AND H. A. SIMON, *Organizations*. New York: John Wiley & Sons, Inc., 1958.

MARCUS, PHILIP M., "Supervision and Group Process," *Human Organization*, XX, No. 1 (1961), 15–19.

MARROW, ALFRED J., *Behind the Executive Mask*. New York: American Management Association, 1965.

————, *Practical Theorist: The Life and Work of Kurt Lewin*. New York: Basic Books, Inc., Publishers, 1969.

————, BOWERS, D. G., AND SEASHORE, S. E., eds., *Strategies of Organizational Change*. New York: Harper & Row, Publishers, 1967.

MASLOW, ABRAHAM H., *Eupsychian Management*. Homewood, Ill.: Richard D. Irwin, Inc., and The Dorsey Press, 1965.

————, *Motivation and Personality*. New York: Harper & Row, Publishers, 1954.

————, *New Knowledge in Human Values*. Scranton, Pa.: Harper and Row, Publishers, 1959.

————, *Toward a Psychology of Being*. Princeton, N.J.: D. Van Nostrand Co., Inc., 1962.

MAYO, ELTON, *The Human Problems of an Industrial Civilization*. New York: The Macmillan Company, 1933.

————, *The Social Problems of an Industrial Civilization*. Boston: Harvard Business School, 1945.

McCLELLAND, DAVID C., *Personality.* New York: Holt, Rinehart & Winston, Inc., 1951.

————, *Studies in Motivation.* New York: Appleton-Century-Crofts, 1955.

————, *et al., The Achievement Motive.* New York: Appleton-Century-Crofts, 1953.

————, *et al., The Achieving Society.* Princeton, N.J.: D. Van Nostrand Co., Inc., 1961.

McGREGOR, DOUGLAS, "Conditions of Effective Leadership in Industrial Organization," *Journal of Consulting Psychologists,* 8 (1944), 56–63.

————, *The Human Side of Enterprise.* New York: McGraw-Hill Book Company, 1960.

————, *Leadership and Motivation.* Boston: MIT Press, 1966.

————, *Professional Manager.* New York: McGraw-Hill Book Company, 1967.

McMURRY, R. N., "The Case for Benevolent Autocracy," *Harvard Business Review,* 36 (1958), 82–90.

MEDALIA, NAHUM Z., "Unit Size and Leadership Perception," *Sociometry,* 17 (1954), 64–67.

————, DELBERT C. MILLER, "Human Relations Leadership and the Association of Morale and Efficiency in Work Groups," *Social Forces,* 33 (1955), 348–52.

MELLINGER, G. D., "Interpersonal Trust as a Factor in Communication," *Journal of Abnormal and Social Psychology,* LII, No. 3 (1956), 304–9.

MELTZER, LEO, AND JAMES SALTER, "Organizational Structure and Performance Job Satisfaction," *American Sociological Review,* 27 (1962), 351–62.

MEYERS, SCOTT M., "Who Are Your Motivated Workers," *Harvard Business Review,* January–February 1964, pp. 73–88.

MILGRAM, STANLEY, "Group Pressure and Action against a Person," *Journal of Abnormal and Social Psychology,* 69 (1964), 137–43.

MILLER, J. G., "Toward a General Theory for the Behavioral Sciences," *American Psychologist,* 10 (1955), 513–31.

MILLER, WALTER B., "Two concepts of Authority," *American Anthropologist,* 57 (April 1955), 271–89.

MINER, JOHN B., AND JOHN E. CULVER, "Some Aspects of the Executive Personality," *Journal of Applied Psychology,* 39 (1955), 348–53.

MORSE, NANCY, AND R. WEISS, "The Function and Meaning of Work and the Job," *American Social Review,* XX, No. 2 (1955), 191–98.

NAGLE, BRYANT F., "Productivity, Employee Attitude and Supervisor Sensitivity," *Personnel Psychology,* 7 (1954), 219–33.

National Training Laboratories, *Explorations in Human Relations Training.* Washington, D.C.: National Education Association, 1953.

NEWCOMB, T. M., *Social Psychology.* New York: Holt, Rinehart & Winston, Inc., 1950.

NEWMAN, WILLIAM H., CHARLES E. SUMMER, AND E. KIRBY WARREN, *The Process of Management* (2nd ed.), Englewood Cliffs, N.J.: Prentice-Hall, Inc., 1967.

OAKLANDER, HAROLD, AND EDWIN A. FLEISHMAN, "Patterns of Leadership Related to Organizational Stress in Hospital Settings," *Administrative Science Quarterly,* 8 (1964), 520–32.

OBROCHTA, RICHARD J., "Foreman-Worker Attitude Patterns," *Journal of Applied Psychology,* 44 (1960), 88–91.

ODIORNE, GEORGE S., *Management by Objectives.* New York: Pitman Publishing Corp., 1965.

O'DONNELL, C., "The Source of Managerial Authority," *Political Science Quarterly,* 67 (1952), 573.

OWENS, ROBERT G., *Organizational Behavior in Schools.* Englewood Cliffs, N.J.: Prentice-Hall, Inc., 1970.

PACKARD, VANCE, *The Status Seekers.* New York: David McKay Co., Inc., 1959.

PARKER, T. C., "Relationships among Measures of Supervisory Behavior, Group Behavior, and Situational Characteristics," *Personnel Psychology,* 16 (1963), 319–34.

PATCHEN, M., "The Effect of Reference Group Standards on Job Satisfactions," *Human Relations,* XI, No. 4 (1958), 303–14.

PEARLIN, LEONARD I., "Sources of Resistance to Change in a Mental Hospital," *American Journal of Sociology,* 68 (1962), 325–34.

PELZ, D. C., "Influence: A Key to Effective Leadership in the First-Line Supervisor," *Personnel,* November 1952, pp. 3–11.

———, "Leadership within a Hierarchial Organization," *Journal of Social Issues,* 7 (1951), 49–55.

———, "Motivation of the Engineering and Research Specialist," American Management Association, *General Management Series* (186), 1957, 25–46.

———, "Some Social Factors Related to Performance in a Research Organization," *Administrative Science Quarterly,* I, No. 3 (1956), 310–25.

PERES, SHERWOOD H., "Performance Dimensions of Supervisory Positions," *Personnel Psychology,* 15 (1962), 405–10.

PERROW, CHARLES, "The Analysis of Goals in Complex Organizations," *American Sociological Review,* 26 (December 1961), 854–66.

———, *Organizational Analysis: A Sociological View.* Belmont, Calif.: Wadsworth Publishing Co., Inc., 1970.

PETER, LAWRENCE J., AND RAYMOND HULL, *The Peter Principle.* New York: William Morrow & Co., Inc., 1969.

PFIFFNER, J. M., "The Effective Supervisor: An Organization Research Study," *Personnel,* 31 (1955), 530–40.

PORTER, DONALD E., AND PHILLIP B. APPLEWHITE, *Studies in Organizational Behavior and Management.* Scranton, Pa.: International Textbook Company, 1964.

PORTER, LYMAN W., "A Study of Perceived Need Satisfactions in Bottom and Middle Management Jobs," *Journal of Applied Psychology,* 45 (1961), 1–10.

PRYER, MARGARET W., AUSTIN W. FLINT, AND BERNARD M. BASS, "Group Effectiveness and Consistency of Leadership," *Sociometry,* 25 (1962), 391–97.

REDDIN, WILLIAM J., *Managerial Effectiveness.* New York: McGraw-Hill Book Company, 1970.

————, "The 3-D Management Style Theory," *Training and Development Journal,* April 1967, pp. 8–17.

REID, P., "Supervision in an Automated Plant," *Supervisory Management,* August 1960, pp. 2–10.

REISMAN, DAVID, *The Lonely Crowd.* New Haven, Conn.: Yale University Press, 1950.

REVANS, R. W., "The Analysis of Industrial Behavior," *Automatic Production-change and Control.* London: Institution of Production Engineering, 1957.

RICE, A. K., *Productivity and Social Organization.* London: Tavistock Publications, 1958.

ROACH, DARRELL E., "Factor Analysis of Rated Supervisory Behavior," *Personnel Psychology,* 9 (1956), 487–98.

ROETHLISBERGER, F. J., *Management and Morale.* Cambridge: Harvard University Press, 1941.

————, AND W. J. DICKSON, *Management and the Worker.* Cambridge: Harvard University Press, 1939.

ROGERS, C. R., *Counseling and Psychotherapy.* Boston: Houghton Mifflin Company, 1942.

RONKEN, H. O., AND P. R. LAWRENCE, *Administering Changes.* Boston: Harvard Graduate School of Business Administration, 1952.

ROSS, I. C., AND A. ZANDER, "Need Satisfactions and Employee Turnover," *Personnel Psychology,* X, No. 3 (1957), 327–38.

RUBENSTEIN, ALBERT H., AND CHADWICK J. HABERSTROH, *Some Theories of Organization.* Homewood, Ill.: Richard D. Irwin, Inc., 1960.

SANFORD, FILLMORE H., *Authoritarianism and Leadership.* Philadelphia: Institute for Research in Human Relations, 1950.

————, "Leadership Identification and Acceptance," *Groups, Leadership and Men,* Harold Guetzkow, ed. Pittsburgh: Carnegie Press, 1951.

SCHACHTER, STANLEY, *The Psychology of Affiliation.* Stanford, Calif.: Stanford University Press, 1959.

SCHAFFER, R. H., "Job Satisfaction as Related to Need Satisfaction in Work," *Psychological Monographs,* 67, No. 14 (1953).

SCHEIN, EDGAR H., *Organizational Psychology.* Englewood Cliffs, N.J.: Prentice-Hall, Inc., 1965.

————, "Management Development as a Process of Influence," *Industrial Management Review,* II, No. 2 (May 1961), 59–77.

————, AND WARREN G. BENNIS, *Personal and Organizational Change through Group Methods.* New York: John Wiley & Sons, Inc., 1965.

SCHLEH, E. C., *Management by Results.* New York: McGraw-Hill Book Company, 1961.

SELZNICK, P., *Leadership in Administration.* Evanston, Ill.: Row, Peterson & Company, 1957.

SHARP, LAURISTON, "Steel Axes for Stone Age Australians," in *Human Problems in Technological Changes,* Edward H. Spicer, ed., pp. 69–94. New York: Russell Sage Foundation, 1952.

SHARTLE, C. L., *Effective Performance and Leadership.* Englewood Cliffs, N.J.: Prentice-Hall, Inc., 1956.

SHERIF, M., *et al., Intergroup Conflict and Cooperation: The Robbers Cave Experiment.* Norman, Okla.: Book Exchange, 1961.

SHULTZ, G. P., "Worker Participation on Production Problems," American Management Association, *Personnel,* XXVIII, No. 3 (1951), 202–11.

SIMON, H. A., *Administrative Behavior.* New York: The Macmillan Company, 1947.

————, *Models of Man, Social and Rational.* New York: John Wiley & Sons, Inc., 1957.

SKINNER, B. F., *Science and Human Behavior.* New York: The Macmillan Company, 1953.

————, *Analysis of Behavior.* New York: McGraw-Hill Book Company, 1961.

SPECTOR, AARON J., "Expectations, Fulfillment, and Morale," *Journal of Abnormal and Social Psychology,* 52 (1956), 51–56.

STAGNER, ROSS, "Motivational Aspects of Industrial Morale," *Personnel Psychology,* 11 (1958), 64–70.

————, "Psychological Aspects of Industrial Conflict: Perception," *Personnel Psychology,* 1 (1948), 131–43.

STANTON, ERWIN S., "Company Policies and Supervisors' Attitudes Toward Supervision," *Journal of Applied Psychology,* 44 (1960), 22–26.

STEINER, IVAN D., AND HOMER H. JOHNSON, "Authoritarianism and Conformity," *Sociometry,* 26 (1963), 21–34.

STEWART, MICHAEL, "Resistance to Technological Change in Industry," *Human Organization,* XVI, No. 3 (1957), 36–39.

STOGDILL, R. M., *Individual Behavior and Group Achievement.* New York: Oxford University Press, 1959.

————, AND C. L. SHARTLE, *Methods in the Study of Administrative Leadership.* Columbus, Ohio: Ohio State University, Bureau of Business Research, 1956.

————, *Patterns of Administrative Performance.* Columbus, Ohio: Ohio State University, Bureau of Business Research, 1956.

————, "Personal Factors Associated with Leadership: A Survey of the Literature," *Journal of Psychology,* 25 (1948), 35–71.

SUOJANEN, WAINO W., *The Dynamics of Management.* New York: Holt, Rinehart & Winston, Inc., 1966.

————, "The Span of Control—Fact or Fable?" *Advanced Management,* XX, No. 11 (1955), 5–13.

SUTERMEISTER, ROBERT A., *People and Productivity.* New York: McGraw-Hill Book Company, 1963.

TALACCHI, SERGIO, "Organization Size, Individual Attitudes and Behavior," *Administrative Science Quarterly,* 5 (1960), 398–420.

TANNENBAUM, A. S., "The Concept of Organizational Control," *Journal of Social Issues,* XII, No. 2 (1956), 50–60.

————, "Personality Change as a Result of an Experimental Change of Environmental Conditions," *Journal of Abnormal Social Psychology,* 52 (1957), 404–6.

————, AND F. H. ALLPORT, "Personality Structure and Group Structure: An Interpretative Study of Their Relationship through an Event-Structure

Hypothesis," *Journal of Abnormal Social Psychology,* LI, No. 3 (1956), 272–80.

TANNENBAUM, ROBERT, AND WARREN H. SCHMIDT, "How to Choose a Leadership Pattern," *Harvard Business Review,* March–April 1958, 95–102.

————, IRVING R. WESCHLER, AND FRED MASSARIK, *Leadership and Organization: A Behavioral Science Approach.* New York: McGraw-Hill Book Company, 1959.

TAYLOR, FREDERICK W., *The Principles of Scientific Management.* New York: Harper & Brothers, 1911.

TERRY, GEORGE R., *Principles of Management* (3rd ed.). Homewood, Ill.: Richard D. Irwin, Inc., 1960.

THELEN, H. A., *Dynamics of Groups at Work.* Chicago: University of Chicago Press, 1954.

THIBAUT, JOHN W., AND HAROLD H. KELLEY, *The Social Psychology of Groups.* New York: John Wiley & Sons, Inc., 1959.

THOMAS, EDWIN J., "Role Concepts and Organizational Size," *American Sociological Review,* 24 (February 1959), 30–37.

THOMPSON, JAMES D., "Common and Uncommon Elements in Administration," *The Social Welfare Forum.* New York: Columbia University Press, 1962.

————, AND FREDERICK L. BATES, "Technology, Organization, and Administration," *Administrative Science Quarterly,* 2 (December 1957), 325–42.

————, AND WILLIAM J. McEWEN, "Organizational Goals and Environment: Goal-Setting as an Interaction Process," *American Sociological Review,* 23 (February 1958), 23–31.

TOWNSEND, ROBERT C., *Up the Organization.* New York: Alfred A. Knopf, Inc., 1970.

TROW, DONALD B., "Autonomy and Job Satisfaction to Task Oriented Groups," *Journal of Abnormal and Social Psychology,* 54 (1957), 204–9.

TRUMBO, DON A., "Individual and Group Correlates of Attitudes toward Work-Related Change," *Journal of Applied Psychology,* 45 (1961), 338–44.

TURNER, ARTHUR N., "Interaction and Sentiment in the Foreman-Worker Relationship," *Human Organization,* XIV, No. 1 (1955), 10–16.

VITELES, M. S., *Motivation and Morale in Industry.* New York: W. W. Norton & Company, Inc., 1953.

VROOM, V. H., "The Effects of Attitudes on the Perception of Organizational Goals," *Human Relations,* XIII, No. 3 (1960), 229–40.

————, "Employee Attitudes," in *Frontiers of Industrial Relations,* R. Gray, ed. Pasadena, Calif.: California Institute of Technology, 1960.

————, *Some Personality Determinants of the Effects of Participation.* Englewood Cliffs, N.J.: Prentice-Hall, Inc., 1960.

————, AND F. C. MANN, "Leader Authoritarianism and Employee Attitudes," *Personnel Psychology,* XIII, No. 2 (1960), 125–40.

WALKER, C., AND H. GUEST, *The Man on the Assembly Line.* Cambridge: Harvard University Press, 1952.

WARNER, W. LLOYD, *Social Class in America.* New York: Harper & Row, Publishers, 1960.

————, AND NORMAN H. MARTIN, eds., *Industrial Man.* New York: Harper & Brothers, 1959.

WEITZ, JOSEPH, AND ROBERT C. NUCKOLS, "Job Satisfaction and Job Survival," *Journal of Applied Psychology*, 39 (1955), 294–300.

WESTERLUND, G., *Group Leadership and Field Experiment*. Stockholm: Nordisk Rotogravyr, 1952.

WHITE, HARRISON, "Management Conflict and Sociometric Structure," *American Journal of Sociology*, 67 (September 1961), 185–99.

WHITE, ROBERT W., "Motivation Reconsidered: The Concept of Competence," *Psychological Review*, LXVI, 5 (1959).

———, AND R. LIPPITT, *Autocracy and Democracy: An Experimental Inquiry*. New York: Harper & Row, Publishers, 1960.

WHYTE, WILLIAM F., "Human Relations Theory—A Progress Report," *Harvard Business Review*, XXXIV, No. 5 (1956), 125–34.

———, *Man and Organization*. Homewood, Ill.: Richard D. Irwin Inc., 1959.

———, ed., *Money and Motivation*. New York: Harper & Row, Publishers, 1955.

WHYTE, W. H., JR., *The Organization Man*. New York: Simon and Schuster, Inc., 1956.

ZALEZNIK, A., *Worker Satisfaction and Development*. Boston: Harvard Business School, 1956.

ZANDER, A., E. J. THOMAS, AND T. NATSOULAS, "Personal Goals and the Group's Goals for the Member," *Human Relations*, XIII, No. 4 (1960), 333–44.

index

A

Achievement, motivation characteristics, 35–37
Achievement Motive, The, 41, 148
Achieving Society, The, 148
Activities
    categories of, 15–16
    definition, 49
Activity, as basic unit of behavior, 10
Adaptability
    definition, 121
    demands, low and high, 122–23
Adaptive leader behavior, 79–81
Adler, Alfred, 33, 41
Administrative Theory in Education, 131

Administrator, relationships of, 141, 142
Aggression, 13
Alcoholics Anonymous, 162
American Management Association, 7
Anomie, 46
Ansbacher, H.L., 41
Ansbacher, R.R., 41
Argyris, Chris, 51, 52, 53, 54, 59, 65, 108, 113, 114, 131, 134, 148, 174, 175
Ās, Dagfinn, 104, 108
Asch, S.E., 50, 65
Assembly line experiment, 53
Associates' personalities and expectations, 118
Athos, Anthony G., 65
Atkinson, J.W., 41, 148

Attempted leadership, 93
Attitudinal changes, 158
Attitudinal dimensions, 86
Attitudinal vs. behavioral models, 86
Authoritarianism and Leadership, 131, 147
Availability, 20

B

Bandura, A., 170
Barker, H., 14, 41
Barnard, Chester I., 69, 77, 87
Bass, Bernard M., 93, 107
Behavior, 9–15, 80, 155
  changes in, 2–3, 16
Behavioral Concepts in Management, 66, 170
Behavior in Organizations: A Multi-dimensional View, 65
Behavior modification, 178
  basic premise, 152
  compared with psychotherapy, 158
  example of, 156–57
  as means of changing maturity, 152–58
Behavior Therapy: Appraisal and Status, 170
Benne, Kenneth D., 112, 131
Bennett, Henry, 126
Bennis, Warren G., 77, 131
Bergen, Garret L., 8
Blake, Robert R., 75, 77, 88, 131, 171
Blanchard, Kenneth H., 147, 148
Blocking needs satisfaction, 12
Bowers, D.G., 66
Bradford, Leland P., 112, 131
Breman, N., 65
Brigham Young University, 148
Brown, J.A.C., 14, 41, 170
Brown University, 141
Bureau of Business Research, Ohio State University, 73

C

Cain, Stephen R., 169, 171
Cartwright, Dorwin, 65, 72, 77, 88, 108

Case-Western Reserve University, 54
Causal variables, 96, 97
Change
  examples of process, 161, 164–67
  impact on total system, 169–70
  levels of, 2, 158–59
  in people, 2–3
  in personality, 21–22
  in situational variables, 127–28
Clark, R.A., 41, 148
Coch, L., 103, 104, 108
Coerced change, 160–61
Coerced change cycle, 159, 179
Coffey, Robert E., 65
Cognitive dissonance, theory of, 13
Communication and Organizational Behavior: Text and Cases, 148
Comparative Analysis of Complex Organizations, A, 107
Compensation, 33
Competence, 34–35
Complex man, 176, 177
Concepts of Air Force Leadership, 41
Conceptual skill, 6
Consideration, 77, 79, 86, 105, 134, 140, 141, 142
  definition, 73
  examples, 74
Continuous reinforcement, 163, 164
Controlling, as management function, 5
Coons, Alvin E., 88
Coping behavior, 12
"Corporate image," 118
Cultural change, influence of, 143–47
Cycling function, of goal-directed activity, 18

D

Day, Jesse H:, 148
Dembo, T., 14, 41
Development of strategies, 123–28
DEW Line, 139
Diagnostic ability, of leader, 122, 133, 149
Dickson, W.J., 65
Disruptive worker, approaches used with, 153–54
Dissonance, definition, 13
Driving forces, 100, 101, 162, 179

Drucker, Peter F., 28, 29, 41, 67, 87, 148
Dynamics of Management, The, 132

E

Effective cycle, spiraling effect of, 150
Effective style, 84–85
Effectiveness dimension, 83, 84, 86, 87, 149–52
Effectiveness formula, 87
Effectiveness variables, 95–99
Ego and the Id, The, 40
Employee orientation, 72
End-result variables, 96–97
Environment diagnosis, case history, 129–30
Environmental variables, 109–111, 129
Equilibrium, 100
Esteem, 31–33
Etzioni, Amitai, 92, 107
Eupsychian Management, 108
Expectancy and availability, 19–21
Expectations
  compatibility of, 126
  definition, 111
Extinction, 157, 163

F

Feedback model, 125
Ferster, C.B., 170
Festinger, Leon, 13, 41
Fiedler, Fred E., 80, 81, 88, 96, 98, 107, 108, 119, 123, 127, 132
Fixation, symptoms of, in industry, 14
Floor, Lucretia G., 87
Followers, 116, 117, 134
  importance in leadership event, 115
  personalities and expectations, 115–16
Force, as mechanism of change, 163
Force field analysis, 100–01, 162
Ford, Henry, 126
Ford Motor Company, 118
Franks, C.M., 170
French, J.R.P., 103, 104, 108
Freud, Sigmund, 10, 13, 40

Frustration, 13
Frustration, 41
Frustration and Aggression, 41
Functions of the Executive, The, 69, 88

G

Gandhi, Mahatma, 25
Gellerman, Saul W., 28, 29, 38, 41, 108, 124, 131, 132
General Electric Company, 124, 125
Getzels, Jacob W., 111, 131
Gibb, C.A., 87, 108
Gibb, Jack R., 131
Goal activity, compared to goal-directed activity, 16
Goals, definition, 11
Group changes, 158, 159
Croup competition, consequences of, 167–68
Group Dynamics, 65
Group Dynamics: Research and Theory, 88, 108
Group dynamics studies, 72–73, 75
Groups, Leadership, and Men, 65
Guba, Eugene G., 131
Guest, Robert H., 117, 132, 151, 171
Guetzkow, Harold, 65
Gurin, G., 87

H

Halpin, Andrew W., 77, 79, 88, 131, 144
Hampton, David R., 66, 170
Handbook of Small Group Research, 108
Handbook of Social Psychology, 108
Haney, William V., 8, 143, 148
"Hard sciences," 3
Hare, A.P., 108
Hartley, E., 108
Harvard Graduate School of Business Administration, 43
Harvard research team, interviews, 44–45
Harvey, O.J., 171
Hawthorne studies, 44–46

Hemphill, John K., 87
Henry, William E., 132
Hersey, Paul, 88, 104, 147, 148
Herzberg, Frederick, 54, 55, 56, 58, 65, 174
Hierarchy of needs, 22–27, 174
High adaptability job, 123
High flexibility demands, 122
High organizational accomplishment, 103
Holsinger, Glenna G., 170
Homans, George C., 48, 65
Hood, W.R., 171
Houk, Clifford, 148
House, R.J., 7
Hull, Raymond, 132
Human group, 48–50
Human Group, The, 65
Human Organization, The, 66, 107, 108
Human Problems of an Industrial Civilization, The, 41, 65
Human relations movement, 43, 70
"Human relations skills," 116
Human Side of Enterprise, The, 65, 108
Human skill, 6, 7
Hygiene factors, 54–56, 174

I

Identification, 162–63, 165
Immaturity-maturity continuum, 134, 174, 175
Immaturity-maturity theory, 50–53
Incentives, definition, 11
Individual behavior changes, 158, 159
Individual goals, 92
Individual Psychology of Alfred Adler, The, 41
Industrial Worker, The, 65
Ineffective cycle, 150
  how to break it, 152
  spiraling effect of, 151
Ineffective style, 85
Inferiority complex, 33
Informal work groups, 31
Initiating structure, 77, 79, 86, 105, 134, 141
  definition, 73
Institutionalization, 118

Integrating the Individual and the Organization, 65, 108, 148
Integration of goals and effectiveness, 101–3
Interaction-influence system, 160
Interactions
  amount of, 120
  definition, 49
Intergroup conflict, management of, 167–69
Intergroup Conflict and Cooperation: The Robbers Cave Experiment, 171
Intermittent reinforcement, 163, 164
Internalization, 162–63, 165, 166
Interpersonal Competence and Organizational Effectiveness, 65, 131, 148
Intervening variables, 96, 99, 100, 103, 105, 119, 179
  indications of deterioration, 98
Intervention Theory and Method: A Behavioral Science View, 65
Israel, Joachim, 104, 108

J

James, William, 5
Jennings, Eugene E., 68, 87
Job demands, 119–20
"Job enlargement," 58
Job enrichment, examples, 58–59
Johnson, Dewey E., 41

K

Katz, D., 87
Katz, Robert L., 8
Kelman, H.C., 170
Key subordinates, selection of, 126–27
Knowledge changes, 158
Koontz, Harold, 4, 7, 68, 87, 88, 144, 148
Korman, A.K., 105, 106, 107, 108, 134

L

LBDQ (*See* Leader Behavior Description Questionnaire)

Leader behavior, 70–72, 134
Leader Behavior Description Questionnaire, 73, 74, 77, 79, 106
Leader Behavior: Its Description and Measurement, 88, 89
Leader behavior style, conclusions on, 106–07, 116, 138
Leader Effectiveness Model, 84–87
Leader-member relations, 127
Leader personality, 82
Leadership, 68, 92
Leadership and Motivation, 65, 108
Leadership and Organization: A Behavioral Science Approach, 87
Leadership Behavior of Airplane Commanders, The, 88
Leadership Behavior of School Superintendents, The, 88
Leadership contingency model, 80–81, 127
Leadership Opinion Questionnaire, 106
Leadership process, 69–76
Leadership, Psychology, and Organizational Behavior, 107
Leadership study, trait vs. situational approach, 68–69
Leadership style, 75–76, 86, 112, 119, 120, 123, 144, 174
Leadership Style and Employee Morale, 132
Least preferred co-worker, 89
Lewin, Kurt, 14, 41, 108, 161, 170
Life cycle theory of leadership, 134–43, 147, 152, 161, 173, 174, 175, 176, 177, 178
  parent-child relationship as illustration, 135–38
  as related to leader behavior, 135
  as related to management styles, 175–77
  as related to motivation, 174–75
  as related to nature of man, 175–77
  as related to process of change, 177–79
Lighting power experiment, 44
Likert, Rensis, 60, 61, 62, 64, 66, 77, 78, 79, 88, 95, 96, 98, 99, 104, 107, 150, 170, 175
Lindzey, Gardner, 108
"Linking pin" activities, 147
  definition, 146
  role, 147

Lippitt, R., 108, 112
Lonely Crowd, The, 41
Long-range goals, 99, 103
Long-run goals, 119
Long-term goals, 179
  vs. short-term goals, 97
Low adaptability job, 123
Lowell, E.L., 41, 148
Low flexibility demands, 122
LPC (*See* Least preferred co-worker)

M

McClelland, David C., 35, 36, 37, 41, 148
Maccoby, N., 87
McGregor, Douglas, 46, 47, 50, 53, 54, 65, 101, 108, 175, 176
Machiavelli, Niccolo, 92, 107
Maier, Norman R.F., 14, 41
Making of a Moron, The, 65
Management, 92, 101, 102, 106
  definition, 3–4
  effectiveness, compared to leadership, 91–92
  by objectives, 104
  process, 4–5
Management and the Worker, 65
Management behavior, 147
Management by Motivation, 41, 108
Management by Objectives, 108
Management Concepts and Behavior: Programmed Instruction for Managers, 88
Management Development: Design, Implementation, and Evaluation, 7
Management systems, 60–64, 175
  system 4, example, 64
  variety of, 61–62
  role, 146
  skills necessary, 6–7
Managerial Grid, 75–76, 77, 86, 87
Managerial Grid, The, 88
Managers, 103, 104, 105
Mann, Floyd C., 120, 132
Marrow, A.J., 66
Maslow, Abraham, 22, 24, 25, 26, 27, 34, 38, 40, 56, 108, 143, 174, 175
Massarik, Fred, 68, 87

Maturity, 134–35, 177
  levels of, 142–43
Mausner, Bernard, 65
Mayo, Elton, 1, 2, 7, 30, 38, 41, 43,
  44, 45, 46, 50, 65, 70, 87
Measures of effectiveness, 106
Meyers, Scott, 55, 66
Michigan Leadership Studies, 72, 75,
  77
Money and Motivation, 41
Money, as associated with physical
  needs, 27
Money motive, 38
Morrow, R.G., 148
Morse, Nancy C., 87, 108
Motivating situation, 16–19
Motivating the Reluctant Learner, 170
Motivation
  definition, 10
  as function of management, 5
Motivation and Productivity, 41, 108,
  131, 132
Motivation-Hygiene Theory, 54–60,
  174
Motivation research, 5, 27–38
Motivation to Work, The, 65
Motivators, 54–55, 174
Motive strength, 11–12, 15
Mouton, Jane S., 77, 88, 171

N

Narrow span of control, 145
National Training Laboratories, 162
Nature of man, assumptions, 176–77
Needs
  definition, 10
  esteem, 24, 27
  physiological, 23
  safety, 23
  satisfaction, 12
  self-actualization, 24–25
  social, 23–24
Negative behavior consequences, 155,
  156
*New Introductory Lectures on Psycho-
  analysis*, 40
New Patterns of Management, 66, 88,
  108, 132, 148, 170
Newcomb, T., 108
Newman, William H., 7

Non-linear systems, 104
Nova educational complex, 148

O

Observed behavior, dimensions of, 86
Odiorne, George S., 108
O'Donnell, Cyril, 4, 7, 68, 87, 88, 144,
  148
Ohio State, 134
Ohio State behavior dimensions, 105
Ohio State Leadership model, 75, 86
Ohio State Leadership Studies, 73–74,
  75, 77, 81
Ohio University, 148
Ohio University Center for Leader-
  ship Studies, 147
*Organizational Analysis: A Socio-
  logical View*, 132
*Organizational Change: The Effect of
  Successful Leadership*, 132, 171
Organizational dilemma, 97–99
Organizational effectiveness, determi-
  nation of, 95–99
"Organizational engineering," 127
Organizational goals, 92, 102, 103,
  119
Organizational Psychology, 147, 171,
  176, 179
*Organizational Relations and Manage-
  ment Action*, 8
Organizational structures, 147
Organization's personality and expec-
  tations, 118–19
"Other-directed individuals," 32
Output or end-result variables, 96, 97,
  99, 103, 105, 108, 119, 150
Overload principle, 35

P

Packard, Vance, 32, 41
Parris Island, 165, 166
Participation and Effectiveness, 103–
  06
Participative change cycle, 159–60,
  179
  compared to coerced change cycle,
  161

Pelz, D.C., 108
People and production, concern for, 87
Perrow, Charles, 132
Personal and Organizational Change through Group Methods, 131
Personal power, 92
Personal relationships, development of, 75
Personality, 21
  definition, 82, 110
  development, 21–22
  and expectations, 111–19
Personality and Organization, 65, 148
Peter, Lawrence J., 130, 132
Peter principle, definition, 130
Peter Principle: Why Things Always Go Wrong, The, 132
Physical stature, of leader, 120
Physiological needs, 27
Placement, problem of, 59–60
Position power, 92, 127
Positive behavior consequences, 155, 156
Positive reinforcement, 178
Power, 32–33, 92–93
Practice of Management, The, 87, 148
Predisposition, 86
Prestige, 31–32
Prince and The Discourses, The, 92, 107
Principles of Behavior Modification, 170
Principles of Management, 7, 87, 88, 148
Principles of Scientific Management, The, 87
Process of Management, The, 7
Production orientation, 72
Productivity, Supervision, and Morale among Railroad Workers, 88
Productivity, Supervision, and Morale in an Office Situation, 88
Project cycle, 139–40
Psychological Service of Pittsburgh, 54
Psychology of Affiliation, The, 41

R

"Rabble hypothesis," 46
Ranking of job attributes, 39–40

"Rate-busters," 31
Rational-economic man, 176
Rationalization, 14
Readings in Social Psychology, 108
Reddin, William J., 83, 88, 96, 108, 131
Refreezing, 163–64
Regression, 14
Reimer, E., 108
Reinforcement, 155, 157
Relationship between variables, 96–97
Relationships behavior, 82, 83, 86
  definition, 83
Relationships-orientation
  behavior, 116, 120
  goals, 119
  leaders, 81, 127
  style, 122, 124
Research and development personnel, 138
  management of, 140
Research Center for Group Dynamics, 72
Resignation, 14–15
Restraining forces, 100, 101, 162, 179
"Revisionists," 77
Riesman, David, 32, 41
Roethlisberger, F.J., 65

S

Safety, 28–30
Sanford, Fillmore, 115, 131, 134, 147
Schachter, Stanley, 30, 31, 41
Schedules of Reinforcement, 170
Schein, Edgar H., 131, 133, 147, 162, 163, 165, 167, 168, 170, 171, 176, 177, 179
Schmidt, Warren H., 71, 87
Science and Human Behavior, 170
Scientific management, concepts of, 52
Scientific management movement, 69–70
Seashore, S.E., 66
Security motives, 29
Self-actualizing man, 176, 177
Self-paced learning curricula, 148
Semantic differential type scales, 89
"Sensitivity training," 112–15
Sentiments, definition, 49
Sharp, Lauriston, 171

Sherif, Carolyn, 171
Sherif, M., 167, 171
Short-range goals, 99, 103
Short-term goals, 101
Short-term output, 179
"Situational determinants," 130, 131, 134
Situational Factors in Leadership, 88
Situational variables, 119–121, 127
Skinner, B.F., 170
Slattery, Patrick D., 170
Social affiliation, 30–31
Social Class in America, 148
Social Interest, 41
Social man, 176–77
Social Problems of an Industrial Civilization, The, 7, 41, 88
Social Psychology of Industry, The, 41, 170
Social skills, need for, 1
Social system, elements in, 49
Some Personality Determinants of the Effects of Participation, 131
Span of control, 144–45
Status Seekers, The, 41
Stogdill, Roger M., 87, 88
Strategies of Organizational Change, 66
Structure, 136, 137, 138, 139, 140, 142
Structured jobs, 120
Stutz, F.H., 148
Style, 110, 112, 116, 121, 122, 123, 124, 126, 127, 134, 139, 141, 142, 146, 177
    adaptability, 121–23
    changes, 125
    determining range, 121–22
    and effectiveness, 84–86, 105–107
    expectations, 117, 118, 125
    of leadership, 84, 85
    related to personality, 83
Subordinates, 101, 102, 103, 104, 105, 106, 112, 115, 116, 138, 144, 145, 146, 147, 150, 152
Successful and effective leadership continuums, 94
Successful Leadership vs. Effective Leadership, 93–95
"Successful sciences," definition, 2
Sum of past experience, 22
Summer, Charles, E., 7
Suojanen, Waino W., 132

Superior, 118, 138, 150, 152
    personalities and expectations, 116–18
    responsibilities of, 146–47
Supervisors, task-oriented, 120
Survey Research Center, University of Michigan, 72
Swanson, G., 108
Synderman, Barbara, 65

T

Tannenbaum, Robert, 68, 71, 87
Task accomplishment, 75
Task behavior, 82, 83, 86
    definition, 83
Task-orientation
    behavior, 116, 120, 139
    goals, 119
    leaders, 81, 127
    planning, 123
    style, 124
Task structure, 119, 120
Taylor, Frederick Winslow, 69, 70, 87
Technical skill, 6
Telephone relay girls, experiment, 44
Terry, George R., 68, 87
Texas Instruments study, 55
T-Group Theory and Laboratory Method, 131
T-group training (*See also* Sensitivity training), 113–14
"Thawing out" process (*See* Unfreezing process)
Theory of Cognitive Dissonance, A, 41
Theory of Leadership Effectiveness, A, 89, 108, 132
Theory X, 46–48, 175, 176
    assumptions about human nature, 111
Theory Y, 46–48, 175–76
3-D Management Style Theory, 83, 108
3-D Management Style Theory, The, 89, 131, 132
Time, as factor in decision-making, 120, 139
Tri-Dimensional Leader Effectiveness Model, 79–87, 91, 108, 109, 133, 134, 137–38

U

Unfreezing process, 165
  common elements of, 162
Union Carbide, 104
University of Michigan, Institute for
  Social Research, 60
Unstructured jobs, 120
"Unsuccessful sciences," definition, 2

V

Valley High School, 148
Variables, 96–97
Vroom, Victor H., 115, 120, 131, 132

W

Warner, Lloyd, 137, 148
Warren, E. Kirby, 7

Weschler, Irving R., 68, 87
Western Electric Company, research
  program, 43
West Point, 139
White, B.J., 171
White, Robert W., 34, 41, 108
Whitehead, T.N., 65
Whyte, William F., 38, 41
Winer, Ben J., 79, 88
Work and the Nature of Man, 65
Work group, as motivation factor, 38
"Work maps," 4
Wriston, Henry, 141, 148

Y

Yale University, 50

Z

Zander, Alvin, 65, 72, 77, 88, 108